OTHER BOOKS BY IRENA CHALMERS

The Confident Cook
American Bistro
The Great American Food Almanac
The Great American Christmas Almanac
The Great American Baby Almanac
Good Old Food
Award Winning Recipes
Working Family's Cookbook
Food Professional's Guide

IRENA CHALMERS'

ALL-TIME

FAVORITES

A LIFETIME OF RECIPES
FOR THE FIRST-TIME COOK

IRENA CHALMERS

PRENTICE
HALL
PRESS

NEW YORK   LONDON   TORONTO   SYDNEY   TOKYO   SINGAPORE

Prentice Hall Press
15 Columbus Circle
New York, New York 10023

PRENTICE HALL PRESS and colophons are registered
trademarks of Simon & Schuster, Inc.

Library of Congress Cataloging-in-Publication Data

Chalmers, Irena.
  Irena Chalmers' All-Time Favorites / Irena Chalmers.
    p.   cm.
  ISBN 0-13-082405-4
  1. Cookery.   I. Title.
TX652.C478   1990
641.5—dc20   89-38542
                                       CIP

Designed by Barbara Cohen Aronica

Manufactured in the United States of America

10 9 8 7 6 5 4 3 2 1

First Edition

For my children,
Hilary, Philip, and Wendy
who ate all this food

CONTENTS

INTRODUCTION

I have had infinite pleasure compiling this group of recipes, for this is the food that I love most and cook again and again. As each recipe was revisited, I conjured up all the many happy evenings when guests have come and sat for hour upon hour with elbows on the table, talking, eating, drinking long into the night.

The only difficult thing about cooking is deciding what it is that I want to cook. Almost always I spend ages sifting through dozens of ideas before arriving at what I think will be the best possible menu. Then I usually change my mind again once I unexpectedly see something at the store.

One of my greatest pleasures is gathering together all the ingredients from many markets. Often I shop as my mother did, carrying a big round-bellied shopping basket and filling it to overflowing. When I get home, I arrange all the vegetables and fruits in big wicker trays so I can see and reach everything easily. It is a great game to transform everything from one form into another until there is a parade of finished dishes running along the kitchen counter.

I delight in all these steps: the shopping, the cooking, the arranging of the table and the flowers—and then the quiet moment before the guests arrive when there is time to ask myself if I invited them for tonight or if I got the date wrong and they are supposed to come tomorrow!

I have no memory at all for some things. I can't remember songs or jokes or the names of movie stars; but, oddly, I can recall with utmost clarity what I served to whom years and years ago. I remember dinners at other people's homes, too.

Many years ago, I was invited by a gorgeous man to have dinner in his Manhattan brownstone apartment. I was rapturous with anticipation. I arrived tarted up to the gills and was greeted by Himself, dressed in a decrepit old sweater and jeans and bare of foot. He led me to his garden where we drank vast quantities of champagne and smoked innumerable cigarettes, depositing the ashes in a rolled-back sardine can. Dinner was delivered from the neighborhood Chinese take-out store. We married, briefly, and though I have now forgotten most of the details of that particular dinner and exactly what delicate morsels we extracted from the little white metal-handled boxes, I remember that dear little sardine can with great affection.

Such little touches, I strongly believe, make meals memorable. The presentation of the food is almost as important as the cooking, so I have made some suggestions about serving the food throughout the book. At the end, too, you will find some ideas of what foods I think complement each other.

Like you, I am working all day and so have little time to make dinner, but I find that if I shop one evening and cook the evening that guests are coming, entertaining can be managed easily and without feeling pressed for time. For weekday evenings I choose simple recipes that are easy to make. I cook stews, slow-simmered soups, and more complicated dishes the night before or save them for the weekend.

I adore going out to eat and delight in all the intricate and dazzling tastes and contrasting textures that professional chefs are constantly creating. But that is not the way I cook at home. For family and friends I prefer familiar dishes and never tire of poached salmon, roast chicken, and freshly made salads. The advantage of making something you know well is that you hardly need to glance at the recipe and feel completely confident about the results.

One of the most difficult things to do is to time the cooking so that everything is finished at the same moment. I think you will be able to achieve this if you take an extra minute or two and make a plan for yourself, applying the same principles that you would use when you undertake a project during your working day. It is enormously important to be organized in the kitchen in order to spare yourself the anxiety of last-minute crises.

I have added a chapter of tips in the front of the book that will answer some of the questions that may arise when you are cooking. I hope you will find them helpful. They are separated from the body of the specific recipes because they have many applications.

I am convinced that if you want to cook well, you will do so. If you can read, you can cook—and the more you cook, the more you will enjoy it, for it is a never-ending hobby that will bring as much pleasure to you as it will to those who share your table.

PART ONE

- -

TIPS AND TECHNIQUES:
From Anchovies to Wine

- -

ANCHOVIES

- To remove the excess salt and some of the "edge" from anchovies, soak them in enough milk to cover them for 10 minutes. Drain before using.

APPLES

- When you peel and slice apples or pears ahead of time, sprinkle them with lemon juice to prevent discoloration.
- When preparing apple and other fruit pies, thicken the juices by adding 2 tablespoons of cornstarch dissolved in 2 tablespoons of cold water, or use 3 tablespoons of instant tapioca sprinkled over $\frac{1}{3}$ cup of cold water. The pie can then be cut into compact slices.

ARTICHOKES

- To tell if an artichoke is cooked, remove a leaf after 40 minutes cooking time. If the leaf comes away easily, the artichoke is ready to eat. Drain it upside down to remove the excess water.

ASPARAGUS

- Peel asparagus with a cheese slicer; it is easier than using a potato peeler or a paring knife.
- To keep asparagus fresh, wrap it in wet paper towels and keep it in the refrigerator.
- An ideal way to cook fresh, young asparagus is to wrap the spears in well-moistened paper towels, put them in a microwavable dish and cook in the microwave on High (100 percent power) for 3 to 6 minutes or until they are tender. Serve them with butter, melted in the microwave for just a few seconds.

◼ AVOCADO

- To ripen an avocado, keep it in a brown paper bag at room temperature for a couple of days. The gases that are released from the avocado will help it soften. If it has not ripened in that time, discard it, because it never will.
- Cut avocados with a stainless steel knife; carbon steel will make the flesh discolor.

◼ BACON

- Crumble leftover bacon, and keep it in the refrigerator to use for garnishing soups, salads, and vegetables.

◼ BAKING

- When baking, do not keep opening and closing the oven door to see how things are getting along. Every time you peer into the oven, the temperature drops significantly. You will be able to tell by the fragrant smell when a bread or cake is ready. When it shrinks from the sides of the baking pan and a cake tester or toothpick inserted into the center comes out clean, you can be sure it is completely cooked.
- Tin baking pans are preferable to glass ones for baking cakes because they give an attractively browned surface.

◼ BAKING POWDER

- When baking powder is added to liquid ingredients, carbon dioxide is formed (you can see the bubbles rising). Bake the dough for quick breads immediately to take advantage of this action before the gas dissipates.
- When cooking with baking powder, sift it with the other dry ingredients to distribute it evenly. Handle the dough as little as possible after mixing and bake it at once.

BAKING SODA

- Baking soda is used with acid ingredients such as buttermilk, yogurt, sour cream, brown sugar, molasses, and dried fruits. It combines with the acid to form carbon dioxide, which in turn lightens and aerates the dough. It can be used alone or in combination with baking powder.

BEANS AND PULSES

- Many packaged beans do not require presoaking. Follow the package directions.
- Supermarkets do not always carry the more unusual forms of pulses, such as lentils, black beans, and flageolets, but a good selection can always be found at health-food stores and gourmet/specialty shops.

BEER

- Beer can replace wine or broths in many recipes. Try using it for steaming sausages and shellfish, or as one of the ingredients in a marinade. It also makes wonderfully light pancake and crêpe batters.

BEETS

- Do not cut off the stems of beets too closely. Leave at least an inch of stem and the root intact to prevent the beets from "bleeding" into the cooking water.

BREAD

- Store bread, well wrapped, in the freezer. It will not go stale and defrosts almost instantly.

- Make stale bread into bread crumbs in the food processor or blender, or cut it into croutons and store them in a plastic bag in the freezer.

■ BROTH

- Canned beef broth, to my mind, has too strong a flavor, so I prefer to use chicken broth whenever possible. When a more distinctive taste is needed, use half chicken and half beef broth.
- To remove excessive sweetness from canned bouillon and beef broth, simmer it for 5 minutes with a little chopped onion, garlic, and celery. Do *not* add carrots.

■ BURNS

- If you burn your fingers, hold them under cold running water for a minute or two, until the pain subsides. Make a thick paste of baking soda and cold water and apply to the burn.

■ BUTTER

- Unsalted butter is used in the preparation of fine sauces, cakes, and pastries because it has a better flavor than salted butter.
- A combination of butter and oil is used in a great many recipes because the oil prevents the butter from burning and makes it possible to cook at a much higher temperature than if only butter were used.
- Clarified butter does not burn as readily as whole butter. To make clarified butter, heat the butter until it is foaming, then strain it through several thicknesses of cheesecloth. Leave it to drip slowly. (Do not squeeze the cheesecloth or the butter will become cloudy.) Discard the milky solids and use the golden clarified butter for dipping lobster and artichokes, or for sautéing meats, chicken, and fish. Clarified butter will keep for several weeks in the refrigerator.

- To make butter curls, dip the curler in cold water before drawing it along the stick of butter to make each curl. If the butter does not form a curl correctly, it may be too salty or too cold.

CAKES

- Leave cakes to cool in the cake pans for 10 to 15 minutes before loosening and turning them out to cool completely on wire cake-cooling racks.
- If you are frosting a cake on a plate or cake stand, slip 4 pieces of wax paper beneath the edges of the cake to protect the plate from spills and drips. (You can draw them out after the frosting has set.)

CAKE-COOLING RACKS

- These wire racks are essential, of course, for cooling cakes and other baked goods. It is a good idea to have at least two on hand.
- Cake-cooling racks lined with paper towels can also be used for draining bacon and other fried foods. The circulating air keeps the food crisp.

CAST-IRON PANS

- To season a cast-iron pan, half fill it with vegetable oil and heat the oil until tiny bubbles appear. Remove the pan from the heat and let it stand for 12 hours. Pour out any remaining oil and wipe with paper towels. After cooking with the seasoned pan, do not wash, but wipe it clean with paper towels; if there are any particles of food sticking to the pan, use salt as a scouring powder.
- Season omelette and crêpe pans in the same way.

CHEESE

- Unless it is a gala occasion, serve only the quantity of cheese you estimate will be eaten. If cheese is left at room temperature for too long, it starts to "sweat" butterfat and can deteriorate rapidly.
- Always rewrap cut cheeses in fresh transparent wrap to exclude the air as completely as possible.
- Soft cheeses such as Brie or Camembert have a tendency to sink in the center; avoid this by turning them over each day.
- To extend the life of blue cheeses, wrap them in a cheesecloth drizzled with vinegar or port wine, then overwrap them in aluminum foil.
- Wrap Parmesan and other hard cheeses in plastic wrap and store them in the vegetable drawer of the refrigerator. The humidity will prevent them from drying and cracking.

CHICKEN

- If possible, buy range-fed chickens from a good butcher. They have an incomparable flavor and texture and are worth the extra trouble and cost.
- When frying chicken, cook the legs first and add the breasts to the pan later. Dark meat takes longer to cook than white meat.
- Truss all chicken and other poultry before roasting or the wings and thighs will be overcooked. To tell whether a bird is completely cooked, pierce the thigh with a fork. If the juices run clear, it is done; if they are slightly pink, return it to the oven for another 5 or 10 minutes.
- When preparing a chicken for a salad or sandwiches, poach it in chicken broth; it will be moist and flavorful.
- When chicken is cooked in a casserole, the leg meat shrinks, exposing the bone. To make it look more attractive, trim off the bone ends and wing tips with poultry shears.
- When boning a chicken breast, be sure to remove the white tendon or it will contract during cooking and cause the chicken meat to shrink.

- It is worth keeping frozen chicken breasts on hand to give weight to a quick pasta meal. They are easy to defrost in the microwave. Do take care to barely thaw the breasts; if they are allowed to cook in the microwave, the fast change of temperature toughens the meat terribly. If you cut the breasts into strips while they are still slightly frozen, you can be sure that they will stay tender.

CHILIES

- If fresh chilies are soaked in cold water for 1 hour, they will be slightly less "hot." Remove the ribs and seeds before using them.
- Rinse dried chilies in cold water, remove the ribs and seeds, then cut the chilies into small pieces. Let these soak and soften for 30 minutes before using them.
- Rinse canned chilies in cold water before using them.

CHOCOLATE

- The easiest way to melt chocolate is to put it on a plate over a pan of simmering water. Cover the plate with a saucer. Or you can melt it in the microwave, following the manufacturer's instructions. Be sure to remove the dish with the chocolate *just before* it all seems to have softened; then, as you stir it, the rest will melt too.
- Never let chocolate become too hot or the cocoa butter will be released, making the chocolate hard and grainy. If this begins to happen, tragedy can be averted by beating in a drop or two of salad oil with a wire whisk.
- When chocolate is refrigerated or frozen, it loses its shine—but the taste is unaffected.

CHOPSTICKS

- When eating with chopsticks, imagine you are picking up a

butterfly. This will prevent you from gripping the sticks so firmly that they cross.

◼ COCKTAIL PARTY TIPS

- The fastest way to prepare dozens of canapés is to establish an assembly-line system. Do all the buttering, then all the whatever-comes-next. If you are working with limited counter space, spread out to the living room or bedroom, or erect a series of surfaces to work on.
- Allow a minimum of four canapés for each person.
- The saltier the hors d'oeuvres, the thirstier the guests.
- When serving guests at a large party, prepare several small trays rather than one huge one.
- Place buffet foods on stands at different heights to add interest to the table.

◼ COCONUT

- To toast coconut, spread it on a flat surface and place in a preheated 350-degree oven for 5 minutes until it is lightly browned. Stir it with a fork once or twice while toasting to distribute the heat evenly.

◼ COFFEE

- Store coffee in the refrigerator or, tightly bagged, in the freezer to preserve the flavor. When making coffee in quantity, remember that ½ pound regular (drip-ground) coffee and 4 quarts of water will yield 20 cups.

◼ COOKIES

- Chill cookie dough before baking it; this will prevent the cookies from spreading too quickly on the baking sheets. If you also chill the baking sheets, the cookies will keep their shape even better.

- Remove the cookies from the baking sheet with a metal spatula while they are still quite hot and cool them in a single layer on wire cake-cooling racks. (Don't stack them on top of each other—trapped steam will make the cookies soggy.)
- Store cookies in containers with tight-fitting lids. Do not mix crisp and soft cookies or they will all become soft.

COOKING UTENSILS

- Wooden spatulas are even more useful than wooden spoons. When stirring, food does not become trapped as it does in the bowl of a spoon, and wooden utensils cannot damage the saucepan.
- Use tongs for turning meats—when they are pierced with a fork, the juices are lost. Tongs are also useful when frying bacon or when reaching for items on a high kitchen shelf.
- Keep frequently used small utensils, such as whisks, spatulas, and spoons, in a large pitcher next to the stove—and save time hunting for them in kitchen drawers.

CREAM

- Heavy cream will double in volume when whipped.
- When whipping heavy cream, add 2 tablespoons sugar to 1 cup heavy cream halfway through the whipping time. Add 1 teaspoon vanilla extract when the cream is almost whipped to the correct consistency.
- To make coffee-flavored whipped cream, add 1 teaspoon instant coffee at the same time as the vanilla extract.
- If whipped cream has to be left in a warm place, fold in 1 teaspoon unflavored gelatin heated until dissolved in 2 tablespoons water for each cup of cream. This will prevent the cream from "weeping."
- Heavy cream makes a good substitute for sour cream because it will not curdle even if it boils.

- If cream (or milk) is in imminent danger of boiling over, immediately lift the saucepan away from the source of heat and as you do so, blow gently on the liquid about to bubble over the rim. This alters the surface tension and will probably keep it from spilling (and from filling the kitchen with the ghastly smell of burned cream).

CREAM OF TARTAR

- Cream of tartar, an ingredient in baking powder, can be used on its own to convert fresh milk to buttermilk for cooking. Add 1 teaspoon cream of tartar to every cup of fresh milk.
- Cream of tartar is also used to stabilize egg whites that are to be beaten stiffly. Add ⅛ teaspoon cream of tartar to 4 egg whites.

CRÈME FRAÎCHE

- Crème fraîche can usually be found in the dairy cases of specialty food stores. A cultured cream so thick that it has to be spooned, not poured, it is used to give depth and character to both entrees and desserts. It keeps well in the refrigerator.

CUSTARD

- Custard should never reach the boiling point or it will lose its silken texture. Small holes will appear if a custard becomes too hot, and it will taste "grainy." To prevent overcooking, stand a dish or dishes of custard in a baking dish filled three-quarters of the way up its sides with hot, but not boiling, water.

DEFROSTING POULTRY AND MEAT

- If time permits, leave frozen poultry and meat in the original wrappings to defrost slowly in the refrigerator. Allow 2 days to thaw a turkey weighing less than 12 pounds, 3 days for a turkey weighing between 12 and 16 pounds, and 4 days for a turkey weighing more than 16 pounds.

- If there is no time to allow frozen meats to thaw slowly in the refrigerator, you can rub the meat's surface with oil to prevent excess loss of moisture and leave it to defrost in a colander placed in the kitchen sink. Refrigerate or cook the meat immediately upon thawing, to avoid the growth of bacteria.
- To speed defrosting, put the plastic-wrapped turkey in a bowl of cold water in the kitchen sink. Either let the cold water run slowly over the turkey or change the water several times.
- It is true that you can start cooking a still-frozen bird in a very low, 250-degree oven, but the extended cooking time results in meat that is very disappointingly dry.
- Frozen birds come with suggested cooking times; trust them if you have an accurate oven thermometer.
- It takes 6 hours to defrost a solidly frozen duck at room temperature. If you have time, it is better to defrost it slowly in the refrigerator, where it will take up to 12 hours to thaw completely.
- Before roasting a duck or a goose, prick the skin all over with a fork or the point of a sharp knife to allow the fat to drain freely. Pour off the fat from time to time as the bird cooks.

EGGS

- One of the easiest ways to separate an egg is to break it into your hand and let the white drip between your fingers.
- If a speck of egg yolk drops into the egg white, lift it out with an empty egg shell.
- To store unbroken egg yolks, cover them with cold water and keep them in the refrigerator for up to 2 days.
- Store leftover egg whites in a covered jar, or freeze them. One egg white weighs 1 ounce.
- Beat egg whites in a clean dry bowl. Egg whites beaten in a copper bowl will increase in volume to 7 times their original

size. If you don't have a copper bowl, add ⅛ teaspoon cream of tartar for 4 egg whites.

- Beat egg whites only when you are ready to use them. If beaten egg whites are not used at once, they become watery and the air beaten into them will escape.
- You can poach eggs ahead of time, for convenience, and keep them hot in a bowl of hot, not boiling, water. They will not continue to cook, but will stay soft.
- Boiled eggs should not in fact be boiled but simmered, to prevent the shells from cracking. Start cooking the eggs in cold water and as soon as the water comes to a boil, immediately lower the heat to a simmer and start counting. In 4 minutes, the egg whites will be firm and the yolks still runny.
- If you are putting an egg into a pan of boiling water, pierce the round end with a pin to prevent the shell from cracking as a result of the sudden increase in the internal pressure.
- To make hard-cooked eggs, simmer them for 12 minutes and then place them under cold running water. If you peel them as soon as they are cool enough to handle, the shells will come off easily.
- To prevent stuffed hard-cooked eggs from sliding on a serving dish, anchor them in place with a touch of the stuffing.
- Store eggs in the refrigerator in the carton; they will stay fresh longer.

FISH

- Fresh fish has no odor. The eyes should gleam and the skin be very shiny.
- There are two classifications for fish: freshwater and saltwater. Fish from either of these two categories may be lean or fatty. Lean fish are generally fried, sautéed in butter, poached, or steamed. Fatty fish are best cooked by dry heat, that is, baked, broiled, or grilled over charcoal. The list on the following page gives some common examples of lean and fatty fish.

LEAN FISH

Bluefish
Cod
Croaker
Flounder
Haddock
Hake
Halibut
Herring
Perch
Pike
Red Snapper
All shellfish
Sole
Swordfish
Whiting

FATTY FISH

Butterfish
Catfish
Chub
Mackerel
Pompano
Salmon
Shad
Smelt
Striped bass
Trout
Turbot
Whitefish

QUANTITIES

For 4 people buy:

$1\frac{1}{2}$ pounds filleted fish

2 pounds fish steaks or cutlets

3 pounds whole fish with head and tail removed

4 pounds whole fish with the head and tail

POACHING

When poaching fish allow:

10 minutes cooking time per pound for whole fish under 2 pounds

8 minutes cooking time per pound for whole fish under 5 pounds

6 minutes cooking time per pound for whole fish over 5 pounds

- Poach fish in water at a bare simmer; to be sure it is cooked, use a fork to part the meat and check that it is opaque all the way to the bone. (This technique can be used to check doneness of fish cooked by methods other than poaching. Test it early on; fish cooks very quickly.) Drain the fish on a wire cake-cooking rack lined with paper towels. Remove the skin by slitting it down the center of the back and peeling it off while the fish is still warm.

HANDLING RAW FISH

- To remove the skin, start at the tail end. Hold the tail firmly in one hand. Use a knife with a thin, flexible blade; with the blade held almost parallel to the counter, work your way toward the head with a sawing motion. (You can use the skin and bones for making a fish broth to use as a foundation for a fish sauce.)
- The most effective way of finding hidden bones in uncooked fish is to run your fingertips from the head end down to the tail. Remove small bones with your fingers or tweezers.
- If you have to freeze raw fish, put it in a well-rinsed milk carton or similar container, fill the container with water and freeze immediately.
- Do not defrost frozen fish fillets for poaching or breaded fish fillets for frying before cooking them. However, whole fish and fish to be broiled, pan-fried, or deep-fat fried should be completely thawed; if the fish is not fully defrosted, the outside will be cooked before the center. Dry the fish thoroughly on paper towels before cooking or fat will splatter over the stove.

FLAMING FOODS

- It is easier to flame brandy and other spirits if they are heated first in a small saucepan. Think of pouring the flames rather than the heated alcohol over the dish. Pour slowly and do not shake the pan, or the flames will be extinguished immediately, leaving behind the taste of raw alcohol.

FLOUR

- Flours cannot be used interchangeably, so recipes should be followed carefully.
- Whole wheat flour, rye, buckwheat, and other flours are all heavier than all-purpose flour. These flours, and cornmeal, are

almost always lightened in recipes by being combined with all-purpose flour. Sift flour to be used for baking to aerate and lighten it.

THE FOOD PROCESSOR

- The food processor is a kitchen "must." It replaces dozens of gadgets and performs many of the grinding, pureeing, chopping, and slicing chores that used to take up major preparation time when cooking. A top-of-the-line mini food processor can be perfectly adequate for a kitchen where most of the cooking is for a couple who only have a few friends dropping in from time to time. Excellent manuals accompany all models and makes.

FORTIFIED WINES

- Madeira, Marsala, sherry, and white vermouth are among the many fortified wines that are extremely useful to have on hand. They keep almost indefinitely and their tastes are so concentrated that just a drop or two will bring a flavor into focus and transform a ho-hum dish into a superb one.

FREEZING

- When freezing foods in jars or rigid containers, allow ½-inch headspace for expansion.
- Freeze liquid preparations such as soups and sauces in plastic freezer bags and stack them in the freezer like the pages of a book; they will take up less space than when packed in boxes.
- Make sauces that are to be frozen slightly thinner than usual because there will be some loss of liquid in the freezer.
- Label and date all foods you put into the freezer and keep a current list of the freezer's contents—or some foods may get overlooked until they are past their prime.

◾ SERVING FRUIT

- Think beyond a hollowed-out melon shell to a halved pineapple as a container for fruit salad; halved oranges and lemons with their centers removed are the ideal size for individual servings of assorted berries.
- For a grand occasion, set the fruit-filled shell on a mound of shaved ice and decorate it with a tiny rosebud.
- Unusual containers also work well; the most spectacular are the massive brandy snifters florists use for making arrangements.

◾ FRYING

- If you chill food thoroughly before frying it, its fibers will be so tightly contracted that the fat cannot penetrate into the food.
- Use 2 forks to dip foods in egg and breadcrumb coating and into batters—it is less messy than using your fingers.
- If you wait until you are ready to cook before dredging foods in flour or breadcrumbs or dipping them in batter, the coating will not become soggy.
- Never fill deep-fat frying pans more than half full so the fat will not spill over the edge when the food is added to the pan.
- Deep-fried foods *must* be cooked at 375 degrees. If the fat is too hot, the outside will be cooked before the inside; if the temperature falls below 340 degrees, the fat will penetrate between the coating and the food itself, with disastrous results. If you do much deep-fat frying, a deep-fat thermometer is an essential piece of equipment.
- Deep-fry a few pieces of food at a time. Don't crowd the pan or steam will be trapped and the fat will become waterlogged, which will prevent the foods from browning and becoming crisp.
- Cook batter-coated shrimp and other small pieces of food directly in the deep fat. If you use a deep-frying wire basket, the batter tends to catch in the mesh and get detached from the food.

- Drain all fried foods on a wire cake-cooling rack lined with paper towels. Do not pile them on top of each other or they will become soggy.
- Serve all fried foods on paper doilies. The paper will absorb any remaining fat and the eye appeal fully repays the small additional effort and cost.

FRENCH FRIES

- When making fresh french fries, dry the cut raw potatoes on paper towels, wrap them in a kitchen towel, and put them in the freezer for half an hour. For best results, the potatoes should be very cold and very dry before frying. Fry in deep fat until they begin to color, then remove the basket from the fat. Reheat the fat to 375 degrees and reimmerse the basket of potatoes slowly. Continue frying until they are crisp and brown. Drain them in a single layer on wire racks lined with paper towels and sprinkle lightly with salt.
- This technique of twice-frying is Chinese in origin; it makes the batter crisp without overcooking the food.

GARLIC

- To peel garlic cloves with ease, smash them lightly with the flat side of a cleaver or the bottom of a small heavy saucepan.
- When chopping garlic, sprinkle a little salt on the chopping board afterward; it will pick up the garlic juice.

GELATIN

- Cut aspic and any preparations containing gelatin with a wet knife; serve them with a spoon dipped into cold water.
- All foods made with gelatin are best eaten the day they are made or they lose their texture and become increasingly rubbery.
- Never let gelatin boil, or when it cools it will form strings and lose its ability to set.

FRESH GINGER

- Keep fresh gingerroot in the freezer and slice off pieces as needed.

GLAZING FOODS

- To give breads and pastry an attractively golden crust, stir together 1 egg yolk and 2 tablespoons cold milk. Use a pastry brush to glaze the surface with this mixture just before baking.
- To enhance open fruit tarts, brush yellow and green fruits with hot strained apricot preserves. Use warm currant jelly to glaze red fruits and black grapes.
- To glaze onions and carrots, sauté them in hot butter and sprinkle them with a couple of teaspoons of granulated sugar.

GUACAMOLE

- To prevent guacamole from darkening, put the avocado pit in the prepared mixture and cover the surface with a thin layer of mayonnaise to exclude the air. Immediately before serving, discard the pit and stir the mayonnaise into the guacamole.

HEATING PLATES

- Heating the plates makes all the difference to a well-cooked meal, as all good restaurants know, since food cools very quickly when served on a cold surface. It is very little trouble to preheat the oven to 350 degrees and warm the plates in it for a few minutes.

HERBS

- To keep the flavor. and color of herbs and spices as long as possible, store them in a cool, dark place.
- When substituting fresh herbs for dried, triple the quantity.
- To keep fresh herbs, put them in ice cube trays, cover them with cold water, and freeze them. When ready to use, melt a cube and you will have "fresh" herbs.
- Smell dried herbs and spices to determine their freshness. If there is no aroma, throw them out and buy a new supply. Suppliers claim that herbs and spices should be replaced every six months.

HOLLANDAISE SAUCE

- Don't be afraid of hollandaise. The secrets of success: invest in a heavy saucepan so that you can control the heat precisely, and don't allow the egg yolks to get too hot.
- To reheat hollandaise sauce, put it in a pan of hot, but not boiling, water and stir it so that the heat will be evenly distributed. Hollandaise and similar butter-based sauces can be kept warm in a wide-necked Thermos flask.
- If you plan to brown hollandaise sauce under the broiler, stir in 1 tablespoon cornstarch dissolved in 3 tablespoons cream for each cup of sauce. This will prevent the sauce from separating.

ICED TEA

- If iced tea turns cloudy, add a little boiling water to make it clear again.

KITCHEN PARAPHERNALIA

- Part of the many pleasures of working in the kitchen is that there are endless fads, trends, and fashions in food demanding that you invest in an ice-cream maker, a bread maker, a fondue pot—or something as yet not dreamed of. Space restrictions may curb your passions, but it can be fun to yield to temptation sometimes. Even if you only make waffles twice a year, the cost of the waffle maker may turn out to be less than the check for going out to brunch a couple of times.

KNIVES

- A chef's knife with an 8-inch blade is essential. Carbon steel holds the sharpest edge, though it will stain if used to cut acid fruit or tomatoes. (It is easy to clean with scouring powder.) Never put a carbon steel knife in the dishwasher—it will become stained, lose its edge, and never be itself again.
- Slice citrus fruits, onions, and avocados with a stainless steel knife. A 4-inch blade is the most useful size.
- Serrated knives are useful because they cut cleanly without squashing the goods. Use a large one for slicing crusty bread or cakes and a smaller one for slicing tomatoes.
- Use a knife with a thin, flexible blade for filleting fish. It is more sensitive than a firm blade and you will be able to reach closer to the bone.
- Buy a carving knife and fork. You will find the long fork will be very handy. The carving knife, on the other hand, may be used only once a year to carve the turkey. The chef's knife, of course, can also double as a carving knife.
- Keep knives on a rack, if possible, rather than in kitchen drawers where the blades can both do and receive damage.

LEEKS

- When washing leeks, cut off the root and the upper two-thirds of the green stem. Make a cut about 3 inches from the root and draw the knife to the top of the leaves; then make a cut perpendicular to it through the leaves. By separating the leaves you will be able to wash away sand and grit more easily.

■ LEFTOVERS

- If you are planning to have leftovers from a roast, slice the meat off from both ends, leaving the rarer center for other uses.
- Wrap and chill leftover cooked foods as soon as possible.
- Reheat leftover cooked meats and vegetables in a microwave oven or stir-fry them in a wok. They need only be *reheated*—not recooked.
- Add mustard, horseradish, capers, herbs, spices, lemon juice, or a freshly cooked vegetable to leftovers to brighten the taste of the preparation.
- It is better to add various leftovers to several new dishes rather than emptying the refrigerator in one impulsive sweep and combining everything in a casserole. Ingenuity rather than enthusiasm pays off here.

■ LEMON JUICE

- To obtain a small amount of fresh lemon juice, make a hole at one end of a lemon. Insert your thumb to enlarge the hole and squeeze out the required amount of juice. Seal the opening with butter.

■ MISSING A LID?

- To make a lid for an oval or oddly shaped pan, heat the pan on a surface burner and cover it with a piece of wax paper or aluminum foil. Press the paper lightly over the rim. An outline of the pan will be formed. Cut the paper with scissors, following the outline, and place the paper lid so that it is touching the surface of the food.

▪ LIVERS

- Save the livers from chickens and other poultry in the freezer until there are enough to make a pâté or to fry with some onions and add to a bowl of spaghetti.

▪ LOBSTER

- When buying live lobsters, select those that look lively in the tank and thrash about when taken from the water. Keep them enclosed in the bag in which they were purchased. In theory they can survive for 12 hours in the refrigerator, but they rarely do, so cook them as soon as possible.
- A 1½-pound lobster is usually sufficient for one person. It can be boiled or steamed in 18 minutes.
- To remove excess water from a boiled lobster, plunge the point of a sharp knife between the eyes and hold the lobster upside down to drain. To prevent the tail from curling, tuck the tip under a heavy chopping block until it cools.
- To serve lobsters, turn them on their backs and cut them lengthwise with a heavy knife or cleaver.

▪ MAYONNAISE

- Use half salad oil and half olive oil for making mayonnaise at home. If you use all olive oil, it has a dominant flavor that limits the mayonnaise's uses.
- Homemade mayonnaise will curdle if the oil is added too quickly. Add the oil a little at a time. If it still separates, or fails to thicken, put an egg yolk and a teaspoon of prepared mustard in a small bowl. Use a wire whisk to beat in the curdled mayonnaise, a tablespoon at a time.
- Stir a tablespoon of mayonnaise into casseroles at the last minute to give flavor and body to a simple sauce.

MEASURING

LIQUID INGREDIENTS
- Use a glass measuring cup and read at eye level.

DRY INGREDIENTS
- Use a dry metal or plastic cup or spoon. Sift the flour or sugar into the cup placed on a piece of wax paper. Level the ingredients in the cup with the back of a knife blade or metal spatula to obtain an accurate measurement.

STICKY INGREDIENTS (HONEY, MOLASSES, AND CORN AND OTHER SYRUPS)
- Put 2 tablespoons of oil or water into a glass measuring cup, roll it around to coat the sides evenly, then pour the oil back into its container or tip out the water. Measure the ingredient. It will slide out of the measuring cup without sticking to the sides (and the cup will be easy to wash).

MEATS

- Remove the transparent wrappings from meat and poultry bought from the supermarket. Wrap the meat or poultry loosely in wax paper or foil to increase its refrigerator life.
- The less ground meat is handled, the lighter it will be. To make even lighter hamburgers, add a tablespoon or two of cold water or red wine. Shape meat patties and hamburgers with wet hands. Ground meat should be eaten within 2 days of being purchased.
- Meat loaf and pâté always taste better when made from two or three meats—veal, ham, and pork or beef, for instance—rather than a single meat.
- Dry meats with paper towels before frying or they will not brown.
- Do not salt meat before frying it. The salt causes the blood to rise to the surface and be lost in the hot fat, and the loss of blood makes the meat dry and stringy and likely to stick to the pan. Wait until the meat is turned before salting it.

- Cook tough meats in a liquid; cook tender meats by dry heat, either by roasting or broiling.
- To test the doneness of meat, press it with your finger. The more "done" it is, the greater the resistance.

LAMB

- When buying a leg of lamb, approximately one third of the weight will be bone. A 6-pound leg of lamb will yield approximately 4 pounds of meat. Allow ⅓ to ½ pound of lamb per person for lamb cooked without the bone; with the bone in, allow ½ to ¾ pound of meat per person.

VEAL

- Veal for scaloppine should be cut across the grain.
- Select veal by its color. The pinker the veal, the older it is and the tougher it will be.
- Pound veal flat between two pieces of wax paper with a cleaver or mallet, being careful not to tear it.

MELBA TOAST

- To make melba toast, toast sliced bread and cut each slice in half vertically. Arrange the halves with the soft sides facing the heating element in the broiler and broil until lightly browned.

MERINGUE

- When making meringues, do not beat the egg whites so stiffly that they can be cut with a knife; beat them just until they are firm enough to support the weight of a whole egg in its shell.
- Add ¼ cup sugar for each egg white when preparing meringues.
- Do not attempt to cook meringue on a wet or humid day; it will absorb the moisture from the air and become soggy.

THE MICROWAVE OVEN

- The larger models that put forth 650 watts are the most useful kind, but there is no real standardization where microwave ovens are concerned. If you have a small one, you will find yourself cooking with the equivalent of a very low flame; if speed is what you need, then you should buy the big one.
- Unless you have kept the manufacturer's documents that came with the microwave oven, it is very hard to discover its wattage. You can, however, figure it out. Place an 8-ounce cup of water in your oven and microwave on High for 3 minutes. If the water boils, your microwave is at least 650 watts.
- Microwave/convection combination ovens are ideal because they offer the advantage of both regular and microwave cooking.

MOLDS

- When preparing cold foods, dip the mold in cold water before filling it, or brush the inside with vegetable oil. If the food does not slide out easily, dip the mold up to the rim in hot, not boiling, water.

MUSHROOMS

- Do not soak mushrooms in cold water or they will become waterlogged. Wipe them clean with a damp cloth.
- Save mushroom stems to use in making stocks and broths.
- When mushrooms are plentiful and good, buy a whole box and fry them quickly in butter. Store them in small batches in zip-lock bags in the freezer. They will defrost in a couple of minutes in the microwave.

NUTS

- To remove the skins from almonds, drop them in boiling water and leave for 5 seconds. Rub the nuts between your finger and thumb and the skins will slip off easily.

- To toast almonds or other nuts, spread them in a single layer on a flat pan. Bake in a preheated 350-degree oven for 8 to 10 minutes or until they are lightly browned. Stir with a fork once or twice while toasting to distribute the heat evenly.
- Nuts will stay fresh longer if stored in a covered jar in the refrigerator. It is useful to keep a variety of nuts—pine nuts, almonds, walnuts, and mixed nuts—in containers in the refrigerator, both for cooking and eating.
- When chopping nuts in the food processor or blender, add a tablespoon of flour to prevent them from forming clumps.

OLIVES

- Cover olives with water or olive oil to prevent them from drying out in the refrigerator.

OMELETTE PANS

- You cannot make an omelette without a well-seasoned cast-iron pan that is used for no other purpose. (A Calphalon or other Teflon-coated surface is an acceptable substitute.) The ideal pan measures 7½ inches across the top. If the pan is too large, the layer of eggs will be too thin and will cook too quickly. For the opposite reason, if you cook a 4-egg omelette in too small a pan, the omelette will be too thick to fold correctly. (See *Cast-Iron Pans* for instructions on seasoning the pan.)

ONION

- Cut a cross in the root end of whole onions so that they will cook evenly and the center will not fall from the outer part.
- It is often quicker to chop just one onion by hand rather than having the additional chore of washing a gadget or food processor.

- Peel the onion, set it on a chopping board, and cut it in half lengthwise with an 8-inch chef's knife. Place it, cut side down, with the root end pointing to the left, if you are right-handed. Make a series of ⅛-inch or ¼-inch horizontal cuts, depending on whether the onion is to be finely or coarsely chopped. Keep the slices attached at the root end. Holding the knife perpendicular to the board, then make a series of cuts running from the root and to the opposite end. Finally, slice the onion vertically to dice it.
- Scrubbing the chopping board with dry mustard helps to remove the oniony smell.

ORANGE AND LEMON RIND

- To remove orange and lemon rind from a grater, bang the grater briskly on the counter or brush the rind from the grater with a pastry brush.

PARSLEY

- Store parsley and other fresh herbs in a covered glass jar in the refrigerator.
- It is easier to chop parsley when it is dry. After chopping, wrap it into a ball in the corner of a kitchen towel and run cold water through it to remove sand and grit.
- Keep a supply of chopped parsley in a covered jar in the refrigerator to use as a last-minute garnish.

PASTA TIPS

- Always add pasta to boiling water a little at a time so that the water remains at a rolling boil.
- Always cook pasta in a large quantity of vigorously boiling salted water. Add a tablespoon of vegetable oil to the water to

prevent the pasta from sticking to itself. At the end of the cooking time, add a cup of cold water to the pot to halt the cooking. Drain the pasta and serve it on hot plates.

- If you keep a supply of various store-bought, fresh-frozen pastas in the freezer, including ravioli and fettuccini, along with three or four cartons of prepared sauces, you will never be at a loss for a quick meal. Remember that partially cooked noodles can also be frozen.

PASTRY

- Do not bake pastry in the same oven with a roast, or the steam in the oven will prevent the pastry from becoming crisp and flaky.
- I always put an old-fashioned funnel-like device in a double-crusted pie while it is baking. These oddly shaped items can be found in specialty cookware stores (or country flea markets); their purpose is to direct the steam through the top crust to prevent it from becoming soggy.

BAKING PASTRY SHELLS "BLIND"
- Fit the rolled pastry into the pie plate, fitting it well into the corners, before trimming. Cover the pastry with a piece of oiled foil, with the oiled side against the pastry. Cover the foil with a single layer of dried beans or pastry weights and fold the edges of the foil over the rim of the pie plate. Bake in a preheated 375-degree oven for 10 minutes or until the pastry has "set." Discard the foil. (The beans or weights can be reused idefinitely.)

    Prick the bottom of the pastry with a fork to prevent air bubbles from forming. Prick the sides to prevent them from sliding down. Return the pastry shell to the oven and bake until crisp. (The time will vary from 8 to 15 minutes, depending on the type of pastry.)

PASTRY BRUSH

- To make a pastry brush flexible, always wet it in cold water and squeeze out the water from the bristles before each use. A paint brush (unused, of course!) can be substituted for a pastry brush.

PÂTÉ

- If you weight cooked pâtés while still warm with unopened cans of food, you will be able to slice them easily when cooled. Almost all pâtés should be allowed to rest in the refrigerator, with the weight still in place, for 24 hours before cutting. Serve them at room temperature.

PEANUT OIL

- Peanut oil reaches the highest temperature of all cooking oils and is the first choice for Chinese cooking and deep-fat frying.

PEAS

- If you keep a big bag of frozen peas in the freezer, you can add a handful to a sauce or provide a little extra color to all kinds of dishes. The peas cook in a moment in a really hot sauce.

PESTO

- Make a large batch of pesto sauce and keep it on hand, chilled, for a last-minute pasta supper. Cover leftover pesto with a thin film of olive oil to prevent the air from discoloring the sauce. When you are ready to use it again, stir the oil into the pesto.

PINEAPPLE

- To test the ripeness of a pineapple, smell the base. It should be redolent of sweetness. If a leaf can be pulled out easily, the fruit will be ripe and ready to eat.

POTS AND PANS

- Buy the very best quality (this always means the most expensive) pots, pans, and skillets that you can afford. Cheap stuff and castoffs from other people's kitchens can be a terrible liability. Kitchen tools are as important to a cook as a tennis racquet is to a star athlete, a Stradivarius to a violinist, or the proper instruments to a surgeon. Buying cookware is no time to economize.
- Pots and pans must be heavy so that the heat is evenly distributed. They should sit squarely on the burner and have tight-fitting lids that will hold in the steam, when necessary.
- You will need some microwave-safe pots and bowls (with lids).
- It is worth investing in a wok and a big pot for cooking spaghetti. The wok will enable you to cook a little meal in no time. (Note that I say cook, not prepare. It takes far longer to cut the ingredients than to cook them.) The big pasta pot could well be a multipurpose casserole that is as useful for cooking vegetables or for making a large quantity of soup, as it is for its true purpose: providing a stew, braised chicken, or risotto for a crowd of friends.

POTATOES

- Maine and Long Island potatoes are used primarily for mashing and frying. Use Idaho potatoes for baking and small new California or Red Bliss potatoes for making potato salad.
- If you peel potatoes in advance, put them in a bowl of lightly salted water in the refrigerator to prevent them from discoloring.
- To prepare old potatoes, peel them and cook them in already boiling salted water. To prepare new potatoes, leave unpeeled and place them in cold salted water; bring to a boil and cook to the desired tenderness. (If you wish, you can slip the skins off easily once the potatoes are cool enough to handle.)

▉ RICE

- Do not raise the lid or stir rice as it cooks, or the grains will stick together.
- To reheat rice, spread it in a buttered shallow dish. Dot the surface with butter and season to taste with salt and pepper. Cover with aluminum foil and place in a preheated 350-degree oven for 15 minutes, or cover with transparent wrap and reheat it in the microwave on High (100 percent power) for 4 minutes. You can also reheat plain boiled rice very successfully in a steamer. Stir the hot rice with a fork to make it fluffy.

▉ ROASTING

- Oven-roast large pieces of meat, whole poultry, or whole fish to obtain a firm exterior and a tender moist interior.
- The larger a roast, the longer its keeping potential. To extend its refrigerator life, marinate it and turn it in the marinade every day for up to 5 days.
- Roasts are always cooked uncovered. Those weighing less than 4 pounds should be basted every 30 minutes with the pan drippings to prevent the meat's becoming dry. (Do not try to roast a piece of meat weighing less than 3 pounds—it will become dry before it is fully cooked.)

TIMES AND TEMPERATURES

- Roasts cooked at 350 or even 300 degrees stay moister than meats cooked at higher tempertaures. There is no need to sear the meat initially. Allow about 20 minutes per pound as a rough rule, and rely on a meat thermometer, inserted into the deepest part of the meat, to establish the internal temperature. (Be sure it is not touching a bone.)

    For rare beef: allow 18 minutes per pound at 350 degrees (internal temperature 115 degrees)

    For medium: allow 20 minutes per pound at 350 degrees (internal temperature 130 degrees)

For well done: allow 25 minutes per pound at 350 degrees (internal temperature 150 degrees)

- A thin, flat piece of meat cooks more quickly than a square, chunky block of meat of the same weight.
- Aged beef takes less time to cook than unaged.
- Meat continues to cook in its own internal heat for at least 5 minutes after being removed from the oven, so to prevent rare meat from becoming medium-rare by the time it is served, err on the side of serving it slightly underdone.
- All roasts benefit from resting, covered in foil, for about 15 minutes after being removed from the oven. This allows the juices that have risen to the surface to redistribute themselves evenly in the meat, making it firmer and easier to carve.
- Suggested temperatures on most charts and thermometers are usually too high.

For beef and lamb, cook to 115 degrees for rare; to 120 degrees for medium-rare; and to 130 degrees for medium.

Cook veal to 155 degrees; pork to 180 degrees; and poultry to 180 degrees.

ROASTING RACK

- Foods to be roasted should always be set on a rack to permit the free circulation of hot air. If the roast is put directly in the pan, the underside will fry and become overcooked. If you don't have a roasting rack, use a wire cake-cooling rack set inside or over a baking pan.

ROLLING PIN

- If you do not have a rolling pin, a tightly capped wine bottle filled with iced water makes a good temporary substitute.

■ SAFFRON

- Soak saffron threads in ¼ cup hot, not boiling, water to cover for 5 minutes. Add the soaking water to the dish along with the saffron.

■ SALAD DRESSINGS

- There are 5 basic ingredients in an oil and vinegar dressing: oil, vinegar, salt, pepper, and mustard. The mustard thickens the dressing and holds it together. Use 1 to 2 parts vinegar to 5 to 6 parts oil, as a general rule of thumb, for the proportions. To make ½ cup you would need 6 tablespoons of oil and 2 tablespoons of vinegar. Add the seasonings to taste.

OIL

- Select the most expensive virgin olive oil you can afford. Buy only a small quantity because the oil will become rancid if you do not use it within a few weeks. Keep the oil at room temperature. If it is chilled, it hardens and loses its flavor.

VINEGAR

- The more flavorful the vinegar, the more its taste will dominate the dressing. Though balsamic, raspberry, and other vinegars have their place, it is useful to keep on hand a good all-purpose wine vinegar, such as Dessaux Fils tarragon vinegar.

OTHER INGREDIENTS

- I like to use coarse kosher salt and freshly ground black pepper.
- A pungent-tasting Dijon mustard should be kept in the refrigerator.
- A clove or two of crushed garlic will give a dressing character.
- Replace the vinegar in your dressing with lemon juice or white vermouth for variety.
- Add some chopped fresh herbs, of any variety except rosemary, which doesn't work because its leaves are too spiky. Use common sense about the quantity—you can hardly add too much.

- Ideally, make only enough dressing for immediate use. Realistically, if you make three times the quantity, you will probably use it within the next few days. Keep it, covered, at room temperature or in the refrigerator.
- Add a drop or two of hot, not boiling, water to oil and vinegar dressings to prevent them from separating.

▪ SALAD GREENS

- There are so many interesting new varieties of greens on the market that it is a pity to remain in a rut and keep buying the same ones.
- To store lettuce and keep it crisp, put the head (unwashed) in a plastic bag along with a paper towel soaked in cold water.
- Prepare all salad greens as close as possible to the time when they are to be eaten. Some people like to cut the leaves; others tear them. Whichever school you follow, do not prepare greens more than 24 hours in advance or the stems will become "rusty."
- To remove the core from a lettuce, cut a V-shaped notch in the base.
- Dry all salad greens thoroughly, either by patting dry or whirling in a salad spinner, so that the dressing will cling to the leaves, not slide like water off a duck's back.
- If you are preparing a salad in advance, put the dressing in the bottom of the bowl, cover it with a piece of transparent wrap, and pile the salad on top. When you are ready to eat, just pull off the wrap and toss the greens in the dressing.
- Don't believe those who tell you that you should never wash a wooden salad bowl. Oil left in the bowl becomes rancid and will spoil the next salad made in it.

▪ SALT

- Cold food needs more salt than hot food.
- None of the many remedies for foods that are too salty really

work if the oversalting is serious, but adding a raw potato (or two) late in the cooking time (to be removed before serving) can moderate oversalting to make the food taste perfectly acceptable. You may want to warn guests to taste their food before they add seasonings.

- Many recipes suggest adding salt to eggplant slices "to draw out the bitter juices." I have never found an eggplant that tasted bitter and believe that adding a layer of salt makes the preparation altogether too salty. This may be another of the culinary myths that are perpetuated from generation to generation.
- It *is* a good idea to sprinkle salt over cucumber and zucchini slices to make the slices crisp when they are to be served raw.

▨ SAUCES

- To prepare a simple sauce, use the same amount of butter as flour. A useful formula to note: I tablespoon of flour combined with I tablespoon of butter or vegetable oil will thicken I cup of liquid to the consistency of a thin sauce.
- To remove the fat from a sauce's surface, place the pan half on and half off the source of heat. The fat drifts to the cooler side and can be lifted off easily with a shallow-bowled spoon.
- To thicken a sauce at the last minute, blend together equal amounts of butter and flour. (You can do this in the palm of a reasonably clean hand. Start with 2 teaspoons of butter and use your thumb to work in 2 teaspoons of flour.) Add a speck of the mixture at a time to the hot sauce, stirring with a wire whisk. The sauce will thicken immediately.
- Sauces can also be thickened by stirring in cornstarch dissolved in cold water. Add I tablespoon cornstarch dissolved in 2 tablespoons cold water per cup of boiling liquid.
- If you can find arrowroot in a specialty store, use it instead of cornstarch for thickening fruit sauces, as it produces a much clearer sauce.
- Avoid adding hollandaise, béarnaise, or similar emulsified sauces to very hot food because they may themselves become so hot

that they separate. Let these sauces cool to room temperature before using them.

- To prevent a skin from forming on hot sauces and cooked custards, cover the surface with transparent wrap so that all the air is excluded.
- To prevent a skin from forming on sauces when heated in the oven, reserve a portion of the sauce, heat it in a small pan and spoon it over the food just before serving.

SAUSAGES

- To prevent bratwurst and similar sausages from squirting in your face when you eat them, hold the sausage steady with a fork and cut it immediately behind, not in front of, the fork.

SHALLOTS

- Store shallots in the refrigerator; they will last longer than at room temperature.

SHELLFISH

CLAMS
- To open clams, slip the clam knife through the shell on the side opposite the hinge. Release the clam from its moorings so that it will be easier to eat on the half shell.
- If clams are very muddy, soak them for an hour in a bowl of cold salted water. Use 1 tablespoon of salt to each quart of water.
- *Never use clams whose shells do not open after cooking.*

MUSSELS
- Farm-raised mussels, now widely available in stores that sell fish,

are very clean and do not require extensive scrubbing. If you are using mussels from the seashore, scrub the mussel shells thoroughly to remove all traces of grit, and remove the "beards" with a sharp knife.

- Never use mussels whose shells are already open or whose shells do not open after cooking.

OYSTERS

- When opening an oyster, protect your hand with an oven mitt. Use an oyster knife and insert the blade at the hinge. This will release the internal pressure.
- If you cannot get an oyster open, pop it into the microwave for a couple of seconds, just until the shell opens. Do not leave it too long or it will cook.
- To test the freshness of an oyster, touch it with the point of a knife or add a drop of lemon juice. If it does not recoil, discard it.
- *Never* use oysters whose shells do not open after cooking.

▨ SHOPPING LISTS

- When preparing a shopping list, divide it into categories, that is, list all the vegetables, dairy products, and so on in separate columns. You will save a lot of shopping time and be much less likely to forget anything.

▨ SILVER TRAYS

- Line silver trays with lettuce leaves when serving acid foods so that the acid does not come in contact with the silver.
- Do not carve on a silver tray. Steel is stronger than silver and will leave cut marks on the tray.

■ SOUP

- If you make soup ahead of time, reheat only the quantity that you anticipate will be eaten. Soups that contain meats, vegetables, rice, or pasta will be overcooked if they are reheated two or three times.
- Almost all homemade soups can be frozen successfully, except those that contain egg yolks and cream, or potatoes. Tomato soup tends to separate if it is frozen.
- To retain a soup's freshness, freeze it as soon as possible after it has been cooked. Add a little extra seasoning because some of the taste is lost after freezing.
- It is a good idea to freeze soup in portions for 2 people that can be quickly reheated in a saucepan or the microwave. Use freezer zip-lock bags that are easy to stack in the freezer; separate the bags with pieces of paper so they do not stick to each other.

■ SOUR CREAM

- Add sour cream to cooked preparations at the last moment. If it is allowed to boil, it will separate and curdle.

■ SPICES

- To obtain the fullest flavor from spices such as paprika, cumin, curry, and chili powder, sauté the spice for a moment or two in hot butter or oil before adding to the dish.

■ SPINACH

- Cook fresh spinach in a covered saucepan over low heat, using only the water that clings to the leaves after you have washed it thoroughly.

STEAKS THAT DON'T CURL UP

- When cooking minute steaks or thin slices of ham, liver, or other meats, cut 2 or 3 notches around the edge of each one to prevent it from curling as the surrounding membrane contracts with the heat.

STEAMING

- Water always becomes steam at 212 degrees, so there is no advantage in turning up the heat under a steamer pan. The food will not cook any more rapidly—though the water will boil away very quickly. Maintain a slow, steady boil and be sure the pan lid fits tightly.

STRAWBERRIES

- Rinse strawberries quickly under cold running water and pat them dry very gently with paper towels. Do *not* immerse them in water or they will become waterlogged.
- Try to buy (or pick) fresh strawberries after a day when the sun has been shining; the fruit will be much sweeter.
- Wait to remove strawberries' stems until just before you are ready to serve them; once hulled, they spill out their juice and soften.

STUFFING

- Do not put hot stuffing inside poultry until just before you are ready to cook it. Stuffing deteriorates very rapidly in this environment, especially if it contains elements such as eggs or giblets that are not fully cooked.
- Avoid packing stuffing too densely into the cavity: leave room for it to expand as it cooks.

- Extra stuffing can be frozen either cooked or uncooked. Just be sure to freeze it promptly.

THERMOMETERS

- The only way to be really sure food is at the correct temperature is to check it with the appropriate thermometer. Oven temperatures are notoriously inaccurate and when cooking meats an internal thermometer is the only reliable guide. Invest in a meat thermometer first, then an oven thermometer, and add a deep-fat thermometer and a candy thermometer as you need them.

TOMATOES

- Don't slice tomatoes until you are ready to use them—the seeds drop out of the slices and the juice makes the plate watery.

TOMATO PASTE

- Transfer tomato paste from an opened can to a covered glass jar and store it in the refrigerator. A small amount of tomato paste added to homemade tomato soups and sauces will give them strength and body.

VANILLA BEAN

- When using a whole vanilla bean, split it in half lengthwise and scrape out the black seeds into the other ingredients—usually milk or cream. The vanilla pod itself is heated with the milk and discarded after it has imparted its flavor.

VEGETABLES

- If you are preparing vegetables in advance, parboil them and drain them in a colander. Rinse immediately under cold running water to stop their cooking and to preserve the bright colors. Reheat them in boiling salted water or sauté them in hot butter just before serving.
- If you split the stems of broccoli, the spears will cook evenly.
- Trim the outer leaves from brussels sprouts and cut a cross in the base of each one so that they will cook evenly.

WATERCRESS

- Immerse watercress, leaves down, in a bowl of cold water until you are ready to use it.

WHISK

- A small wire whisk is as vital a piece of kitchen equipment as a sharp knife. Its use guarantees that all sauces will be smooth and free from lumps and other miseries, and it is also invaluable for making salad dressings.

WHITE VERMOUTH

- A small quantity of white vermouth imparts a lot of flavor and can be used as a substitute for a large quantity of white wine. Replace 1 cup white wine with ¼ cup white vermouth and ¾ cup chicken broth or water.

■ WINE FOR COOKING

- When choosing wine for cooking, select one that tastes good— though it is not necessary to have the finest vintage. A wine that is not good enough for drinking will taste still worse when it has been cooked and will spoil the dish. It is always better to use beef or chicken broth than inferior wine for cooking.
- It can sometimes be nice to use the same wine for cooking as for drinking with dinner.
- If there is leftover wine, add it to commercial unpasteurized vinegar; it will greatly improve the vinegar's taste.

■ WINE FOR DRINKING

- As a general rule, a bottle of wine will serve 4 people happily or 6 people once. On certain occasions, a half bottle of wine at each place setting can be a way to go. The better you know people, the more wine they drink. The more wine they drink, the better you get to know them.
- All red wines except Beaujolais should be served at room temperature and uncorked an hour before they are served. White wines, champagne, and Beaujolais are chilled for 1 to 2 hours before serving. Don't serve champagne too cold—it will give you a headache!
- Don't put white wine in the refrigerator, forget about it, take it out, then change your mind, and put it back again. Too many abrupt changes in temperature will cause the wine to deteriorate.
- Wineglasses should be large enough to invite guests to smell the wine's aroma; all wines, even lesser ones, benefit from being served in a big clear glass that gives the wine a chance to breathe. For this reason the glasses, whatever their size, should be only half filled.

PART TWO

RECIPE ROUNDUP

I

STARTERS AND SMALL MEALS

ARTICHOKES WITH GREBICHE DRESSING

STUFFED ARTICHOKES

STUFFED MUSHROOMS

MARINATED MUSHROOMS

TOMATO TARTARE

STUFFED CHERRY TOMATOES

AVOCADO HALVES WITH CRABMEAT

PROSCIUTTO WITH FIGS

GUACAMOLE

BASIC DIP

CHEDDAR CHEESE SPREAD

TAPENADE

SAUTÉED ALMONDS

GREEN FETTUCCINI WITH PESTO AND ZUCCHINI

GREEN FETTUCCINI WITH PROSCIUTTO AND CREAM

FETTUCCINI IN A WARM BATH

LINGUINI WITH A TEMPEST OF MIXED VEGETABLES

SHINY FRESH VEGETABLES

LIVER PÂTÉ WITH VERMOUTH AND CURRANTS

FRENCH COUNTRY TERRINE

BAY SCALLOPS WITH LIME AND CREAM

MOUSSE OF SMOKED TROUT

HOT SHRIMP WITH COARSE SALT

CURRIED MUSSELS AND CUCUMBER POLONAISE

SMALL SALADS FOR TWO

MUSSEL SALAD

HERRING SALAD

CHICK-PEA SALAD

RICE SALAD

COLD PASTA SALAD

WATERCRESS AND ENDIVE SALAD

POTATO SALAD I

POTATO SALAD II

AVOCADO AND LOBSTER SALAD

APPLE AND CHEESE SALAD

RED ON RED SALAD

YELLOW ON YELLOW SALAD

GREEN ON GREEN SALAD

MELON SALAD

PEAR AND PROSCIUTTO SALAD

LICHEE AND MUSHROOM SALAD

SLICED RADISH AND MUSHROOM SALAD

COLD BEEF SALAD

ARTICHOKES WITH GREBICHE DRESSING

Serves 6

6 large globe artichokes

7 to 8 quarts water

1 tablespoon salt

Juice of ½ lemon

DRESSING

¾ cup Homemade Mayonnaise (see page 186)

¼ cup milk

1 teaspoon mild Dijon mustard

1 tablespoon olive oil

1 tablespoon wine vinegar

1 Hard-cooked Egg (see page 227), finely chopped

2 scallions, finely chopped

1 tablespoon finely chopped sweet gherkins

2 teaspoons drained capers

2 tablespoons finely chopped fresh parsley

Cut off the artichoke stems so that the artichokes will stand without tipping over. Discard the lowest row of leaves. Lay the artichokes on their sides and cut off ½ inch from the top of each one. Trim ½ inch from the tip of each leaf, using a pair of scissors.

Pour water into a large pot. Add the salt. Squeeze the lemon juice into the water. Add the artichokes. Cover the pot and cook over gentle heat for about 50 minutes. Test for doneness by pulling out a leaf; it should come away easily. Drain the artichokes upside down on paper towels spread over a wire cake-cooling rack and squeeze each one gently to remove all the water. Serve on individual plates.

Combine all the ingredients for the dressing. Serve the dressing in small individual dishes alongside the artichokes so that people can dip the leaves into the dressing.

■ STUFFED ARTICHOKES

Serves 6

6 large globe artichokes

STUFFING
½ pound pork sausage
1 small onion, finely chopped
½ cup finely chopped mushrooms
¼ cup tomato puree
1 teaspoon sage
2 tablespoons finely chopped fresh parsley
1 teaspoon salt
Freshly ground black pepper
1 cup white wine or water
3 thin slices lemon

Cook the artichokes as directed in the preceding recipe. Then, using a small teaspoon, scoop out the center "choke" carefully and discard it.

To prepare the stuffing, crumble the pork sausage into a skillet and cook until all the fat is rendered, about 5 minutes. Drain off the fat. Add the onion, mushrooms, tomato puree, sage, parsley, salt, and pepper to taste; cook over low heat for 10 minutes. Remove the skillet from the heat and allow the sausage mixture to cool slightly.

Preheat the oven to 350 degrees.

Distribute some of the sausage mixture between the leaves of the artichokes, and fill the center cavity of each with the remainder. Tie each artichoke around the middle with a piece of string to close the leaves over the stuffing. Arrange the artichokes in a large baking dish and add the wine or water and lemon slices. Cover the dish with foil and bake for 40 minutes. Uncover and serve hot or at room temperature.

STUFFED MUSHROOMS

Serves 6

1 pound white button mushrooms
4 tablespoons butter
1 small onion, finely chopped
Juice of ½ small lemon
1 tablespoon all-purpose flour
⅓ cup heavy cream
Salt
Freshly ground black pepper
2 tablespoons finely chopped fresh parsley, for garnish

Preheat the oven to 350 degrees.

Wipe the mushrooms with a damp paper towel and rinse them briefly under cold running water. Remove the stems and set aside the caps. Use a food processor to finely chop the stems and about one third of the mushroom caps.

Heat the butter in a skillet and add the onion and the chopped mushroom caps and stems; fry them over moderate heat until the mushrooms have softened, about 3 minutes. Add the lemon juice. Add the flour and stir until thick. Add the cream, season to taste with salt and pepper, and simmer gently until the mixture has thickened again, about 5 minutes.

Fill the reserved mushroom caps with the mixture. Butter a baking sheet and arrange the filled caps on it. Bake for 15 minutes. Sprinkle with the parsley and serve hot.

MARINATED MUSHROOMS

Serves 4

2 tablespoons tarragon vinegar
6 tablespoons light olive oil
Salt
Freshly ground black pepper
1 teaspoon mild mustard
¼ teaspoon dried tarragon
3 tablespoons finely chopped fresh parsley
4 scallions, thinly sliced
½ pound uniformly sized small white button mushroom caps, left whole

Make a French dressing by whisking together all of the ingredients except the mushrooms. Add the raw mushrooms, cover, and leave them to marinate in the refrigerator for 24 hours. Drain off the dressing and reserve it to use for a salad or for serving with cold vegetables. Serve the mushrooms while still cold.

■ TOMATO TARTARE

Serves 2

2 large ripe tomatoes

Salt

¼ pound sirloin steak, trimmed of all fat and freshly ground twice by the butcher

2 tablespoons finely chopped scallions

I clove garlic, finely chopped

I teaspoon Worcestershire sauce

Salt

Freshly ground black pepper

I egg white, slightly beaten

4 tablespoons finely chopped fresh parsley, for garnish

Capers, for garnish

Slice each tomato in half and remove the pulp with a teaspoon. Sprinkle the cavities with salt and invert the halves on paper towels to drain the excess juice.

Combine the uncooked ground steak with the stallions, garlic, Worcestershire sauce, salt and pepper to taste, and about half the egg white, then form it into 4 balls about the size of the tomato cavities. Roll the steak balls in the remaining egg white, then in the chopped parsley.

Place one steak tartare ball in each tomato half and garnish with capers. Cover and place in the refrigerator to chill. Serve very cold.

■ STUFFED CHERRY TOMATOES

Makes 12 cherry tomatoes

12 cherry tomatoes

BLUE CHEESE FILLING
½ cup cottage cheese
⅓ cup crumbled blue cheese
1 teaspoon grated onion
¼ teaspoon salt
Freshly ground black pepper
2 to 3 tablespoons sour cream

Prepare the tomatoes by cutting a thin slice from the top of each one and scooping out the pulp with a small spoon or a melon-ball cutter. Sprinkle the shells with salt and invert them onto a paper towel to drain for 15 minutes.

Meanwhile, combine all the ingredients for the filling in a bowl; mix thoroughly. Using a small spoon or a pastry bag fitted with a plain tube, fill the tomato shells with the blue cheese mixture. Chill before serving.

VARIATION: Goat cheese or any other soft cheese can be substituted for the blue cheese.

AVOCADO HALVES WITH CRABMEAT

Serves 2

1 large ripe avocado
Juice of ½ lemon
6 ounces fresh backfin crabmeat, picked over carefully to remove any cartilage
2 tablespoons Homemade Mayonnaise (see page 186)
1 tablespoon Dijon mustard
Pinch of salt
Freshly ground black pepper
1 Hard-cooked Egg (see page 227), finely chopped, for garnish

Cut the avocado in half and remove the pit. Carefully peel away the avocado skin and sprinkle the halves with lemon juice to prevent discoloration. Cut a thin slice from the bottom of the avocado half so it will be flat without tipping over.

Combine the crabmeat, mayonnaise, and mustard in a bowl and season to taste with salt and pepper. Divide the crabmeat mixture between the avocado halves. Garnish with chopped egg and serve chilled, but not icy cold.

NOTE: Backfin crabmeat can be found fresh almost everywhere. Don't use frozen crabmeat because it is stringy and has no taste.

PROSCIUTTO WITH FIGS

Serves 6

12 fully ripened green or black figs
12 slices prosciutto

Chill the figs before attempting to peel them. Cut off the pointed end and make 4 light cuts into the skin of the fig, cutting from top to bottom as if to divide it into quarters. Use a sharp paring knife to remove the skin, cutting as close to the surface as possible.

Roll up each slice of prosciutto. Arrange the figs and the prosciutto rolls alternately on a plate lined with fig leaves or tender lettuce leaves. No dressing is needed.

■ GUACAMOLE

Makes about 2 cups

2 medium ripe avocados
4 scallions, thinly sliced
1 teaspoon salt
2 tablespoons lime or lemon juice
A few drops Tabasco

Peel and pit the avocados and cut them into small pieces. Put the avocado pieces in a food processor or blender and add the remaining ingredients. Process until the mixture is still slightly chunky, or until it reaches the consistency you prefer. Serve with tortilla chips.

■ BASIC DIP

Makes about 1½ cups

8 ounces cream cheese
⅓ cup plain yogurt or sour cream
1 teaspoon Dijon mustard
Salt and freshly ground black pepper, to taste

Put all the ingredients in a food processor or blender and process until smooth.

◼ CHEDDAR CHEESE SPREAD

Makes about 1 ½ cups

1 pound Canadian or New York State white cheddar cheese, cut into small pieces
6 scallions, finely chopped
2 tablespoons finely chopped chives
1 teaspoon Dijon mustard
2 tablespoons butter, softened
2 tablespoons dry cocktail sherry
Dash of Tabasco or hot pepper sauce
1 teaspoon Worcestershire sauce

Put all the ingredients in the food processor or blender and process until combined. Transfer to a small bowl, cover, and refrigerate until chilled. Let the mixture come to room temperature before spreading on crackers or freshly made toast.

◼ TAPENADE

Makes ¾ cup

1 cup Greek Calamata or other, preferably wrinkled, black olives, pitted
2 2-ounce cans Portuguese anchovy fillets, with the oil from the can
1 3½-ounce can tuna (preferably Italian), drained
½ cup capers
1 teaspoon dry English mustard
1 cup light olive oil
1 tablespoon lemon juice
2 tablespoons brandy

Tapenade is made like mayonnaise. Put the olives, anchovies, tuna, capers, and mustard into the food processor or blender and process into a smooth puree. Add the oil slowly through the top, with the motor running, then add the lemon juice and brandy with the motor still on. Spoon the tapenade into a container, cover, and chill in the refrigerator for 4 hours to allow all the flavors to intermingle.

The tapenade will be fairly thin when it is first made but will thicken and become quite firm when it is chilled. Serve on crackers or freshly made toast.

SAUTÉED ALMONDS

Serves 6

3 tablespoons vegetable or peanut oil
2 cups shelled whole almonds
2 teaspoons Worcestershire sauce
Coarse kosher salt

Remove the skins from the almonds by dropping them in boiling water and then rubbing each nut between your thumb and fingers.

Heat the oil in a skillet and fry the almonds gently over moderate heat until they are nicely browned, about 5 minutes. Add the Worcestershire sauce and toss to distribute it evenly. Remove the nuts and drain them on a cake-cooling rack lined with paper towels. Roll the almonds in the salt and serve them while they are still warm.

GREEN FETTUCCINI WITH PESTO AND ZUCCHINI

Serves 2 as a first course

½ pound green fettuccini
½ cup Pesto (see page 189)
2 thin zucchini, cut into thin strips
½ cup white wine

Cook the pasta according to package directions or to taste.

While the pasta is cooking, heat the pesto very gently, so that it is just warm and will not chill the noodles.

Pour the wine in a saucepan and heat. Put the zucchini pieces in a steamer basket in the pan and steam over moderate heat for 4 minutes.

Drain the fettuccini and toss with the warm pesto and hot zucchini. Serve immediately.

GREEN FETTUCCINI WITH PROSCIUTTO AND CREAM

Serves 4 as a first course

½ pound green fettuccini
4 tablespoons unsalted butter
¼ pound prosciutto, cut into small pieces
¾ cup heavy cream
I cup shelled fresh peas, parboiled, or I cup frozen peas, defrosted
¼ cup chopped fresh chives or fresh Italian parsley
½ cup grated Parmesan cheese

Cook the pasta according to package directions or to taste.

Meanwhile, melt the butter in a skillet and heat the prosciutto gently for 3 minutes. Stir in the cream, then add the peas and heat until hot.

Drain the fettuccini. Return the pasta to the pan in which it was cooked and toss with the prosciutto mixture and chives. Serve immediately and pass the Parmesan cheese separately.

■ FETTUCCINI IN A WARM BATH

Serves 6 as a first course

1½ cups heavy cream or 1 cup crème fraîche
4 tablespoons unsalted butter
4 cloves garlic, finely chopped
1 2-ounce can flat anchovies, drained and mashed
1 fresh white truffle
Dash of cayenne pepper
1 pound fettuccini

Simmer the cream very gently until it has thickened slightly and reduced to about 1 cup, about 15 minutes. Watch it carefully because it has a great tendency to boil over. Add 2 tablespoons of the butter to the cream.

Heat the remaining 2 tablespoons butter over low heat in a small skillet and "stew" the garlic, taking great care not to let either ingredient burn. Add the garlic-flavored butter to the hot cream. Stir in the mashed anchovies. Grate the truffle and add it to the cream. Add a dash of cayenne.

Cook the pasta according to package directions or to taste.

Toss the sauce with the hot, drained fettuccini. Serve immediately.

NOTE: The sauce can be prepared in advance and reheated—cautiously—as the fettuccini cooks.

LINGUINI WITH A TEMPEST OF MIXED VEGETABLES

Serves 8 as a first course

1 pound pancetta; cooking prosciutto; fresh ham or bacon, sliced and diced (optional); or
   2 tablespoons vegetable oil

8 shallots, finely chopped

3 cloves garlic, finely chopped

2 thin carrots, peeled and diced

1 green bell pepper, cut into small strips

1 yellow bell pepper, cut into small strips

1 red bell pepper, cut into small strips

¾ pound fresh green beans, cut into 1-inch pieces

3 thin green zucchini, julienned

2 thin yellow squash, julienned

1 pound fresh peas, shelled

A few asparagus spears, cut into 1-inch pieces

1 pound plain linguini

1 pound green linguini

Salt

1 pint box cherry tomatoes, each cut in half

⅓ cup chopped fresh basil leaves

Freshly ground black pepper

1 cup freshly grated Parmesan cheese

Prepare the vegetables you have selected in advance or buy them already prepared from a salad bar. If you are using pancetta fry it in a skillet until it is hot, remove and set aside to keep warm or heat the vegetable oil. Add the shallots and garlic and fry until softened, about 3 minutes.

Cook the carrots, peppers, and green beans in boiling salted water for 5 minutes. Add the zucchini, squash, peas, and asparagus and continue cooking until each is crisp-tender and bright in color, about another 5 minutes. Drain and rinse the vegetables under cold running water until quite cold. Their color will brighten significantly.

Cook the pasta according to package directions or to taste. While the pasta is cooking, reheat the vegetables for barely 2 minutes in a large pot of boiling water. Drain the pasta and add the pancetta, shallots, garlic, and vegetables, then toss with the tomatoes and fresh basil. Season with freshly ground black pepper. Serve on warmed plates and pass the Parmesan cheese separately.

■ SHINY FRESH VEGETABLES

Serves 12 or more

3 small yellow onions, each cut into 4 wedges
1 pound carrots, sliced into rounds or cut diagonally
2 green bell peppers, seeded and cut into small triangles or strips
2 red bell peppers, seeded and cut into small triangles or strips
1 bunch broccoli, separated into florets
½ pound snow peas, trimmed
½ cup olive oil
Salt

Fill a large saucepan with boiling salted water. Cook each vegetable until it is crisp-tender, as follows: First, boil the onions for 2 minutes (they will separate into strips in the water). Add the carrots and cook for 3 minutes. Add the peppers and cook for 2 minutes. Add the broccoli and cook for 2 to 3 minutes until tender but still crisp. Lastly, add the snow peas and cook for only 1 minute.

Drain the vegetables in a colander. Plunge the colander into a bowl of very cold water to stop the vegetables from cooking further and to brighten their color. Shake the vegetables free from all water, toss them in just enough oil to moisten them and season with salt to taste. Serve at room temperature in a big bowl or in a basket lined with a brightly colored napkin.

LIVER PÂTÉ WITH VERMOUTH AND CURRANTS

Makes 2 cups

7 tablespoons butter
I small onion, finely chopped
I clove garlic, finely chopped
I teaspoon sage
I pound calf liver, or duck or chicken livers, cut into small pieces
¼ cup dry white vermouth
Salt
Freshly ground black pepper
¼ cup currants, soaked in hot water for 10 minutes and drained

Heat 3 tablespoons of the butter in a skillet and fry the onion, garlic, and sage slowly for 5 minutes. Add the liver. Increase the heat and cook the liver until lightly browned but still pink in the center, about 5 minutes. Add the vermouth and cook for a few minutes longer.

Put the ingredients in the food processor and process until very smooth. Melt the remaining 4 tablespoons of butter; add the butter to the pureed liver and mix well. Season to taste with salt and pepper. Stir in the currants and pour into small crocks or a terrine. Cover with transparent wrap and chill for at least 4 hours before serving.

NOTE: The currants add texture and an interesting flavor to this delicately seasoned pâté; if you cannot find currants easily, leave them out, but do not feel tempted to substitute raisins, which are not the same thing at all.

FRENCH COUNTRY TERRINE

½ pound thinly sliced bacon

1 yellow onion, cut into quarters

1 clove garlic

1 pound chicken livers

2 pounds pork butt or fatty pork loin, cut into small pieces, or ground pork

⅓ cup Madeira or port wine

2 teaspoons thyme

½ teaspoon nutmeg

1 teaspoon salt

Freshly ground black pepper

2 teaspoons Dijon mustard

2 eggs, beaten

½ cup bread crumbs

Preheat the oven to 325 degrees.

Line a 2-quart terrine or loaf pan with bacon slices, setting a few slices aside to cover the terrine later. Chop the onion and garlic finely in a food processor and transfer them to a large bowl.

Place the uncooked chicken livers in a food processor and process until smooth. Add them to the bowl.

Chop the pork coarsely in the food processor and add it to the bowl along with all the remaining ingredients. Combine them thoroughly and fill the terrine with the mixture. Bang the pan against the kitchen counter to smooth the mixture and to remove any air pockets. Cover the top with more slices of bacon and bake in the preheated oven for 1½ hours, or until the internal temperature reading is 165 degrees on a meat thermometer.

Let the terrine cool, and then cover it with foil and weight it (see page 30) so that it will be easy to slice later. Refrigerate for 1 to 4 days to allow the flavors to mature. Let the terrine sit out of the refrigerator an hour or so before serving time.

▪ BAY SCALLOPS WITH LIME AND CREAM

Serves 6

1½ pounds fresh bay scallops
3 tablespoons fresh lime juice
1 cup crème fraîche or lightly whipped cream
Freshly ground black pepper
Lettuce leaves, for serving
Watercress, for garnish

Put the scallops in a bowl and pour the lime juice over them. Chill in the refrigerator for 2 hours. Drain the scallops and fold in the crème fraîche. Season with pepper (do *not* add salt).

Serve on a bed of lettuce leaves and garnish with 2 or 3 sprigs of watercress. Serve slightly chilled.

▪ MOUSSE OF SMOKED TROUT

Serves 12

2 6-ounce smoked whole trout
3 ounces cream cheese
¼ cup chopped onion
1 tablespoon fresh lemon juice
Dash of hot pepper sauce
1 long, thin unpeeled cucumber, sliced
Lemon wedges, for garnish
Fresh parsley or watercress, for garnish

Reserve 1 whole trout to put in the center of the serving platter. Remove the skin and bones from the second trout and put the fish in the food processor with the cream cheese, onion, lemon juice, and hot pepper sauce. Process until smooth, then mound it on the individual cucumber slices.

For a very grand presentation, put the whole smoked trout in the center of a fairly small serving tray, preferably a footed silver one, and arrange slices of cucumber topped with the smoked trout mousse around the edge of the dish, interspersed with lemon wedges and sprigs of parsley.

■ HOT SHRIMP WITH COARSE SALT

Serves 3

1 pound jumbo shrimp, with shells on (allow 3 shrimp per person)
Vegetable oil
Coarse kosher salt
Fresh parsley or watercress, for garnish
Lemon wedges, for garnish

Preheat the broiler or charcoal grill.

Roll the shrimp in oil and then in salt. Arrange them in a single layer on an oiled broiler pan and broil them 4 inches from the source of heat, turning once, until small black blisters form and the shrimp are firm, about 5 minutes. Garnish with sprigs of parsley and lemon wedges and eat the shrimp the second they are cooked. Part of the pleasure is to burn your fingers!

CURRIED MUSSELS AND CUCUMBER POLONAISE

Serves 6

3 pounds fresh mussels (see pages 37–38), preferably farm-raised

1 long, thin cucumber, or 2 smaller cucumbers, peeled and seeds removed

2 teaspoons salt

2 tablespoons fresh lemon juice, strained

⅓ cup heavy cream

½ cup sour cream

4 tablespoons vegetable oil

1 tablespoon cider vinegar

¾ teaspoon curry powder

1 teaspoon salt

½ teaspoon freshly ground black pepper

2 teaspoons fresh tarragon leaves, or 1 teaspoon dried tarragon

½ cup Homemade Mayonnaise (see page 186)

2 tablespoons finely chopped parsley, for garnish

Radicchio or Bibb lettuce leaves

Remove all traces of the mussel "beards" and wash the mussels thoroughly to remove any tiny grains of sand. Bring about 1 inch of water to a boil in a large casserole. Put a steamer basket in the casserole and steam the mussels, covered, until they have opened, about 5 minutes. Set aside to cool completely.

Slice the cucumbers thinly. Toss with the salt and chill for 1 hour. Drain the liquid that will have formed. Rinse the cucumber slices quickly under cold running water and pat dry with paper towels. Stir in the lemon juice and heavy cream. In a separate bowl, combine the sour cream, oil, vinegar, curry powder, salt, pepper, tarragon, and mayonnaise; add to the cucumber mixture, stirring until mixed. Remove the mussels from their shells and fold them into the cucumber mixture. Serve the Polonaise on lettuce leaves garnished with chopped parsley, and accompany it with thinly sliced French or sourdough bread.

SMALL SALADS FOR TWO

MUSSEL SALAD

36 steamed Mussels (see page 156)
4 small potatoes, boiled, peeled, and sliced
¼ cup Homemade Mayonnaise (see page 186)
1 teaspoon Dijon mustard
2 tablespoons chopped fresh chives, for garnish

Toss the mussels and sliced potatoes with the mayonnaise and mustard. Garnish the salad with chopped chives.

HERRING SALAD

2 filleted herrings in sour cream
6 scallions, finely chopped
Grated rind of 1 orange

Toss all the ingredients together.

CHICK-PEA SALAD

1 cup cooked chick-peas
¼ pound cubed salami
6 cherry tomatoes, cut into quarters
½ green bell pepper, seeded and diced
¼ cup oil and vinegar dressing (see pages 34–35)

Toss all the ingredients together.

NOTE: You can use chick-peas from the salad bar or canned ones, drained.

RICE SALAD

½ cup cold cooked rice
6 scallions, finely chopped
½ green bell pepper, seeded and diced
½ cup diced cooked ham
¼ cup oil and vinegar dressing (see pages 34–35)

Toss all the ingredients together.

NOTE: Use Carolina, Basmati, or wild rice, as you prefer.

COLD PASTA SALAD

1 cup cooked macaroni shells or other pasta shapes
¾ cup cooked shellfish, chicken, or cold meat, cut into bite-size pieces
1 cup cut-up vegetables, freshly cooked until crisp-tender and cooled
½ cup Pesto (see page 189)

Toss all the ingredients together.

NOTE: You can use one kind of fresh, colorful vegetable or a combination, as you prefer.

If you prefer, you may substitute for the pesto ½ cup each mayonnaise (see page 186) and chopped fresh basil; combine them in the food processor until the basil is finely chopped.

WATERCRESS AND ENDIVE SALAD

1 bunch watercress
2 heads endive
¼ cup Homemade Mayonnaise (see page 186)
2 tablespoons milk
1 teaspoon Dijon mustard

Trim the watercress. Remove and discard the core of the endive; slice the endive thinly. Combine the mayonnaise with the milk and mustard. Pour this dressing over the watercress and endive, and toss.

POTATO SALAD I

4 small potatoes, boiled, peeled or unpeeled
4 chestnuts in brine, drained
4 scallions, finely chopped
¼ cup oil and white vermouth dressing (see pages 34–35)

Slice the potatoes; crumble the chestnuts. Toss all the ingredients together.

POTATO SALAD II

4 small potatoes, boiled, peeled or unpeeled
4 strips bacon, fried until crisp
4 scallions, finely chopped
¼ cup Homemade Mayonnaise (see page 186)
¼ cup mashed blue cheese

Slice the potatoes and crumble the bacon. Combine the potatoes, bacon, and scallions. Stir together the mayonnaise with the mashed blue cheese; pour this dressing over the potato mixture and toss.

AVOCADO AND LOBSTER SALAD

½ cucumber, peeled, seeded, and cut into bite-size pieces
1 fully ripe avocado
½ cup Homemade Mayonnaise (see page 186)
¼ cup chopped fresh herbs, such as basil, oregano, or cilantro, or a combination
1 cup cooked lobster meat, cut into bite-size pieces

(continued on next page)

AVOCADO AND LOBSTER SALAD *(cont.)*

Steam the cucumber pieces until crisp-tender, about 5 minutes. Set aside to cool.

Halve the avocado; discard the pit and remove the skin carefully. Cut a thin slice from the rounded side of each half so that it will lay flat without tipping.

Combine the mayonnaise and chopped herbs. Toss the cooled cucumber pieces and the lobster meat with the herb mayonnaise. Spoon half the mixture into the cavity of each avocado half.

APPLE AND CHEESE SALAD

1 bunch watercress or 1 head Radicchio
1 crisp apple, unpeeled, cut into bite-size pieces
3 stalks celery, finely chopped
½ cup Swiss cheese, cut into cubes
¼ cup chopped walnuts, toasted
¼ cup oil and vingear dressing (see pages 34–35)

Trim and separate the watercress leaves. Toss all the ingredients together.

RED ON RED SALAD

1 red bell pepper, seeded and diced
12 cherry tomatoes, quartered or halved
¼ cup oil and vinegar dressing (see pages 34–35)

Steam the diced pepper until crisp-tender, about 5 minutes. Set the pepper aside to cool. Combine the cooled pepper with the tomatoes, and toss the vegetables with the dressing.

YELLOW ON YELLOW SALAD

1 yellow bell pepper, seeded and diced
1 cup canned whole-kernel corn, or the kernels scraped from 2 ears sweet corn, freshly
    cooked and cooled
¼ cup oil and vinegar dressing (see pages 34–35)

Steam the diced pepper until crisp-tender, about 5 minutes. Set the
pepper aside to cool. Combine the cooled pepper with the corn
kernels, and toss the vegetables with the dressing.

GREEN ON GREEN SALAD

1 green bell pepper, seeded and diced
1 cup green peas, freshly cooked and cooled
¼ cup oil and vinegar dressing (see pages 34–35)

Steam the diced pepper until crisp-tender, about 5 minutes. Set the
pepper aside to cool. Combine the cooled pepper with the green
peas, and toss the vegetables with the dressing.

MELON SALAD

1 small cucumber, peeled and diced
2 cups melon balls from a variety of melons (Persian, Cranshaw, cantaloupe, or any other)
8 ounces plain yogurt
Mint leaves, for garnish

Steam the diced cucumber until crisp-tender, about 5 minutes. Set
aside to cool. Combine the cooled cucumber with the melon; toss the
mixture with the yogurt and garnish with mint leaves.

PEAR AND PROSCIUTTO SALAD

4 slices prosciutto
4 pear halves, freshly poached or canned (drained)
½ cup Homemade Mayonnaise (see page 186)
1 tablespoon chopped fresh tarragon

Thoroughly combine all the ingredients.

LICHEE AND MUSHROOM SALAD

½ cup fresh green beans, cut into 1½-inch-long pieces
6 fresh lichees
4 fresh white mushrooms
¼ cup oil and lemon juice dressing (see pages 34–35)

Steam the green beans just until crisp-tender, about 5 minutes. Set the beans aside to cool.

Meanwhile, peel and slice the lichees, discarding the pits. Slice the mushrooms thinly. Combine the lichees and mushrooms with the cooled green beans; toss the mixture with dressing.

SLICED RADISH AND MUSHROOM SALAD

Serves 6

1 clove garlic, peeled
4 scallions, sliced
6 medium mushrooms
12 large red radishes

DRESSING
¼ cup parsley sprigs
½ teaspoon salt
Freshly ground black pepper
¼ cup lemon juice
¾ cup light olive oil

Chop the garlic and scallions and slice the mushrooms and radishes in the food processor. Put all these ingredients in an attractive salad bowl.

To make the dressing, chop the parsley in the food processor. Add the remaining dressing ingredients and process for 2 seconds. Pour the dressing over the vegetables in the salad bowl and toss.

COLD BEEF SALAD

Serves 4

3 cups thin strips of cold roast beef
2 medium whole potatoes, boiled with the skins on and cooled
½ tablespoon chopped dill or other fresh herb
1 head Boston lettuce
2 medium very ripe tomatoes, peeled and sliced, for garnish

DRESSING
1 tablespoon prepared horseradish
1 tablespoon red wine vinegar
3 tablespoons olive oil
Salt and freshly ground black pepper, to taste

Put the beef strips in a bowl. Peel the potatoes (or leave them unpeeled, if you wish) and slice them into the bowl with the beef. Combine the ingredients for the dressing and toss with the beef and potatoes until thoroughly combined.

Line a salad bowl with lettuce leaves and heap the beef and potato mixture in the center. Garnish the salad with thin slices of tomato.

2

SOUPS—HOT AND COLD

CHICKEN SOUP WITH RICE

BILLI BI SOUP WITH CRAB

MANHATTAN CLAM CHOWDER

NEW ENGLAND CLAM CHOWDER

CREAM OF ASPARAGUS SOUP

PEAR AND TURNIP SOUP

BLACK BEAN SOUP

CREAM OF CHESTNUT SOUP

MUSHROOM AND BARLEY SOUP

WINTER TOMATO CONSOMMÉ

ONION SOUP

POTATO SOUP

FISH SOUP

FRESH TOMATO SOUP

CLEAR VEGETABLE SOUP

PUMPKIN SOUP WITH LEEKS

COLD CURRIED AVOCADO SOUP

CHILLED CLARET CONSOMMÉ

VICHYSSOISE

CHICKEN SOUP WITH RICE

Serves 6

FOR THE BROTH

1 3-pound chicken, with giblets

1 medium yellow onion, sliced

1 carrot, peeled and sliced

2 stalks celery, sliced

1 bay leaf

½ teaspoon thyme

1 teaspoon peppercorns

4 sprigs fresh parsley

8 cups water

½ cup uncooked rice

2 carrots, peeled and cut into 2-by-⅛-inch strips

1 teaspoon sage

1 teaspoon salt

Freshly ground black pepper

1 cup peas

½ cup heavy cream (optional)

2 tablespoons finely chopped fresh parsley, for garnish

To make the broth, put the chicken and the giblets into a large saucepan. Add the onion, carrot, celery, bay leaf, thyme, peppercorns, parsley, and water. Adjust the lid so that the saucepan is three-quarters covered. Bring to a boil over high heat. Lower the heat and simmer for 45 minutes.

Remove the chicken from the broth and set it aside until it is cool enough to handle. Separate the meat from the skin and bones; cut the meat into bite-size pieces and set aside, covered, in the refrigerator. Return the skin and bones to the saucepan, partially cover the pan again, and simmer for 1½ hours.

Strain the broth, discarding the skin, bones, and vegetables; cool the broth slightly, then refrigerate it for 8 hours. Remove and discard the fat that will have risen to the surface.

Pour the broth into a saucepan and bring it to the boiling point. Stir in the rice, carrot strips, sage, and salt; add pepper to taste. Lower the heat, cover the pan, and simmer for 15 minutes. Add the peas and reserved chicken meat and simmer for 5 minutes more. Stir in the cream. Pour into a tureen, sprinkle the soup with chopped parsley and serve.

VARIATIONS: Substitute a handful of any kind of cooked pasta—spaghetti, small bow-ties, or even macaroni—for the rice; add it to the soup at the last minute.

▪ BILLI BI SOUP WITH CRAB

Serves 4

1 10½-ounce can condensed tomato soup
1 10½-ounce can condensed pea soup
2 cups light cream
2 teaspoons curry powder
1 12-ounce container pasteurized backfin crabmeat
Grated rind of 1 lemon

Combine all the ingredients in a heavy saucepan and heat gently, stirring frequently. Take care not to let the soup boil.

MANHATTAN CLAM CHOWDER

Serves 6

2 tablespoons butter

2 medium onions, chopped

2 small carrots, chopped

2 stalks celery, chopped

1 medium green bell pepper, seeded and chopped

7 medium boiling potatoes, peeled and chopped

About 24 fresh hard-shelled clams (see page 37), shucked, or 1 14-ounce can shucked
    clams, or 1 14-ounce package frozen shucked clams

4 medium ripe tomatoes, peeled, seeded, and chopped, or 1 16-ounce can whole tomatoes,
    with liquid, chopped

2 cups water

Freshly ground black pepper

Heat the butter in a large heavy saucepan; sauté the chopped vegetables until softened, but not browned.

Drain the clams and reserve the liquor. Chop the clams into small pieces; set them aside. Add the reserved clam liquor, the tomatoes, and the water to the vegetable mixture; simmer uncovered for 45 minutes. Season to taste with salt and pepper. Add the clams just before serving; heat them just until they are warmed through or they will become tough.

NEW ENGLAND CLAM CHOWDER

Serves 4 to 6

About 24 hard-shelled clams (see page 37), shucked, or 1 pint chopped fresh clams
2 slices bacon, or 2 ounces salt pork, diced
1 medium onion, finely chopped
1½ cups diced uncooked potatoes
1 cup water
Salt
Freshly ground black pepper
1 cup light cream
½ cup milk
2 tablespoons butter

Drain the clams and reserve their liquor. Wash and chop the clams; set aside.

Fry the bacon in a saucepan over medium-high heat. Sauté the onion in the bacon grease until softened. Add the potatoes, water, and the reserved clams and their liquor; and season to taste with salt and pepper. Simmer uncovered for 15 minutes, then stir in the cream and milk and dot with butter. Serve immediately and pass a pepper mill at the table.

NOTE: This is not a time when you can substitute canned clams. The essence of this chowder lies in the taste of the sea the fresh clams impart to it.

CREAM OF ASPARAGUS SOUP

Serves 4

3 cups chicken broth (see page 5)
1 pound young, tender asparagus spears
2 tablespoons butter
1 small onion, finely chopped
4 inside stalks celery, finely chopped
2 tablespoons all-purpose flour
Grated rind of 1 lemon
Salt
Freshly ground black pepper
½ cup plain yogurt

Heat the chicken broth and set aside.

Wash the asparagus carefully to remove any trace of sand. Trim the stalks and cut into small pieces.

Heat the butter in a heavy saucepan and sauté the onion and celery over low heat until softened, about 5 minutes. Stir in the flour, then add the warm chicken broth and the asparagus, setting aside a few tips for garnishing the soup, if desired. Cover and simmer over low heat for 20 minutes. Add the grated lemon rind and season to taste with salt and pepper. Puree the soup in a blender or food processor and strain. Pour the soup into warmed bowls, top each serving with a spoonful of yogurt, and garnish with the reserved asparagus tips.

PEAR AND TURNIP SOUP

Serves 6

4 cups chicken broth (see page 5)
Salt (optional)
2 medium potatoes, peeled, and chopped into small pieces
2 small yellow onions, chopped
2 firm, ripe Anjou pears, unpeeled, cored and chopped
I small turnip, peeled and chopped
I teaspoon dried winter savory or dill
I cup light cream
Freshly ground black pepper
½ cup finely chopped celery, for garnish

Heat the chicken broth to boiling in a large heavy saucepan. Add salt to taste. Add the potatoes, onions, pears, turnip, and winter savory. Cover and simmer over low heat for 20 minutes.

Transfer the soup to a food processor; process it until smooth. Strain it into a clean saucepan to remove any fragments of the pear skin. Stir in the cream, then reheat the soup until hot—do not let it boil. Season to taste with pepper and garnish with chopped celery.

◾ BLACK BEAN SOUP

Serves 12

2 pounds dried black beans

1 2-pound smoked ham on the bone, or 2 pounds smoked pork hocks

8 cups water, initially

3 large yellow onions, finely chopped

4 stalks celery, with the leaves, finely chopped

3 cloves garlic, finely chopped

½ teaspoon allspice or powdered cloves

4 bay leaves

Several dashes of cayenne pepper

⅓ cup Madeira wine

2 Hard-cooked Eggs (see page 227), chopped, for garnish

1 cup sour cream, for garnish

12 lemon slices, for garnish

Soak the beans in cold water to cover for 24 hours. Drain the beans and put them in a large heavy casserole. Add the ham bone and the remaining ingredients except the Madeira and the garnishes. Simmer uncovered over low heat for 3 hours, adding water as necessary to keep the bone and beans covered. At the end of this time, the beans should be very soft. Remove the pan from the heat.

Discard the bay leaves and remove the bone. Reserve some of the cooked beans to add texture to the soup. Puree the remaining soup in a blender or food processor (do this in batches or it will overflow).

Return the pureed soup to the large heavy casserole. Add the Madeira and reheat the soup gently until it is very hot, adding more water or some chicken broth if it has become too thick.

Garnish each bowl of soup with some of the chopped eggs and sour cream, and top each serving with a lemon slice.

■ CREAM OF CHESTNUT SOUP

Makes 6 cups

4 medium mushrooms

I medium onion, peeled and quartered

½ medium tart apple, peeled and cored

2 tablespoons butter

I 15½-ounce can unsweetened chestnut puree

I I-ounce (square) semisweet baking chocolate

2 teaspoons tomato paste

I tablespoon lemon juice

4 cups beef broth (see page 5)

Chop the mushrooms, onion, and apple in the food processor. Heat the butter in a large saucepan; sauté the mushroom mixture over gentle heat for 5 minutes. Add the remaining ingredients and heat until hot, stirring frequently.

MUSHROOM AND BARLEY SOUP

Serves 6

1 tablespoon butter
1 large yellow onion, finely chopped
1 carrot, finely chopped
2 stalks celery, finely chopped
1 pound mushrooms, finely chopped (in the food processor)
4 cups beef broth (see page 5)
3 cups chicken broth (see page 5)
½ cup pearl barley, washed
½ teaspoon salt
Freshly ground black pepper
1 tablespoon vinegar (optional)
2 tablespoons finely chopped fresh parsley, for garnish

Heat the butter in a saucepan until it is bubbling; sauté the onion, carrot, and celery in the butter for 3 minutes. Add the mushrooms. Lower the heat, cover the pan, and steam the vegetables for 10 minutes. Add the broths, barley, salt, and pepper to taste. Simmer, uncovered, until the barley is soft, about 30 minutes. For a sharper flavor, stir in the vinegar at the last minute. Garnish with chopped parsley.

■ WINTER TOMATO CONSOMMÉ

Serves 8

4 cups chicken broth (see page 5)

4 cups tomato juice

1 cup finely chopped shallots or scallions

2 teaspoons tomato paste

½ teaspoon dried thyme

½ teaspoon dried basil

½ teaspoon ground allspice

2 teaspoons freshly squeezed lemon juice

2 tablespoons dry sherry or Madeira

2 tablespoons finely chopped fresh chives or fresh parsley

2 paper-thin lemon slices, each cut into 4 pieces, or finely diced avocado, for garnish

Combine the broth, tomato juice, shallots, tomato paste, thyme, basil, and allspice in a saucepan; over low heat, gently simmer the soup, uncovered, for 15 minutes; strain. Stir in the lemon juice, sherry, and chives; reheat just until hot. Garnish each serving with lemon and serve with freshly made toast triangles, with the crusts removed.

ONION SOUP

Serves 6

3 tablespoons butter

4 large yellow onions, thinly sliced

2 tablespoons all-purpose flour

Salt

Freshly ground black pepper

3 cups beef broth (see page 5)

3 cups chicken broth (see page 5)

1 teaspoon dried thyme

¼ cup Calvados or other apple brandy

6 slices firm-textured French bread

1 cup grated Gruyère or other good-quality Swiss cheese

¼ cup freshly grated Parmesan cheese

Heat the butter in a saucepan; slowly cook the onions in the butter over low heat, stirring occasionally, until they are just beginning to brown and caramelize, about 15 minutes. Stir in the flour and 1 teaspoon salt and season with pepper to taste. Gradually add the beef and chicken broths, stirring constantly, and bring the soup to a boil. Add the thyme. Reduce the heat and simmer, uncovered, over low heat for 40 minutes, watching the pan from time to time to make sure it is not boiling too quickly. Add the Calvados during the last 10 minutes of cooking. Add more salt and pepper to taste.

Meanwhile, preheat the oven to 325 degrees. Place the slices of bread on a baking sheet and bake until they are completely dry, about 15 minutes.

Place the oven rack in its lowest position. Preheat the broiler.

Ladle the soup into bowls. Float a slice of bread in each bowl and sprinkle each piece with some cheese. Put the bowls on a baking sheet; broil the soup until the cheese has melted and is lightly browned, about 3 or 4 minutes. Serve immediately.

POTATO SOUP

Serves 6

5 cups chicken broth (see page 5)

½ teaspoon salt

4 medium potatoes, peeled and cut into small pieces

2 large yellow onions, chopped

6 fat leeks, well washed, chopped (including part of the green stems)

1 teaspoon dried chervil or oregano

3 tablespoons finely chopped fresh parsley

½ cup heavy cream, or more as needed

2 tablespoons butter

Bring the chicken broth to a simmer in a large saucepan; add the salt. Add the potatoes, onions, and leeks; cover the pan and simmer over low heat for 20 minutes. Using a potato masher, mash the potatoes into the broth until it becomes a coarse-textured soup. Add the chervil, parsley, heavy cream, and butter; simmer for 5 minutes more. Pass a pepper mill at the table.

FISH SOUP

Serves 8

3 pounds assorted fish fillets, such as bass, halibut, and cod

½ pound raw shrimp

1 pound any other raw shellfish, such as sea scallops or pasteurized backfin crabmeat

2 cups clam broth

4 cups chicken broth (see page 5)

1 pound leeks, well washed, trimmed, and chopped

2 small yellow onions, chopped

1 teaspoon dried thyme

Grated rind of 2 oranges

⅛ teaspoon saffron threads

½ cup Pernod (optional)

1 pound fresh plum tomatoes, peeled, seeded, and chopped

Cut the fish into 2-inch pieces, discarding any remaining bones, and set aside. Place the shrimp in a steam basket; steam the shrimp over an inch of boiling water until they are firm and pink, about 4 minutes. Peel the shrimp and pick over the seafood to remove any stray pieces of grit, shell, or cartilage; set the shrimp and seafood aside.

Pour the clam and chicken broths into a large casserole. Add the leeks, onions, and thyme. Simmer uncovered over low heat until the leeks and onions have softened, about 20 minutes. Stir in the grated orange rind and saffron, then add the fish and seafood; simmer over low heat until the fish is opaque, about 8 minutes. Stir in the Pernod and chopped tomatoes; simmer for 4 minutes more.

VARIATION: Add 4 diced boiled potatoes to the soup.

■ FRESH TOMATO SOUP

Serves 6

2 tablespoons vegetable oil
1 onion, finely chopped
2 cloves garlic, finely chopped
3 pounds very ripe red tomatoes, halved or cut into medium-size wedges
1 tablespoon tomato paste
4 cups chicken broth (see page 5)
½ cup packed fresh basil leaves, or 1 teaspoon dried basil
2 tablespoons finely chopped fresh parsley, chives, or basil leaves, for garnish
Plain yogurt, for garnish (optional)

Heat the oil in a saucepan, sauté the onion and garlic in the oil over moderate heat until softened, about 3 minutes. Add the tomatoes and tomato paste, then stir in the chicken broth and basil. Cover the pan and simmer for no longer than 20 minutes (longer cooking causes the soup to lose its color). Puree the soup in a food processor, then strain it to remove the tomato skin and seeds.

Serve it hot in bowls, garnished with chopped parsley, or serve it cold in tall glasses, each topped with a spoonful of plain yogurt.

VARIATIONS: Add orange rind cut into pieces about the size of tomato seeds, chopped clams, a variety of chopped fresh herbs, or sherry or Madeira.

CLEAR VEGETABLE SOUP

Serves 8

6 cups chicken broth (see page 5)
1 tablespoon tomato paste
2 thin carrots, thinly sliced
1 stalk celery, thinly sliced
4 leeks or 12 scallions, thinly sliced
¼ of a 10-ounce package frozen chopped spinach
½ of a 10-ounce package frozen peas
1 teaspoon lemon juice
2 teaspoons frozen chopped fresh chives, or ½ teaspoon oregano

Heat the broth in a large saucepan. Stir in the tomato paste. Add the carrots, celery, and leeks; cook over moderate heat for 5 minutes. Add the spinach, peas, lemon juice, and chives; cook for 5 minutes more.

PUMPKIN SOUP WITH LEEKS

Makes 8 cups

2 tablespoons butter
1 pound leeks, washed and thinly sliced
1 16-ounce can solid-pack pumpkin
5 cups chicken broth (see page 5)
¼ teaspoon dried crushed red pepper
1 small tomato, diced

Heat the butter in a saucepan; sauté the leeks in the butter gently until softened but not browned, about 5 minutes. Add the remaining ingredients. Heat, stirring occasionally, until the leeks are tender, about 5 minutes.

■ COLD CURRIED AVOCADO SOUP

Serves 8

2 tablespoons butter
2 bunches scallions, finely chopped
1 tablespoon curry powder
2 medium fully ripe avocados, peeled and chopped
8 cups chicken broth (see page 5)
½ cup plain yogurt
Grated rind of 1 lemon
Juice of 1 lemon, strained
½ teaspoon salt
1 tablespoon chopped fresh dill, chives, or parsley, for garnish

Heat the butter in a small skillet. Gently sauté the scallions in the butter until softened but not browned, about 4 minutes. Add the curry powder and stir for 1 minute to release its flavor. Puree the curried scallions, avocados, 1 cup of the broth, yogurt, lemon rind, lemon juice, and salt in the food processor or blender. Transfer the puree to a bowl and gradually add as much of the remaining chicken broth as is needed to make the soup of a pouring consistency. (It will thicken slightly as it stands.)

Chill the soup in the refrigerator for at least 2 hours. Sprinkle the chopped dill over the soup just before serving.

CHILLED CLARET CONSOMMÉ

Serves 2

1½ cups canned beef consommé with gelatin added
½ cup good-quality red wine
1 teaspoon unflavored gelatin
1 teaspoon very finely chopped fresh parsley or chives, for garnish
2 thin lemon wedges, for garnish

Pour the consommé and wine into a small saucepan. Sprinkle the gelatin over the surface of the liquid and let it set, without stirring, for 2 minutes. Over moderate heat, bring the mixture just to a simmer, stirring once or twice. Remove the pan from the heat.

Pour the soup into bowls and refrigerate for 3 hours. To serve, garnish each bowl with a small sprinkling of chopped parsley and a wedge of lemon.

NOTE: All foods made with the addition of gelatin are best eaten the day they are made or they become rubbery.

■ VICHYSSOISE

Serves 6

4 cups chicken broth (see page 5)
4 medium potatoes, peeled and chopped into small pieces
3 leeks, washed and sliced
2 small yellow onions, chopped
1 teaspoon chervil
1 cup light cream
Salt
Freshly ground black pepper
2 tablespoons finely chopped fresh chives, for garnish

Heat the chicken broth to the boiling point in a large heavy saucepan. Add the potatoes, leeks, onions, and chervil. Cover and simmer over low heat for 20 minutes.

Transfer the soup to a food processor and process until it is smooth. Stir in the cream, then refrigerate the soup for 4 hours. Before serving, add salt and pepper to taste. Garnish each bowl of soup with chopped chives.

NOTE: Vichyssoise thickens after it has been chilled, so thin it before serving to the consistency you prefer with the addition of a little extra milk or cream.

VARIATION: Add a bunch of chopped watercress to the recipe and garnish the completed soup with a few reserved watercress leaves. Serve the soup hot or cold.

3

■ ■■■■■■■■■■■■■■■■■■■■ ■

MAIN COURSE DISHES—
HEARTY AND LIGHT

■

SAUERBRATEN

BELGIAN CARBONNADE OF BEEF

BRATWURST IN BEER

BEEF IN RED WINE (BOEUF BOURGUIGNON)

NEW ENGLAND BOILED DINNER

FLANK STEAK WITH MUSHROOMS

BROILED BARBECUED SPARERIBS

MEAT LOAF

PEPPER STEAK

CHILI

BRAISED VEAL SHANKS (OSSO BUCO)

CALVES' LIVER WITH LEMON AND THYME SAUCE

VEAL AND PROSCIUTTO ROLLS (SALTIMBOCCA ALLA ROMANA)

BAKED VEAL CHOPS WITH HAM AND CHEESE

VEAL WITH LEMON AND BRANDY

VEAL IN WINE SAUCE

FRUIT-STUFFED PORK LOIN WITH RED CABBAGE

SAUTÉED PORK LOIN

LAMB STEW

LAMB SHANKS WITH YELLOW SPLIT PEAS AND LEMON

ROAST LEG OF LAMB WITH GARLIC AND ROSEMARY

CHICKEN IN THE POT

CHICKEN POTPIE

CHICKEN WITH CITRUS FRUITS

FRIED CHICKEN IN BEER BATTER

BROILED CHICKEN WITH MUSTARD

CHICKEN IN CHAMPAGNE

CHICKEN IN RED WINE (COQ AU VIN)

STIR-FRIED TURKEY BREAST WITH SESAME OIL

STIR-FIRED CHICKEN WITH WALNUTS

CHICKEN PAPRIKASH

CHICKEN WITH PROSCIUTTO

CHICKEN WITH ALMONDS AND GARLIC

SUNDAY NIGHT CHICKEN SUPPER

CHICKEN WITH RICE (ARROZ CON POLLO)

GINGERED CHICKEN

CHICKEN BREASTS STUFFED WITH RICOTTA AND HERBS

POT-ROASTED ROULADE OF TURKEY

CHICKEN WITH LEMON AND HERBS

CURRIED CHICKEN

CRISP-FRIED TURKEY BREAST

BROILED SWORDFISH WITH MUSTARD BUTTER

SMOKED FISH CASSEROLE

SWORDFISH WITH CAPERS

TUNA WITH RED WINE AND TOMATOES

FOIL-BAKED FISH WITH FENNEL

LOBSTER MAYONNAISE

POACHED TROUT

BAKED SHAD

LOBSTER NEWBURG

RED SNAPPER WITH TOMATOES

BAKED RED SNAPPER WITH TARRAGON SAUCE

POACHED SALMON STEAKS

GRAVAD LAX

SWORDFISH STEAK WITH SHRIMP

SHRIMP IN CRISP BATTER

BROILED SHRIMP WITH GARLIC

CIOPPINO

MOULES MARINIÈRES

TORTELLINI WITH SCALLOPS AND BACON

LASAGNE

SPAGHETTI WITH GARLIC AND HERBS

SPAGHETTI WITH BUTTER AND CHEESE

FETTUCCINI WITH CHICKEN BREASTS

GREEN FETTUCCINI WITH TOMATOES AND MOZZARELLA

FETTUCCINI WITH CLAMS AND SHRIMP

PASTA PRIMAVERA

LINGUINI WITH MUSSELS AND PEAS

ZITI WITH MEAT AND TOMATO SAUCE

HOMEMADE PASTA

SAUERBRATEN

Serves 8

MARINADE
2 cups red wine vinegar
1 cup red wine
1 cup water
1 onion, finely chopped
1 clove garlic, finely chopped
2 carrots, finely chopped
2 stalks celery, finely chopped
1 tablespoon pickling spice

4 pounds eye round or chuck steak, at least 4 inches thick
1½ cups crushed gingersnaps

Combine the marinade ingredients in a large baking dish and place the beef in the marinade. Cover the dish loosely with transparent wrap and refrigerate the meat for at least 24 hours, turning it in the marinade twice.

Preheat the oven to 350 degrees.

Transfer the beef with the marinade and vegetables into a large casserole (a Crockpot is ideal for this purpose). Cover and cook gently for 2½ hours. Remove the beef from the casserole and keep it warm.

Strain the marinade and juices into a saucepan and add the gingersnap crumbs. Simmer over moderate heat until the sauce has thickened, about 5 minutes.

BELGIAN CARBONNADE OF BEEF

Serves 6

2½ pounds best-quality boneless chuck
Vegetable oil
4 medium onions, sliced
I clove garlic, finely chopped
2 tablespoons all-purpose flour
1½ cups beer, preferably dark (definitely *not* lite)
I cup beef broth (see page 5)
¼ teaspoon nutmeg
½ teaspoon salt
I teaspoon sugar
I teaspoon Dijon mustard

BOUQUET GARNI
3 sprigs fresh parsley
I bay leaf
½ teaspoon dried thyme
I teaspoon peppercorns

6 3-inch rounds of French or other firm-textured bread, toasted

Preheat the oven to 350 degrees.

Trim all the fat from the beef and cut the meat into 2-inch cubes. Heat 2 tablespoons vegetable oil in a skillet over high heat and fry the cubes, a few at a time, turning until browned on all sides. Transfer the beef to a casserole.

Lower the heat to moderate. Sauté the onions and garlic until softened, about 3 minutes, adding more oil if necessary. Stir in the flour, then add the beer gradually, stirring until thickened. Pour the mixture over the beef in the casserole and add the beef broth, nutmeg, salt, sugar, and mustard.

Tie the herbs for the bouquet garni in a cheesecloth bag and add it to the casserole. Cover the casserole and bake for 1½ hours. Discard the herb bag. Let the casserole cool, then refrigerate it overnight.

About 50 minutes before you are ready to serve the carbonnade, preheat the oven to 350 degrees; reheat the stew in the oven until the gravy is hot and bubbling, about 30 minutes. Coat one side of each bread round with mustard and place the slices, mustard side down, on top of the meat, pushing the bread down partially into the sauce.

Return the casserole to the oven and continue cooking with the casserole uncovered, until the bread is crusty brown, about 15 minutes more.

■ BRATWURST IN BEER

Serves 8

2 pounds bratwurst
1 cup beer
1 teaspoon peppercorns
2 tablespoons butter

Prick the skins of the bratwurst with a fork in several places. This will prevent them from bursting when the heat causes the insides to expand. Put the bratwurst, beer, and peppercorns in a saucepan and simmer, uncovered, over low heat for 20 minutes. Remove the bratwurst and drain them on paper towels.

Heat the butter in a skillet, add the bratwurst, and cook over moderate heat for a few minutes until the skin is lightly browned.

■ BEEF IN RED WINE (BOEUF BOURGUIGNON)

Serves 6

4 slices bacon

2½ pounds boneless chuck, trimmed and cut into 2-inch cubes

2 tablespoons brandy (optional)

2 yellow onions, finely chopped

1 clove garlic, finely chopped

2 tablespoons all-purpose flour

1½ cups red wine

½ cup beef broth (see page 5)

½ teaspoon salt

4 tablespoons butter

1 pound small white onions, peeled

1 teaspoon sugar

½ pound mushrooms, quartered

2 tablespoons finely chopped fresh parsley

BOUQUET GARNI

3 sprigs fresh parsley

1 bay leaf

½ teaspoon dried thyme

1 teaspoon peppercorns

Fry the bacon in a skillet over medium-high heat until it is almost crisp and all the fat has been rendered. Drain the bacon, reserving 3 tablespoons of the fat in the pan. Fry the beef cubes, a few at a time, in very hot bacon fat, transferring them to a casserole as soon as they have browned on all sides.

If you are using brandy, heat it in a small saucepan. Remove it from the heat, ignite it, and pour it, flaming, over the beef in the casserole.

Fry the yellow onions and garlic in the fat remaining in the skillet until softened, about 3 minutes. Stir in the flour, then add the red wine and beef broth gradually, stirring with a wire whisk to form a smooth sauce. Pour the mixture over the beef in the casserole.

Tie the herbs for the bouquet garni in a cheesecloth bag and bury this among the beef cubes. Add the salt. Cover and cook in the preheated oven for 1½ hours. Allow the casserole to cool and discard the bag of herbs.

When you are getting ready to serve, heat 2 tablespoons of the butter in a small heavy skillet. Sauté the white onions in the butter over low heat for 15 minutes. Sprinkle them with the sugar and continue cooking until the sugar has caramelized and formed a light brown glaze over the onions, about 5 minutes more. Add the onions to the casserole.

Heat the remaining 2 tablespoons butter. Sauté the mushrooms in the butter over medium-high heat until they are lightly browned, about 4 minutes. Stir them into the beef in the casserole and sprinkle the chopped parsley over the top.

NEW ENGLAND BOILED DINNER

Serves 6

2½ pounds corned beef
3 sprigs fresh parsley
1 bay leaf
1 teaspoon dried thyme
1 teaspoon peppercorns
2 carrots, sliced
2 onions, sliced
2 stalks celery, sliced

VEGETABLES
1 small head green cabbage, cut into 8 wedges
5 carrots, sliced
6 small boiling potatoes
3 medium parsnips, sliced
1 small turnip, cut into small pieces

DRESSING
1 cup whipped cream or sour cream
1 tablespoon prepared horseradish
Juice of ½ lemon

Preheat the oven to 325 degrees.

Put the corned beef in a casserole just large enough to hold it. Cover the corned beef with water, and add the remaining first group of ingredients. Cover and cook in the preheated oven until the beef is fork-tender, about 2½ hours.

Tie each cabbage wedge in 2 places with string so that it will retain its shape. Cook the cabbage and each of the remaining vegetables in separate pans of salted water until tender. (The vegetables are cooked separately so that each will retain its color and because the cooking time for the vegetables varies.)

Thoroughly combine the dressing ingredients.

Slice the corned beef and arrange the vegetables around it. Serve the dressing separately.

■ FLANK STEAK WITH MUSHROOMS

Serves 3 to 4

2 pounds flank steak

2 tablespoons butter

I medium onion, chopped

6 mushrooms, thinly sliced

I tablespoon Worcestershire sauce

I teaspoon tomato paste

I teaspoon freshly grated horseradish

I tablespoon all-purpose flour

I cup beer

Salt

Freshly ground black pepper

Preheat the broiler or charcoal grill.

Broil the steak for 8 minutes; turn it, and broil it for 5 minutes more. Keep it hot while you prepare the sauce.

Heat the butter in a saucepan; sauté the onion in the butter over moderate heat until softened, about 5 minutes. Add the mushrooms and sauté until they are lightly browned. Stir in the Worcestershire sauce, tomato paste, horseradish, and flour. Add the beer gradually, stirring until well incorporated. Season to taste with salt and pepper. Simmer the sauce for 5 minutes.

Slice the steak across the grain and serve covered with the mushroom sauce.

BROILED BARBECUED SPARERIBS

Serves 6

½ cup cider vinegar

¼ cup water or pineapple juice

½ cup sugar

1 clove garlic, finely chopped

3 tablespoons sherry, optional

3 tablespoons soy sauce

1 tablespoon cornstarch, dissolved in 2 tablespoons cold water

6 pounds country-style spareribs

2 tablespoons vegetable oil

To prepare the marinade, combine the vinegar, water, and sugar in a small saucepan; simmer over low heat until the sugar has dissolved. Add the garlic, sherry, and soy sauce; simmer for 3 minutes more. Add the dissolved cornstarch and stir until the mixture has thickened into a sauce. Let the sauce cool.

Meanwhile, trim any excess fat from the spareribs. Place the ribs in a large shallow dish. Pour the sauce over the ribs and cover the dish. Let the spareribs marinate in the sauce in the refrigerator for at least 2 hours.

Preheat the broiler or charcoal grill.

Brush the broiler rack with the oil. Remove the spareribs from the marinade and broil them 6 inches from the heat for 20 minutes on each side. Baste the ribs with the remaining sauce every 6 minutes.

NOTE: This marinade can also be used for broiled chicken and pork chops.

■ MEAT LOAF

Serves 4

1 pound ground beef
½ teaspoon salt
Freshly ground black pepper, to taste
2 slices firm-textured bread, crusts removed
½ cup packed sprigs fresh parsley
1 teaspoon oregano
1 egg, slightly beaten
2 tablespoons vegetable oil
1 small onion, finely chopped
1 clove garlic, finely chopped
1 tablespoon tomato paste
1 tablespoon soy sauce
4 slices bacon

Preheat the oven to 350 degrees.

Put the ground beef in a bowl and break it up, but do not handle it too much or the meat loaf will become compact and heavy. Add the salt and pepper. Working with ½ slice of bread at a time, tear it into small pieces and put these in the food processor or blender and pulse to form crumbs. Add the parsley to the food processor, and process until it is chopped.

Stir the bread crumb mixture into the beef. Stir in the oregano; fold in the egg.

Heat the oil in a skillet; sauté the onion and garlic in the oil until softened, about 3 minutes. Add the onion and garlic, tomato paste, and soy sauce to the beef; mix gently. Press the mixture into a 7-by-4-inch loaf pan. Cover the meat loaf with the bacon slices and cook in the preheated oven for 1 hour.

Discard the fat that will have formed. Serve the meat loaf as it is or with fresh tomato sauce (see page 188).

PEPPER STEAK

Serves 6

4 tablespoons vegetable oil
6 6-ounce strip steaks
3 tablespoons cracked pepper
2 tablespoons butter
1 teaspoon salt
¼ cup Cognac
1 cup heavy cream
Watercress sprigs, for garnish

Reserve 2 tablespoons of the oil and brush each steak all over with the remaining oil. Press the cracked pepper onto the surface of both sides of the steaks, using the heel of your hand.

Heat the butter and the reserved oil in a large heavy skillet until very hot; fry the steaks, 3 at a time, over high heat for 4 minutes on each side. The surface of the steaks should be well browned and the center rare. Remove the steaks, season them with salt and let them rest on hot plates while you prepare the sauce.

Add the Cognac and cream to the juices in the pan and boil over high heat, stirring, until the cream has thickened slightly, about 2 or 3 minutes. Spoon the sauce over the steaks and serve immediately. Garnish the plates with watercress.

CHILI

Serves 8

2 tablespoons vegetable oil

I large onion, finely chopped

I clove garlic, finely chopped

2 medium carrots, finely chopped

2 pounds top-quality ground beef

3 tablespoons chili powder

Dash of cayenne pepper

A few drops Tabasco

I½ teaspoons salt

I teaspoon sugar

I 32-ounce can Italian plum tomatoes, with their liquid

2 bay leaves

I 32-ounce can red kidney beans, drained

Taco shells or tortillas, for serving

Heat the oil; sauté the onion, garlic, and carrots over moderate heat until softened, about 5 minutes. Stir in the ground beef and cook over low heat until all the fat has been rendered. Drain and discard the fat. Transfer the drained mixture to a heavy casserole or large saucepan. Stir in all the remaining ingredients except the beans and taco shells. Simmer, uncovered, over very low heat for 4 hours, adding a little water if the chili is becoming too thick. Add the kidney beans and continue cooking until they have heated through. Discard the bay leaves and serve with tacos shells or tortillas.

BRAISED VEAL SHANKS (OSSO BUCO)

Serves 6

6 veal shanks, cut 2 inches thick and each tied with string to hold its shape

3 to 4 tablespoons vegetable oil

2 medium onions, finely chopped

4 cloves garlic, finely chopped

1 carrot, diced

2 stalks celery, finely chopped

2 tablespoons all-purpose flour

Pared rind and juice of 1 orange

Pared rind and juice of 1 lemon

1 16-ounce can Italian plum tomatoes, with their juice, or 1 pound very ripe tomatoes, peeled and cut into pieces

2 teaspoons tomato paste

1 cup red wine

1 cup chicken broth (see page 5)

¼ cup chopped fresh basil leaves, or 1 teaspoon dried oregano

Salt

Freshly ground black pepper

3 tablespoons finely chopped fresh parsley

Preheat the oven to 350 degrees.

Dry the veal shanks on paper towels so that they will brown well. Heat the oil in a heavy casserole; brown the shanks, 2 or 3 at a time, on all sides. Remove the veal from the casserole. Sauté the onions, garlic, carrot, and celery in the oil remaining in the casserole for 5 minutes. Discard all but 1 tablespoon of the oil. Stir in the flour, return the veal shanks to the casserole, and add the remaining ingredients except the salt, pepper, and parsley.

Cover and cook in the preheated oven until the veal is very tender, about 1½ hours.

Remove the veal to a serving platter and keep it warm. Strain the pan juices; cook the juices until reduced to 1¼ cups. Season with salt and pepper to taste. Spoon the sauce over the veal and garnish with parsley.

■ CALVES' LIVER WITH LEMON AND THYME SAUCE

Serves 4

8 thin slices calves' liver (about 1½ pounds)
1 cup all-purpose flour
2 tablespoons butter
1 tablespoon vegetable oil

S A U C E
1 medium onion, finely chopped
2 tablespoons all-purpose flour
1 cup beef broth (see page 5)
¼ cup lemon juice
1 teaspoon dried thyme
1 teaspoon tomato paste

Dredge the liver in the cup of flour and shake off the excess. Heat the butter and oil in a large skillet until very hot; fry the liver, a few pieces at a time, for 3 minutes on each side. Take great care not to overcook it or it will become tough. Take the liver out of the pan and keep it warm.

To make the sauce, add the onion to the skillet and sauté it for 3 minutes. Stir in 2 tablespoons flour. Then, using a wire whisk, stir in the beef broth, lemon juice, thyme, and tomato paste. Lower the heat, return the liver to the pan, and simmer it in the sauce until it is very hot again—but it should remain pink on the inside—about 2 minutes.

NOTE: Beef liver does not taste good; if you can't get the best calves' liver, have a sandwich instead.

VEAL AND PROSCIUTTO ROLLS (SALTIMBOCCA ALLA ROMANA)

Serves 6

12 thin slices veal, cut for scaloppine

12 slices prosciutto

2 teaspoons dried sage

2 tablespoons olive oil

2 tablespoons butter

¼ cup Marsala wine

Cut the veal and ham slices so that are the same size. Sprinkle each veal slice with sage, set a ham slice on top, and roll it up, securing the ham inside the veal with a toothpick. Repeat until you have 12 veal and ham rolls.

Heat the oil and butter in a large heavy skillet; fry the rolls over medium-high heat until they are lightly browned and tender, about 4 minutes. Do not overcook them or the veal will become tough. Transfer the rolls to a hot serving platter.

Add the Marsala to the pan juices and cook over high heat, stirring to pick up the browned pieces clinging to the pan, until reduced by half. Pour the sauce over the veal.

◼ BAKED VEAL CHOPS WITH HAM AND CHEESE

Serves 4

2 tablespoons butter

1 tablespoon vegetable oil

4 veal loin chops, cut ¾ inch thick

Salt

Freshly ground black pepper

4 slices mozzarella cheese

4 slices boiled ham

1 1-pound jar top-quality marinara sauce, heated

2 tablespoons chopped fresh basil

¼ cup heavy cream

Preheat the oven to 400 degrees.

Heat the butter and oil in a heavy skillet until very hot—but do not let the butter turn brown. Add the veal chops and cook over medium-high heat, turning occasionally, until browned on both sides. Season with salt and pepper to taste. Cover each chop with a slice of cheese and a slice of ham.

Pour the hot marinara sauce into a baking dish. Add the basil and cream and stir to combine. Arrange the chops in the dish and spoon the sauce over them. Cover the dish with foil and bake until the cheese has melted, about 35 minutes.

VEAL WITH LEMON AND BRANDY

Serves 2

¾ pound veal scaloppine, cut from the top of the leg and flattened by the butcher
2 to 3 tablespoons butter
½ cup all-purpose flour
1 tablespoon lemon juice
2 tablespoons brandy
1 tablespoon finely chopped fresh parsley, for garnish
Lemon slices, for garnish
Watercress, for garnish

Dry the veal with paper towels. Heat 2 tablespoons of the butter in a 10-inch skillet until it is very hot but not brown. Dredge the veal scaloppine in the flour, patting off the excess flour between your hands. Slide 2 pieces of veal at a time into the hot butter and brown them quickly over moderately high heat, for about 3 minutes on the first side and 2 minutes on the second side. Continue, adding more butter if necessary and working quickly, until all the veal is cooked. Transfer each batch onto a very hot serving plate.

Add the lemon juice and brandy to the butter in the skillet, stirring to scrape up any brown bits. Simmer for 2 minutes, then pour the sauce over the veal. Sprinkle with chopped parsley and garnish with lemon slices and watercress.

■ VEAL IN WINE SAUCE

Serves 2

1 pound veal, cut from the leg

2 tablespoons butter

2 shallots or scallions, finely chopped

3 medium mushrooms, sliced

1 teaspoon paprika

1 tablespoon all-purpose flour

Salt and pepper

¾ cup white wine or chicken broth (see page 5)

¼ cup heavy cream

2 tablespoons finely chopped fresh parsley, for garnish

Cut the veal into thin strips and set aside.

Heat the butter in a saucepan, sauté the shallots in the butter until they are soft and transparent. Add the veal strips and fry over high heat for 2 minutes, folding the veal over and over as though you were stir-frying it. Toss in the mushrooms and cook for another 2 minutes. Stir in the paprika and flour and season to taste with salt and pepper. Add the wine or chicken broth, stirring to form a medium-thick sauce. Stir in the cream and cook for 1 minute more.

Serve sprinkled with the parsley.

NOTE: It is particularly difficult to give precise cooking times for veal. The meat varies so widely in age and quality that the only test is to taste a small piece and see if it is done. You may need another couple of minutes' cooking time for this recipe, but that should be sufficient.

FRUIT-STUFFED PORK LOIN WITH RED CABBAGE

Serves 6

1 3-pound head red cabbage, shredded

4 slices uncooked bacon, diced

1 cup red wine

2 tablespoons port wine

¼ cup red wine vinegar

Salt

Freshly ground black pepper

¼ pound dried apricots, finely chopped

¼ pound dried apples, finely chopped

1 cup apple cider or water

2 tablespoons apricot preserves

2 tablespoons applesauce

4 teaspoons Dijon mustard

1 3½-pound boneless pork loin, with a pocket cut in it to hold the stuffing

Preheat the oven to 350 degrees.

Combine the cabbage, bacon, wines, and vinegar with the salt and pepper to taste; spread the mixture over the bottom of a large roasting pan.

Soak the apricots and apples in cider for 15 minutes. Stir in the apricot preserves and applesauce. Season to taste with salt and pepper. Spread 1 teaspoon of the mustard into the pocket of the pork; fill the pocket with the fruit mixture. Tie the loin with string at 2-inch intervals to form a compact roll. Place the pork on top of the cabbage mixture, cover the pan with aluminum foil, and cook in the preheated oven for 1¾ hours.

Remove the meat from the oven, take off the foil, and brush the surface of the pork with the remaining 3 teaspoons of mustard. Return the meat to the oven and continue cooking, uncovered, until the pork is golden brown, about 30 minutes more.

■ SAUTÉED PORK LOIN

Serves 6

2 tablespoons butter

1 tablespoon vegetable oil

2 pounds boneless pork loin, cut into ½-inch-thick slices

½ cup chopped onion

1 teaspoon Dijon mustard

1 tablespoon paprika

2 tablespoons all-purpose flour

½ cup chicken broth (see page 5)

½ cup apple juice

3 tablespoons Calvados or other apple brandy

½ cup heavy cream

Heat the butter and oil in a large skillet until sizzling hot; fry the pork slices quickly over medium-high heat until lightly browned, about 3 minutes on each side. Remove the pork and set aside. Add the chopped onion to the skillet; sauté it until softened, about 5 minutes, then stir in the mustard, paprika, and flour. Add the remaining ingredients, stirring with a small wire whisk to form a smooth sauce. Return the pork slices to the skillet and simmer over low heat, uncovered, until the pork is white and tender, about 8 minutes.

■ LAMB STEW

2½ pounds stewing lamb, trimmed and cut into 2-inch cubes

3 tablespoons vegetable oil

2 onions, finely chopped

2 cloves garlic, finely chopped

2 carrots, chopped

2 stalks celery, chopped

2 tablespoons all-purpose flour

1 cup red wine

1 cup chicken broth (see page 5)

1 teaspoon tomato paste

1 teaspoon dried rosemary

1 bay leaf

½ teaspoon salt

Freshly ground black pepper

1 cup green peas, cooked

1 16-ounce can white beans, drained

2 tablespoons finely chopped fresh parsley

Preheat the oven to 350 degrees.

In a large skillet, fry the lamb cubes, a few at a time, in the oil until lightly browned. Transfer the lamb to a casserole. Sauté the onions, garlic, carrots, and celery in the fat remaining in the skillet until softened, about 3 minutes. Stir in the flour and add the wine and broth (or use 2 cups broth). Stir in the tomato paste, rosemary, bay leaf, salt, and pepper to taste. Pour the sauce over the lamb. Cover the casserole and cook in the preheated oven until the lamb is tender, about 1½ hours.

Add the peas and beans. Continue cooking for 5 minutes until the peas and beans are hot, about 5 minutes more. Sprinkle with parsley and serve.

NOTE: The stew may be made a day ahead and refrigerated. Gently reheat it before serving.

LAMB SHANKS WITH YELLOW SPLIT PEAS AND LEMON

Serves 6 to 8

1 pound dried yellow split peas
4 cloves garlic, finely chopped
2 onions, finely chopped
2 carrots, finely chopped
4 stalks celery, finely chopped
2 teaspoons dried rosemary
½ ounce dried mushrooms
1 lemon
4 cups beef broth (see page 5)
3½ pounds lamb shanks, each cut in half through the joint

Preheat the oven to 350 degrees.

Rinse the dried peas in a colander and put them in a large casserole that has a tight-fitting lid. Add the garlic, onions, carrots, celery, rosemary, and mushrooms. Grate the rind of the lemon and add it to the pot, then cut the lemon in half and bury the halves among the peas. Add the beef broth. Arrange the lamb shanks on top of the peas. Cover the pot and put it in the preheated oven. Cook until the lamb is tender and the peas have absorbed all the liquid, about 2 hours.

VARIATION: Green split peas or lentils may be substituted for the yellow split peas.

ROAST LEG OF LAMB WITH GARLIC AND ROSEMARY

Serves 8

MARINADE

1 teaspoon salt

Freshly ground black pepper, to taste

1 small onion, finely chopped

1 clove garlic, finely chopped

2 teaspoons dried rosemary

Pared rind of 1 lemon

Juice of 1 lemon

1 cup red wine

1 4-pound boned leg of lamb

Combine the marinade ingredients in a shallow dish just large enough to accommodate the lamb. Place the lamb in the marinade and cover the dish with transparent plastic wrap. Refrigerate the marinating lamb for up to 3 days, turning it from time to time to coat the lamb thoroughly with the marinade.

Preheat the broiler or charcoal grill.

Remove the lamb from the marinade and broil it for 15 minutes on the first side and 10 minutes on the second side. Brush the lamb with the marinade while it broils.

CHICKEN IN THE POT

Serves 8

1 5-pound chicken or capon, trussed
8 cups chicken broth, or 4 cups chicken broth and 4 cups dry white wine (see page 5)
8 carrots, cut into 1½-inch lengths
8 leeks, washed carefully and sliced
4 onions, finely chopped
6 sprigs fresh parsley
1½ teaspoons dried tarragon, or 1 tablespoon fresh tarragon leaves
16 tiny new potatoes
1 pound fresh green beans
2 cups fresh peas

Put the chicken or capon in a 5- or 6-quart casserole and cover it with the chicken broth. Bring the broth to a simmer and skim off the foam that rises to the surface. When the broth is completely clear, cover the casserole and simmer over very low heat for 1 hour. Add the carrots, leeks, onions, parsley, and tarragon; simmer for 40 minutes more. Remove the chicken from the casserole, cut it into serving pieces, and set the pieces aside. Discard the parsley. Add the potatoes and beans to the broth. Cover and simmer for 15 minutes more. Return the chicken to the pot and add the peas. Cover and simmer for another 10 minutes.

Serve the chicken and vegetables in the broth in deep soup bowls, or reserve the broth and serve it separately.

CHICKEN POTPIE

Serves 4

2 cups cooked chicken, cut into cubes

2 cups cooked ham, cut into cubes

2 cups mixed cooked vegetables, such as peas and carrots or celery and onions

2 tablespoons butter

2 tablespoons all-purpose flour

2 cups chicken broth (see page 5)

Baking Powder Biscuits (see page 242), slightly undercooked

Preheat the oven to 350 degrees.

Combine the chicken, ham, and vegetables in a bowl.

Heat the butter in a saucepan until it is hot and bubbling. Stir in the flour and add the chicken broth gradually, stirring, to form a smooth sauce. Simmer over low heat until the sauce has thickened and reduced slightly, about 15 minutes. Stir the sauce into the ingredients in the bowl and combine thoroughly. Transfer the mixture to a 9-inch baking dish or divide it among 4 individual baking dishes. Top the filling with the biscuits, cover the dish with foil, and bake for 20 minutes. Uncover and continue baking until the biscuits are crisp and well browned, about 10 minutes.

NOTE: The biscuits can be made ahead of time or you can bake them while you are preparing the potpie filling. If you do this, you will then need to reduce the oven temperature to bake the pie since the biscuits bake at 450 degrees.

CHICKEN WITH CITRUS FRUITS

Serves 4

1 3½-pound roasting chicken
1 teaspoon salt
2 lemons, thinly sliced and each slice halved
2 limes, thinly sliced and each slice halved
1 thick-skinned orange, thinly sliced and each slice quartered
1 tablespoon vegetable oil
1 teaspoon paprika

Preheat the oven to 350 degrees.

Season the inside of the chicken cavity with salt and add some of the lemon, lime, and orange slices. Arrange half of the remaining fruit slices in a baking dish. Truss the chicken, brush it with the oil, sprinkle it with paprika, and put it in a baking dish. Bake the chicken for 55 minutes or until done (see page 7).

Discard the fruit inside the cavity and cut the chicken into serving pieces and garnish the platter with the remaining citrus slices.

FRIED CHICKEN IN BEER BATTER

Serves 2

I cup all-purpose flour
I teaspoon paprika
Salt
Freshly ground black pepper
½ cup beer
I 2½-pound frying chicken, cut into serving pieces
Peanut oil or vegetable shortening
Coarse kosher salt
Marmalade Sauce (see page 190)

Combine ½ cup of the flour, the paprika, and salt and pepper to taste in a small bowl. Stir in the beer with a wire whisk to make a batter slightly thinner in consistency than pancake batter.

Pat the chicken pieces dry with paper towels. Dredge the chicken in the remaining ½ cup of flour, shake off the excess, and then coat each piece with the batter.

Half fill a deep-fat fryer with the oil; heat the oil to 375 degrees. Place as many of the chicken pieces in the fryer basket as possible without crowding; deep fry them for 25 minutes, then lift the frying basket from the oil. Reheat the oil until it is again 375 degrees. Lower the basket carefully into the hot fat (the chicken will splutter and protest quite a lot) and continue frying until the chicken pieces are brown and crisp, about 5 minutes more. Continue with any remaining chicken.

Remove the chicken and drain well on paper towels spread over a wire cake-cooling rack. (This will allow the air to circulate around the chicken and keep it crisp; if you put it directly on paper towels on the counter, the steam will become trapped and the batter will almost certainly become soggy and unappetizing.)

Sprinkle the pieces with coarse salt and serve on paper doilies, which will absorb any remaining fat. Serve with marmalade sauce on the side.

BROILED CHICKEN WITH MUSTARD

Serves 4

1 2½-pound broiling chicken, cut into serving pieces
1 tablespoon vegetable oil

BASTING SAUCE (FLAVORED BUTTER)
4 tablespoons butter, melted
2 tablespoons Dijon mustard
2 tablespoons finely chopped fresh parsley
2 tablespoons chopped chives
1 tablespoon chopped fresh mint, or 1 teaspoon dried marjoram
1 tablespoon lemon juice

Preheat the broiler or charcoal grill.

Dry the chicken thoroughly with paper towels. Brush the broiling rack with the oil to prevent the chicken from sticking to it.

Combine the ingredients for the basting sauce and brush the chicken all over with part of the flavored butter.

Set the chicken on a rack 6 inches from the heat to allow the air to circulate so the skin will become crisp. Broil for 20 minutes on each side, basting every few minutes with the remaining flavored butter.

CHICKEN IN CHAMPAGNE

Serves 2

3 tablespoons butter
1 2½-pound chicken, preferably range-fed, cut into serving pieces
Salt
Freshly ground black pepper
4 cloves garlic, unpeeled
1 bottle champagne (reasonably good quality)
1 tablespoon cornstarch dissolved in 2 tablespoons cold water
1 tablespoon finely chopped fresh parsley, or 1 thinly sliced truffle, for garnish

Preheat the oven to 325 degrees.

Heat the butter in a deep skillet. Lightly brown the chicken, a few pieces at a time, on all sides. (If the butter browns, discard it, clean the skillet with paper towels and start again, using fresh butter for the next batch.) Then remove the chicken from the skillet and drain on paper towels while cooking the rest. Season to taste with salt and pepper.

Remove the outer peeling of the garlic cloves but leave the inner peel intact (in order to give just a hint of garlic). Add the garlic to the skillet.

Return all the chicken pieces to the skillet. Add 1 cup of the champagne to the skillet; cover and cook over medium-high heat for 15 minutes. Remove the lid and add another cup of champagne. Cover the skillet again and cook for 15 minutes more. Repeat the process with the third and fourth cups of champagne. Remove the chicken pieces and keep them warm in the oven.

Remove the garlic cloves from the skillet and discard them. Boil the champagne over high heat until the liquid is reduced to 1 cup. Stir the dissolved cornstarch into the liquid in the skillet, and continue stirring until the liquid is thickened and a sauce has formed, about 2 minutes. Pour the sauce over the chicken and garnish with finely chopped parsley.

CHICKEN IN RED WINE (COQ AU VIN)

Serves 4 to 6

2 2½-pound chickens
4 tablespoons butter
1 tablespoon vegetable oil
18 shallots, peeled and left whole, or 10 scallions, cut into 1-inch pieces
10 small white onions, peeled and left whole
1 teaspoon paprika
2 tablespoons all-purpose flour
½ cup red wine
½ cup chicken broth (see page 5)
Salt
Freshly ground black pepper
½ pound button mushrooms, trimmed
¼ pound thinly sliced ham, cut into strips
2 tablespoons finely chopped fresh parsley

Preheat the oven to 350 degrees.

Truss the chickens. Heat 2 tablespoons of the butter and the oil in a large heavy casserole and brown the chickens, breast side first, over medium-high heat. Remove the chickens and set aside. Add the shallots and onions to the casserole; cook until lightly browned, then remove them and set aside. Add the paprika and flour to the butter and oil in the casserole, stirring with a wire whisk. Gradually pour in the wine and chicken broth, and cook, stirring, over medium-high heat until a medium-thick sauce has formed. Then return the chickens, shallots, and onions to the casserole. Cover and simmer over low heat for 50 minutes. Check for doneness (see page 7), and season with salt and pepper to taste.

Heat the remaining 2 tablespoons of butter in a small saucepan; sauté the mushrooms in the butter for about 5 minutes or until soft. Garnish the casserole with the mushrooms, sliced ham, and parsley.

STIR-FRIED TURKEY BREAST WITH SESAME OIL

Serves 4

1 1½-pound boneless, skinless turkey breast, cut into strips
2 tablespoons sesame oil
1 tablespoon soy sauce
1 teaspoon honey
¼ teaspoon dried cumin
Freshly ground black pepper
Pinch of cayenne pepper
Peanut oil
6 scallions, chopped
½ cup peanuts
1 teaspoon cornstarch
¼ cup dry sherry
Salt

Put the turkey strips in a bowl and add the sesame oil, soy sauce, honey, cumin, black pepper, and cayenne pepper. Mix to coat the turkey. Cover the bowl and refrigerate for 2 hours.

Heat the peanut oil in a wok or large skillet over high heat. Add the turkey and stir-fry for 5 minutes. Add the scallions and peanuts; stir-fry for 5 minutes more.

Stir the cornstarch into the sherry to form a smooth paste; add the paste to the pan and cook until the liquid has thickened and glazes the other ingredients. Add salt to taste.

STIR-FRIED CHICKEN WITH WALNUTS

Serves 4

8 dried black mushrooms, or 8 fresh white mushrooms, sliced
2 tablespoons vegetable oil
4 skinless, boneless chicken breasts, cut into strips▪
⅓ cup chicken broth (see page 5)
8 scallions, cut into 2-inch pieces
4 tender stalks celery, cut diagonally into small pieces
1 cup walnuts
2 tablespoons soy sauce
2 tablespoons dark plum sauce
1 cup snow peas or sugar snap peas
Freshly cooked All-Purpose Rice (see page 205)

Put the dried mushrooms in a bowl and cover them with hot water. Let them soak until they are soft, about 15 minutes. Rinse the mushrooms, remove the tough stems, and slice.

Heat the oil in a skillet on high heat. Add the chicken and stir-fry until the meat is white and opaque, about 3 minutes. Add the chicken broth, scallions, celery, walnuts, and mushrooms; stir-fry for 2 minutes.

Add the soy and plum sauces to the skillet. Reduce the heat to moderate and continue to stir-fry the ingredients for about 5 minutes. Add the snow peas and stir-fry for 3 minutes more.

Increase the heat to high and cook until the liquid has been reduced and the vegetables are crisp-tender. Remove the skillet from the heat and serve immediately with hot, freshly cooked rice.

VARIATION: Other green vegetables, such as broccoli florets, sliced zucchini, or cucumber, can be substituted for the snow peas. Cucumber is particularly good served as a hot vegetable.

▪ You can substitute turkey or duck breast for the chicken breasts.

CHICKEN PAPRIKASH

Serves 4

2 tablespoons butter

I tablespoon vegetable oil

2 medium onions

6 mushrooms, sliced

I 3-pound chicken, cut into serving pieces

2 medium tomatoes, peeled, seeded, and chopped

3 teaspoons tomato paste

I green bell pepper, cut into strips

2 tablespoons Hungarian paprika

I teaspoon salt

½ cup chicken broth (see page 5)

2 tablespoons all-purpose flour

¾ cup sour cream

Heat the butter and oil in a heavy casserole over low heat. Sauté the onion until softened, about 5 minutes. Add the mushrooms and sauté them for 3 minutes. Remove the vegetables from the pan.

Increase the heat to moderate. Add the chicken to the casserole and cook, turning occasionally, for 10 minutes.

Reduce the heat to low. Add the tomatoes, tomato paste, and green pepper; stir in the paprika and salt. Add the chicken broth and cook, covered, for 20 minutes, then remove the lid and cook, stirring occasionally, until the chicken is tender, about 10 to 15 minutes more. Transfer the chicken pieces to a serving platter and keep warm.

Stir the flour into the sour cream until well blended. Add the mixture to the pan and cook, stirring occasionally, until the sauce starts to thicken, about 4 to 5 minutes. (Do not let the mixture get too hot or it will curdle.) Pour the sauce over the chicken and serve.

◼ CHICKEN WITH PROSCIUTTO

Serves 4

4 skinless, boneless chicken breasts

8 thin slices prosciutto, halved

½ cup grated Parmesan cheese

½ cup shredded mozzarella cheese

8 fresh sage leaves, or I teaspoon dried sage

2 tablespoons butter

2 tablespoons olive oil

¾ cup white wine

Salt

Freshly ground black pepper

Cut each chicken breast lengthwise into 3 or 4 pieces. Put the pieces between 2 sheets of wax paper and pound them with a rolling pin until they are ⅛ inch thick.

Cover each chicken piece with a half slice of prosciutto, 2 teaspoons of Parmesan, 2 teaspoons of mozzarella and half a sage leaf. Roll each piece up lengthwise and secure with a toothpick.

Heat the butter and oil in a large skillet until bubbling; cook the chicken rolls, 8 at a time, until lightly browned about 4 to 5 minutes. Repeat with the remaining chicken rolls, removing the rolls from the skillet once they are browned.

Add the wine to the skillet and simmer, stirring, over gentle heat, for 2 to 3 minutes. Return the chicken rolls to the pan, season to taste with salt and pepper, and simmer until tender, about 3 to 4 minutes more. Spoon the juices from the pan over the chicken.

CHICKEN WITH ALMONDS AND GARLIC

Serves 4 to 6

1 3½- to 4-pound chicken, cut into serving pieces
¼ cup olive oil
2 cloves garlic, finely chopped
1 large onion, sliced
2 tablespoons all-purpose flour
1½ cups white wine
1 cup chicken broth (see page 5)
Salt
Freshly ground black pepper
1 bay leaf
1 sprig fresh thyme, or ½ teaspoon dried thyme
24 blanched almonds, finely chopped
½ teaspoon ground saffron
2 Hard-cooked Eggs (see page 227), chopped, for garnish
¾ cup toasted bread crumbs, for garnish
1 tablespoon finely chopped fresh parsley, for garnish

Pat the chicken dry with paper towels. Heat the oil in a large heavy skillet and cook the chicken over moderate heat, turning frequently, until golden brown on all sides. Remove the chicken from the pan and set aside. Pour off all but about 2 tablespoons of fat from the pan.

Add the garlic and onion to the skillet and sauté until softened, about 3 to 4 minutes. Return the chicken to the pan and stir in the flour. Stir in the wine and the chicken broth. Season with salt and pepper to taste and add the bay leaf and thyme. Bring the mixture to a boil, then reduce the heat to low and simmer, covered, for 20 minutes.

Add the chopped almonds and saffron and simmer until the chicken is tender, about 20 minutes more. Sprinkle the chicken with the chopped eggs, bread crumbs, and parsley just before serving.

SUNDAY NIGHT CHICKEN SUPPER

Serves 6

1 5-pound chicken or capon

6 cups water

3 onions, cut into pieces

4 carrots, sliced

8 leeks, washed and sliced

4 stalks celery, sliced

1 turnip, sliced

4 cloves

3 sprigs fresh parsley

2 bay leaves

1 teaspoon dried thyme

1 teaspoon peppercorns

6 cloves garlic, peeled and left whole

Truss the chicken and put it in a large clay cooking pot or casserole. Pour in the water. Add a quarter each of the sliced onions, carrots, leeks, and celery and half the sliced turnip. Add the herbs and spices. Cover the casserole and simmer over low heat for 1 ½ hours. Remove the chicken and strain the broth, discarding the vegetables. Return the strained broth and chicken to the casserole. Add the remaining vegetables and continue cooking until the vegetables are tender, about 20 minutes more.

Strain the broth again and serve as a soup. Serve the chicken and vegetables separately with crusty French bread.

CHICKEN WITH RICE (ARROZ CON POLLO)

Serves 4

I 3-pound chicken, cut into serving pieces
Salt
Freshly ground black pepper
¼ cup plus I tablespoon olive oil
I medium onion, coarsely chopped
2 cloves garlic, finely chopped
1½ cups chicken broth (see page 5)
½ cup water
½ cup white wine
¼ teaspoon red pepper flakes
¼ teaspoon ground saffron
I bay leaf
I 16-ounce can plum tomatoes
I cup uncooked rice
½ red bell pepper, seeded and cut into strips
½ yellow bell pepper, seeded and cut into strips
½ green bell pepper, seeded and cut into strips

Preheat the oven to 350 degrees.

Season the chicken pieces with salt and pepper to taste. Heat the ¼ cup of oil in a large heavy skillet over moderate heat. Fry the chicken pieces (do this in batches, to avoid overcrowding the pan), turning once, until golden brown on all sides, about 10 minutes; remove the chicken to a large ovenproof casserole.

Add the onion and garlic to the skillet and sauté until softened, about 3 minutes. Add the broth, water, wine, red pepper flakes, saffron, bay leaf, tomatoes with their liquid, and rice. Season with salt and pepper to taste and bring to a boil.

Pour the liquid mixture over the chicken in the casserole; cover and bake the casserole until both the rice and the chicken are tender, about 25 minutes.

Heat the remaining tablespoon of oil in a small skillet. Add the pepper strips and sauté until they are just tender, about 4 minutes. Stir the pepper strips into the casserole and serve at once.

■ GINGERED CHICKEN

Serves 4 to 6

MARINADE
½ cup soy sauce
¼ cup sherry
2 tablespoons lemon juice
I teaspoon sugar
¼ teaspoon cayenne pepper
I clove garlic
I-inch piece fresh gingerroot, peeled and finely chopped

I 3½- to 4-pound chicken, cut into serving pieces

Combine the marinade ingredients in a saucepan and bring to a boil, then set aside and allow the mixture to cool to lukewarm.

Put the chicken pieces in a bowl, pour the marinade over them and cover. Marinate for about 30 minutes at room temperature (or up to 4 hours if refrigerated), turning the pieces several times to ensure that they are evenly coated.

Preheat the broiler or charcoal grill.

Remove the chicken from the marinade; drain the pieces and pat them dry with paper towels. Cook on a lightly oiled rack, basting frequently with the marinade, until the chicken is done and nicely glazed, about 7 to 8 minutes on each side for white meat, or 15 to 16 minutes for dark meat.

CHICKEN BREASTS STUFFED WITH RICOTTA AND HERBS

Serves 6

MARINADE
1 cup olive oil
¼ cup lemon juice
2 tablespoons Dijon mustard
3 cloves garlic, crushed
Freshly ground black pepper, to taste

6 boneless chicken breasts, with skin on
1 cup ricotta cheese
2 tablespoons chopped fresh basil, or 2 teaspoons dried basil
2 tablespoons grated Parmesan cheese
1 tablespoon fresh bread crumbs
Salt
Freshly ground black pepper

Combine the ingredients for the marinade in a shallow pan large enough to accommodate the chicken breasts; place the chicken in the marinade. Marinate the chicken breasts for about 2 hours at room temperature or up to 8 hours if refrigerated, turning the breasts occasionally.

Preheat the broiler or charcoal grill.

Combine the ricotta, basil, Parmesan, and bread crumbs in a bowl, using a fork. Remove the chicken breasts from the marinade. Slip your fingers between the skin and meat of one of the breasts; stuff the pocket with about one-sixth of the cheese filling; repeat with the remaining breasts. Season to taste with salt and pepper.

Arrange the chicken breasts, stuffed side up, on a lightly oiled rack, and broil for about 4 minutes on each side. Let the breasts stand for a couple of minutes, then slice them diagonally. They can be served hot, warm, or at room temperature.

NOTE: If you are using a charcoal grill, heat the coals to medium-hot and cover the breasts with foil while they are on the grill.

POT-ROASTED ROULADE OF TURKEY

Serves 6 to 8

1 4-pound boned turkey beast, with the skin on

3 teaspoons Dijon mustard

10 to 12 fresh basil leaves, or 10 fresh spinach leaves, washed and stemmed, and 3 tablespoons dried basil

¼ pound Swiss cheese, thinly sliced

¼ pound boneless ham, thinly sliced

Olive oil

Salt

Freshly ground black pepper

½ cup white wine

Preheat the oven to 350 degrees.

Lay the turkey breast, skin side down, on a work surface and pound with a mallet to flatten slightly. Brush the mustard over the surface of the meat and arrange the basil leaves on top of the mustard. (If you are using spinach leaves, sprinkle the dried basil over the leaves.) Arrange the cheese slices over the basil; top with the ham slices. Roll the breast up tightly, starting at the long side, and tie it at 2-inch intervals with kitchen twine. Rub the roll with olive oil and season to taste with salt and pepper.

Pour the wine into a large ovenproof casserole, put the rolled turkey into the casserole, and roast, covered, for about 1½ hours. Let the roulade stand for about 20 minutes before slicing.

CHICKEN WITH LEMON AND HERBS

Serves 6

2 2½-pound roasting chickens
3 tablespoons butter
Pared rind and juice of 2 lemons, strained
24 whole shallots, peeled, or 24 scallions, white part only, cut into 1-inch lengths
2 tablespoons fresh mint leaves, chopped, or 1 teaspoon dried mint
2 tablespoons chopped chives
3 tablespoons finely chopped fresh parsley
¾ cup chicken broth (see page 5)
¼ cup white vermouth
1 teaspoon salt
Freshly ground black pepper
2 tablespoons cornstarch dissolved in ¼ cup cold water
Watercress sprigs, for garnish
Lemon wedges, for garnish

Preheat the oven to 350 degrees.

Truss the chickens so that they will not become dry as they cook. Heat the butter in a large casserole. Add the chickens to the casserole, but do not brown them. Add the lemon rind and strained lemon juice, shallots, mint, chives, and parsley. Add the chicken broth and white vermouth; season with salt and pepper to taste. Cover the casserole and bake the chickens for 50 minutes. Discard the lemon rind. Remove the chickens from the casserole; cut them into serving pieces and keep them warm.

Stir the dissolved cornstarch into the liquid in the casserole. Cook over low heat, stirring, until the liquid thickens and forms a smooth sauce. Arrange the chicken on a hot serving platter and cover it with the sauce. Garnish the platter with watercress and lemon wedges.

NOTE: If you decide to serve the chicken cold, do not thicken the broth into a sauce. Omit the cornstarch and save the cooking liquid to use as the foundation for a soup.

CURRIED CHICKEN

Serves 6

3 tablespoons vegetable oil
2 2½-pound frying chickens, cut into serving pieces
2 small yellow onions, chopped
1 green bell pepper, seeded and chopped
1 tablespoon good Indian (Madras) curry powder
2 teaspoons ground cumin
2 tablespoons all-purpose flour
½ cup tomato puree
1½ cups chicken broth (see page 5)
Juice of ½ lemon

Preheat the oven to 350 degrees.

Heat the oil in a large skillet and fry the chicken pieces until they are lightly browned. Remove the chicken pieces with a slotted spoon and put them in a casserole. Sauté the onions and green pepper in the oil remaining in the skillet for 3 minutes. Stir in the curry powder and cumin; cook over moderate heat for 2 minutes. Stir in the flour and add the tomato puree, chicken broth, and lemon juice.

Pour the sauce over the chicken, cover the casserole, and bake until the chicken is tender, about 50 minutes.

CRISP-FRIED TURKEY BREAST

Serves 4

½ cup all-purpose flour
1 teaspoon dried thyme
1 tablespoon paprika
1 teaspoon salt
Freshly ground black pepper
8 moderately thin slices turkey breast, cooked or raw
2 eggs, lightly beaten
2 tablespoons milk
1 tablespoon Dijon mustard
1 cup fine bread crumbs
2 tablespoons butter
1 tablespoon vegetable oil

Combine the flour, thyme, paprika, salt, and pepper to taste in a large bowl. Dredge the turkey breast slices in the seasoned flour and shake off the excess.

In a separate bowl, combine the eggs, milk, and mustard. Coat the floured turkey slices in the batter, then dredge them in the bread crumbs.

Heat the butter and oil in a large skillet until very hot. Fry the turkey over moderately high heat until the batter is crisp and golden. For leftover cooked turkey, fry for 4 minutes on each side; allow an additional 2 minutes per side for raw turkey slices. Serve immediately.

BROILED SWORDFISH WITH MUSTARD BUTTER

Serves 4

MUSTARD BUTTER

8 tablespoons butter, softened

2 tablespoons Dijon mustard

1 tablespoon freshly squeezed lemon juice

1 tablespoon chopped fresh Italian parsley

4 6-ounce swordfish steaks, about ¾ inch thick

2 tablespoons olive oil

Salt

Freshly ground black pepper

Combine the butter, mustard, lemon juice, and parsley. Roll the mixture up tightly in aluminum foil, making a cylinder, and refrigerate until firm, about 2 hours. Slice the cylinder into ⅛-inch-thick pieces and return it to the refrigerator.

Rub the swordfish steaks with the olive oil and season to taste with salt and pepper. Broil on a lightly oiled rack for 5 to 8 minutes per side or until done (see page 14).

Place a slice of the prepared butter on the center of each piece of hot fish and serve immediately.

SMOKED FISH CASSEROLE

Serves 4

1 pound smoked haddock fillets

1¼ cups milk

½ cup water

2 tablespoons butter

1 small onion, finely chopped

2 strips bacon, cooked and finely crumbled

1 cup drained canned whole kernel corn

Freshly ground black pepper

2 tablespoons all-purpose flour

Preheat the oven to 350 degrees.

Rinse the fish under cold running water. Remove the skin, then pat the fish dry with paper towels and cut it into small pieces.

Reserve 2 tablespoons of the milk; combine the rest of the milk with the water and pour the mixture into a deep ovenproof casserole. Add the butter, onion, bacon, corn, and pepper to taste. Bake, covered, until the onion starts to soften, about 15 minutes.

Add the fish to the casserole; bake, covered, for 10 minutes more.

Combine the flour and the reserved milk in a bowl to form a smooth paste. Beat in a few tablespoons of the hot liquid from the casserole and stir the thickener back into the liquid in the casserole. Bake, covered, until the fish flakes easily with a fork, about 5 minutes more.

■ SWORDFISH WITH CAPERS

Serves 4

½ cup fresh lemon juice
4 6-ounce swordfish steaks
Salt
Freshly ground black pepper
6 tablespoons butter
2 tablespoons capers
1 tablespoon chopped fresh parsley, for garnish

Reserve ¼ cup of the lemon juice; sprinkle remaining ¼ cup of lemon juice over the swordfish. Sprinkle with salt and pepper to taste.

Heat the butter in a skillet over moderate heat; fry the swordfish until browned, about 4 minutes. Turn the steaks and cook them for 3 to 4 minutes more. Do not overcook. Transfer the steaks to a warm platter and keep warm.

Add the capers and the reserved lemon juice to the skillet; heat until bubbling. Pour the sauce over the swordfish and sprinkle with chopped parsley.

TUNA WITH RED WINE AND TOMATOES

Serves 4

2 cups red wine

2 cups clam broth or bottled clam juice

2 cups water

1 small onion, finely chopped

1 clove garlic, peeled

1 bay leaf

½ teaspoon dried thyme

1 celery stalk, chopped

4 6-ounce tuna steaks or fillets

4 tablespoons butter

3 tablespoons all-purpose flour

Pinch of sugar

Salt and freshly ground black pepper

3 medium-size tomatoes, peeled, seeded, and chopped

2 tablespoons finely chopped fresh parsley

4 lemon wedges, for garnish

Combine the wine, clam broth, and water in a fish poacher or large saucepan and bring to a boil. Add the onion, garlic, bay leaf, thyme, and celery. Reduce the heat to low and simmer for 20 minutes.

Strain the poaching liquid through cheesecloth and return it to the pan. Lower the tuna into the stock and bring it to a gentle simmer. Reduce the heat until the liquid is barely moving, cover the pan, and poach the fish until it yields when gently pressed with a finger, about 10 minutes. Drain the fillets, reserving 2 cups of the poaching liquid, and transfer the fish to a warm plate. Cover the fish with foil.

Heat the butter in a heavy saucepan over moderate heat. When the foam has nearly subsided, add the flour and the sugar. Stir until the mixture is just beginning to brown, then remove the pan from the heat and stir in a little of the reserved poaching liquid.

Return the sauce to the heat and cook, stirring, until thickened, then slowly stir in the remaining poaching liquid. Cook until the sauce is thickened, about 5 to 7 minutes. Season to taste with salt and pepper. Stir in the tomatoes and the parsley until just heated through.

Arrange the tuna on a heated serving platter. Spoon a little of the sauce over the fish and pour the rest into a warmed sauceboat to be passed separately. Garnish the platter with the lemon wedges.

FOIL-BAKED FISH WITH FENNEL

Serves 4

4 4-ounce bluefish fillets
4 tablespoons butter
2 tablespoons finely chopped fennel
2 tablespoons finely chopped fresh parsley
4 teaspoons freshly squeezed lemon juice
4 slices lemon, for garnish

Preheat the oven to 375 degrees.

Cut 4 pieces of aluminum foil to about 12 by 9 inches; spread each piece of foil with a little of the butter.

Place a bluefish fillet on each piece of foil. Dot with the remaining butter and sprinkle with half the fennel and half of the parsley. Fold the fillets in half and sprinkle with the remaining fennel and parsley; sprinkle each one with lemon juice. Fold the foil loosely over the fish to form 4 packets and arrange these on a baking sheet.

Bake until the fish flakes easily with a fork, about 10 to 12 minutes. Open each foil packet just before serving and garnish with a slice of lemon.

VARIATION: Substitute scrod or cod for the bluefish, white wine for the lemon juice, orange slices for the lemon slices.

■ LOBSTER MAYONNAISE

Serves 6

3 3-pound live lobsters
1½ cups Homemade Mayonnaise (see page 186)
Bibb or Boston lettuce, for garnish
Cucumber, tomato, and lemon slices, for garnish
3 Hard-cooked Eggs (see page 227), cut into wedges, for garnish

Pour about 2 inches of salted water into a large pot or casserole and add a steamer basket. When the water boils, add the lobsters and steam them for about 18 minutes, regulating the heat so the water does not boil away. Use large tongs to remove the cooked lobsters from the pot and set them aside until they are cool enough to handle.

Turn a lobster onto its back with its legs in the air. Extend the tail and hold it down with a kitchen towel. Using a sharp knife, cut the membrane to which the legs are attached to each side of the back shell. Remove and discard the membrane and lift the tail meat out in one piece. (It will come out very easily.) Cut the meat into slices and set aside in a bowl.

Remove and discard the stomach sac and contents of the head cavity. (The green "tomalley" is used to enrich hot sauces, but cannot be used in this recipe.) Be on the lookout for any red "coral" found at the top of the tail meat; set it aside to be added to the mayonnaise to flavor it and give it a pink cast.

Wrap each claw in a kitchen towel and crack the shell with a heavy rolling pin, a lobster-cracking utensil, or a hammer. Remove the claw meat, cut it into bite-size pieces, and add it to the bowl. Repeat the process with the second lobster.

For the third lobster, leave the head meat inside the cavity and simply fold the membrane back over the body when you have removed the tail meat. Remove the claws and extract the meat as before. Add the meat from the third lobster to the bowl of lobster pieces, but keep the shell intact. (The third lobster will be used to garnish the dish and will become the centerpiece while the dinner is eaten.) Fold the mayonnaise into the lobster meat.

On a large oval or rectangular silver serving tray, lay a trough of lettuce leaves, conforming roughly to the long Y shape of the lobster. Mound the lobster mayonnaise on top of the lettuce, with a greater quantity at the top of the Y to give the presentation some height. Brush the reserved lobster shell with oil to make it shine, and lay it over the meat, placing the head over the higher point of the mound. Fold the membrane and legs back over the empty tail shell and extend the legs over the lobster meat, so the shell is hiding the meat like a chicken sitting on its eggs.

Garnish the tray with alternating slices of cucumber, lemon and tomato and hard-cooked egg quarters. This is the occasion to go to the trouble of making homemade mayonnaise and baking crusty rolls, and to serve champagne or well-chilled white wine.

■ POACHED TROUT

Serves 2

2 8-ounce whole dressed trout
1 cup water
½ cup white wine
1 lemon, cut in half
2 tablespoons finely chopped fresh parsley

Put the trout in a skillet and add the water and wine. Cover with buttered wax paper. Bring to a simmer and poach *very gently* until the fish is opaque and flakes easily with a fork, about 8 minutes. Transfer the fish carefully to hot plates, using 2 slotted spatulas.

BAKED SHAD

Serves 6

2½ pounds shad fillets
¼ teaspoon salt
Freshly ground black pepper
4 tablespoons butter, melted
2 tablespoons freshly squeezed lemon juice

Preheat the oven to 350 degrees.

Butter a large baking dish and put the fish in it, skin side down. Season the fish with salt and pepper to taste. Combine the melted butter and 1 tablespoon of the lemon juice; brush this mixture over the fish. Bake the fish, uncovered, for 10 minutes, basting with the lemon butter after 5 minutes. Sprinkle the remaining tablespoon of lemon juice over the fish just before serving.

LOBSTER NEWBURG

Serves 4

1 2½-pound live lobster
3 tablespoons butter
2½ tablespoons all-purpose flour
1½ cups chicken broth (see page 5)
2 egg yolks
½ cup heavy cream
2 tablespoons dry sherry
½ teaspoon salt
Dash of cayenne pepper
1 teaspoon tomato paste
Freshly made toast, cut into triangles and crusts removed

Cook the lobster in a large pot of boiling salted water for 18 minutes following the directions in the previous recipe. Remove the meat and cut it into bite-size pieces.

Heat the butter in a saucepan and stir in the flour. Stir in the chicken broth. Combine the egg yolks with the cream and add to the chicken broth mixture. Then add the sherry, salt, pepper, and tomato paste, stirring until combined. Add the lobster and simmer the sauce over low heat just until the lobster pieces have heated through, about 5 minutes. Serve immediately on toast triangles.

RED SNAPPER WITH TOMATOES

Serves 2

1½ pounds red snapper fillets
2 tablespoons butter
½ medium onion, chopped
1 cup dry white wine, or ½ cup white vermouth mixed with ½ cup water
Juice of ½ lemon
½ teaspoon salt
4 tomatoes, peeled, seeded, and chopped
2 teaspoons finely chopped fresh parsley, for garnish

Put the fish in a shallow pan just large enough to hold it. Distribute the butter, onion, wine, lemon juice, and salt evenly over the fish. Cover the pan and simmer over low heat, allowing 10 minutes of cooking time for each inch of thickness of the fish. Transfer the fish carefully to a serving dish and keep warm.

Strain the poaching liquid into a saucepan and boil it until it is reduced to about ½ cup. Add the tomatoes and simmer for a couple of minutes until they have heated through. Strain the sauce and spoon it over the fish. Garnish with the parsley.

BAKED RED SNAPPER WITH TARRAGON SAUCE

Serves 4

4 ½-pound whole dressed red snapper, head removed
3 tablespoons butter, melted
1 lemon, thinly sliced, plus lemon wedges for garnish
Fresh parsley sprigs, for garnish
Cherry tomatoes, for garnish

SAUCE
½ cup Homemade Mayonnaise (see page 186)
2 teaspoons lemon juice
1 teaspoon grated lemon rind
1 teaspoon finely chopped fresh tarragon leaves

Preheat the oven to 350 degrees.

Brush some of the melted butter over a shallow baking dish large enough to accommodate the fish in a single layer, or use 2 baking dishes. Brush the fish with the remaining butter and arrange the lemon slices over each fish. Cover with foil and bake for 25 minutes.

To prepare the sauce, whisk all the ingredients together until smooth. (It should be served at room temperature.)

Serve the fish directly from the baking dish, garnished with lemon wedges and sprigs of parsley, interspersed with cherry tomatoes. Pass the sauce separately.

POACHED SALMON STEAKS

Serves 2

2 ½-pound salmon steaks
1 cup cold water
½ cup white wine
1 teaspoon salt
Juice of ½ lemon

BOUQUET GARNI
½ onion, thinly sliced
1 teaspoon whole peppercorns
1 bay leaf
4 sprigs fresh parsley
½ teaspoon dried thyme
Chopped fresh chives, for garnish
Freshly shelled green peas, for garnish

Place the salmon in a large skillet and add the water, wine, salt, and lemon juice. Tie the onion, peppercorns, bay leaf, parsley, and thyme in a piece of cheesecloth to form a bouquet garni and add to the skillet. Simmer the fish gently, over *very* low heat, allowing 10 minutes for each inch of thickness.

Lift the salmon from the water and drain on paper towels spread over a wire cake-cooling rack.

Serve at room temperature, garnished with the chives and peas.

GRAVAD LAX

Serves 6

3 tablespoons coarse kosher salt
3 tablespoons sugar
1½ tablespoons cracked black peppercorns
1 3-pound center-cut salmon, with skin on, cut in half lengthwise and bones removed
1 large bunch fresh dill, chopped

Mix together the salt, sugar, and peppercorns in a small bowl.

Place one piece of the salmon on a flat surface, skin side down, and cover with an even layer of the peppercorn mixture and the dill. Put the other piece of salmon on top, skin side up. Wrap the fish in wax paper to enclose it completely and put it in a shallow dish. Weight the salmon evenly with cans of food. (The heavy weight and the salt will force the water out of the fish, leaving it firm and easy to slice.)

Put the salmon in the refrigerator and leave it to marinate for 3 or 4 days, turning it every other day. Remove the salmon from its wrappings and gently scrape off and discard the seasonings. Pat the fish dry.

Slice the salmon very thinly with a sharp, thin-bladed knife, held almost horizontally, and serve as you would smoked salmon.

NOTE: It is essential to use fresh dill for this recipe.

VARIATION: Cut slightly thicker slices, about the same size as minute steak, and broil or pan-fry them in an oiled Teflon-coated skillet *literally* for no longer than 2 minutes. Serve with a garnish of watercress.

SWORDFISH STEAK WITH SHRIMP

Serves 2

2 scallions, chopped

2 ½-pound swordfish steaks (or one steak weighing about 1 pound)

1 sprig fresh parsley

1 bay leaf

8 peppercorns

½ cup white wine

Juice of ½ lemon

1 tablespoon butter

1 tablespoon all-purpose flour

⅓ cup heavy cream

Salt

Freshly ground black pepper

6 cooked shrimp, shelled and deveined

Lemon wedges, for garnish

Fresh parsley sprigs, for garnish

Preheat the oven to 350 degrees.

Butter an ovenproof dish and sprinkle it with the scallions. Place the fish on top of the scallions and add the parsley, bay leaf, peppercorns, wine, and lemon juice. Bake the fish for 12 to 15 minutes, turning it once. Strain the liquid from the pan; set it aside. Transfer the fish to a serving dish and keep it warm while you make the sauce.

Heat the butter in a small saucepan and stir in the flour. Whisk in the poaching liquid and then the cream. Add salt and pepper to taste. Spoon the sauce over the fish and arrange the shrimp on top of the sauce. Garnish the serving dish with lemon wedges and parsley.

SHRIMP IN CRISP BATTER

Serves 6

BATTER

1 cup sifted all-purpose flour
1 teaspoon salt
1 teaspoon paprika
1 tablespoon fresh lemon juice
1¼ cups beer
Marmalade Sauce (see page 190)

1½ pounds jumbo shrimp
Peanut oil
Juice of 1 lemon
½ cup all-purpose flour

Whisk together the batter ingredients until smooth. Set the batter aside to thicken at room temperature for 1 hour.

Meanwhile, remove the shells from the shrimp leaving the tail shells attached and cut them into fantails by cutting down the back just enough so that you can spread the shrimp out like a fan. When you are ready to cook the shrimp, fill a deep-fat fryer with the peanut oil to a depth of 4 inches. Heat the oil to 375 degrees. Sprinkle the shrimp with lemon juice and dredge them in the flour. Shake off the excess flour and dip the shrimp in the batter. Slide a few shrimp at a time into the hot oil and fry each batch until the batter has puffed, about 3 to 4 minutes. Remove to drain on paper towels and repeat the process until all the shrimp are fried.

When all the shrimp have been fried once, reheat the oil to 375 degrees and repeat the process again, deep-frying them a few at a time until the batter is as crisp as tempura, about 3 minutes. Serve with marmalade sauce.

BROILED SHRIMP WITH GARLIC

Serves 2

¾ pound large fresh shrimp

2 tablespoons butter

2 scallions or shallots, finely chopped

4 cloves garlic, crushed

Juice of ½ lemon

I teaspoon fresh parsley

I teaspoon chives

½ teaspoon fresh tarragon, or ¼ teaspoon dried tarragon or oregano

½ teaspoon paprika

Cook the shrimp in simmering salted water for 3 minutes. Remove and set them aside until they are cool enough to handle. Remove the body shell, but leave the tail intact. Cut each shrimp in half through the length of the back, keeping it attached at the tail. Discard the dark vein running down the back of the shrimp.

Heat the butter in a skillet and sauté the scallions and garlic until soft and transparent. Add the fantailed shrimp, lemon juice, herbs, and paprika. Remove the pan from the heat and turn the shrimp over until they are coated on both sides with the garlic butter. Transfer them to a shallow ovenproof dish with a slotted spoon; reserve the garlic butter.

Preheat the broiler or charcoal grill.

Broil the shrimp for 3 minutes; turn them with tongs and broil for 2 minutes more. Serve very hot, with French bread to dip into the reserved garlic butter.

CIOPPINO

Serves 8

2 dozen littleneck clams (see page 37)

2 dozen mussels (see pages 37–38)

⅓ cup olive oil

2 medium onions, finely chopped

2 cloves garlic, finely chopped

1 medium green bell pepper, seeded and finely chopped

¼ cup finely chopped fresh parsley

3 medium tomatoes, peeled, seeded, and chopped

½ cup dried Italian mushrooms, soaked in warm water to cover for 15 minutes, then drained

2 cups dry red wine

1½ teaspoons salt

Freshly ground black pepper

1 pound medium-shrimp, shelled and deveined

1½-pound live lobster, cut into bite-size pieces

2 tablespoons tomato paste

1½ teaspoons chopped fresh oregano

2½ pounds striped bass or other firm white fish fillets, cut crosswise into 2-inch pieces

Scrub the clams and mussels thoroughly and rinse them in 3 changes of cold water.

Pour about an inch of water into a 5½-quart heavy casserole and bring to a boil. Add the clams and mussels, cover the pan, and steam them until the shells have opened, about 5 minutes. Discard any whose shells have not opened. Strain the broth through 3 thicknesses of cheesecloth and reserve it. Discard the top shell from each clam and mussel; reserve the shellfish on the half shells.

Heat the olive oil in the casserole and cook the onions, garlic, and green pepper over moderate heat until softened, about 5 minutes.

Add the parsley, tomatoes, mushrooms, red wine, salt, and pepper to taste and bring to a boil. Lower the heat and add the shrimp, lobster, tomato paste, and oregano. Add the pieces of fish and the reserved broth from the clams and mussels. Cover the pan and simmer for 8 minutes over very low heat. Add the reserved clams and mussels on the half shell and cook just until hot, about 2 minutes. Take great care not to overcook the fish——it should be just opaque.

NOTE: Have the lobster cut up at the fish market unless you are stout of heart.

VARIATION: You can make a very good variation on this fish stew if you use white wine instead of red and omit the oregano. Instead, add the grated rind of 2 oranges, ¼ teaspoon saffron threads, and ⅓ cup Pernod.

MOULES MARINIÈRES

Serves 6

4 dozen fresh mussels, preferably farm-raised (see pages 37–38)
6 shallots, finely chopped
⅓ cup white wine or white vermouth
1 tablespoon lemon juice
½ cup heavy cream (optional)
1½ tablespoons butter
3 tablespoons very finely chopped fresh parsley

Wash the mussels in cold water. Bring about 1 inch of water to a boil in a large casserole. Put a steamer basket in the casserole and steam the mussels, covered, until they have opened, about 5 minutes. Set aside and discard any whose shell hasn't opened.

Strain the liquor from the casserole through cheesecloth into a saucepan and simmer over low heat until it is reduced to about 1 cup.

Add the shallots and the wine to the mussel broth and cook over low heat until the shallots have softened, about 10 minutes. Add the lemon juice, cream, butter, and parsley; stir to combine.

To serve, discard the top half of each mussel shell. Divide the mussels in half shells among 6 hot plates and pour the sauce around them. Serve them with crusty bread to dip into the tasty sauce.

TORTELLINI WITH SCALLOPS AND BACON

Serves 2

½ pound fresh or frozen tortellini
½ pound bacon, cut into small pieces
¼ cup chicken broth (see page 5)
2 tablespoons white vermouth
2 tablespoons olive oil
½ pound fresh bay scallops
Freshly grated Parmesan cheese

Cook the tortellini according to package directions or to taste.

Meanwhile, fry the bacon in a skillet until crisp. Drain on paper towels and set aside.

Heat the chicken broth, vermouth, and oil in a small saucepan.

Toss the drained tortellini with the hot liquid, bacon pieces, and the scallops. (The scallops will cook in the trapped heat.) Serve with the grated Parmesan, passed separately.

VARIATION: Add quartered cherry tomatoes or cooked and reheated asparagus tips or broccoli florets or a combination.

◼ LASAGNE

Serves 10

1 pound lasagne noodles, preferably fresh
Vegetable oil

FILLING
2 cups ricotta cheese
¼ cup finely chopped green bell pepper
2 tablespoons finely chopped onion
3 eggs
1 teaspoon salt
Freshly ground black pepper, to taste
1 teaspoon dry mustard
2 cups milk
1 pound mozzarella cheese, thinly sliced

SAUCE
4 tablespoons butter
½ cup finely chopped scallions
2 cloves garlic, finely chopped
¼ cup finely chopped green bell pepper
3 tablespoons all-purpose flour
1 14-ounce can Italian plum tomatoes, drained
3 tablespoons tomato paste
1 teaspoon salt
Freshly ground black pepper, to taste
1 teaspoon dried oregano

Preheat the oven to 350 degrees.

Bring a large pot of salted water to a boil and add the lasagne noodles. If you are using fresh pasta, boil it for 4 minutes; if you are using packaged pasta, boil it for 8 minutes. Drain the pasta. Refill the pan with lukewarm water to which you have added 1 tablespoon of vegetable oil (this will prevent the noodles from sticking to each other); add the lasagne noodles.

Combine the ricotta cheese, green pepper, and onion in a small bowl. In another bowl, beat together the eggs, salt, pepper, and mustard; stir in the milk. Butter a 12-inch shallow baking dish and arrange half of the lasagne noodles in it. Cover the noodles with a third of the mozzarella slices and half the ricotta cheese mixture. Arrange half of the remaining mozzarella and then all the remaining lasagne noodles on the top and cover with the remaining ricotta cheese mixture and mozzarella. Pour the egg-milk mixture over all. Put the dish in a large pan of hot water and bake for 1 1/4 hours.

To prepare the sauce, heat the butter in a saucepan; sauté the scallions, garlic, and green pepper in the butter until tender. Stir in the flour and cook for 2 minutes. Add the tomatoes, tomato paste, salt, pepper, and oregano; stir constantly until the sauce has thickened. Simmer the sauce, uncovered, over low heat for 30 minutes.

Cut the lasagna into squares and pour a generous spoonful of the sauce over each serving.

■ SPAGHETTI WITH GARLIC AND HERBS

Serves 2 to 3

½ pound spaghetti, preferably imported Italian
4 tablespoons olive oil
12 cloves garlic, coarsely chopped
½ cup fresh basil leaves, finely chopped
2 tablespoons finely chopped cilantro
3 tablespoons finely chopped fresh chives
A lot of freshly ground black pepper

Cook the spaghetti according to package directions or to taste.

While it is cooking, heat the oil in a skillet and add the garlic. Sauté the garlic over low heat for 8 minutes, then strain the oil. Add the oil to the drained hot spaghetti and toss with the herbs and pepper. Serve immediately.

■ SPAGHETTI WITH BUTTER AND CHEESE

Serves 2 to 3

½ pound spaghetti
6 tablespoons unsalted butter, melted
½ cup freshly grated Parmesan cheese
2 tablespoons finely chopped fresh Italian parsley
Freshly ground black pepper, to taste

Cook the spaghetti according to package directions or to taste.

Lift it from the boiling water, using a spaghetti rake or strainer, and shake it vigorously to get rid of most of the water. Put it into a heated bowl and add the remaining ingredients. Toss with 2 forks until every strand is coated with butter. Serve immediately.

FETTUCCINI WITH CHICKEN BREASTS

Serves 4

1 pound fettuccini

3 tablespoons butter

4 skinless, boneless chicken breast halves, cut into thin strips

6 cloves garlic, peeled and finely chopped

6 scallions, finely chopped

1 tablespoon all-purpose flour

⅓ cup heavy cream

1 tablespoon fresh lemon juice

⅓ cup grated Gruyère or other good Swiss cheese

¼ cup freshly grated Parmesan cheese

½ teaspoon salt

Freshly ground black pepper

3 tablespoons finely chopped fresh parsley

Cook the pasta according to package directions or to taste.

While the pasta is cooking, heat the butter in a large skillet; sauté the chicken strips in the butter over high heat until they are firm and white, barely 4 minutes. Remove the chicken and keep it warm. Stir in the garlic and scallions; sauté over moderate heat for 3 minutes. Stir in the flour. Add the cream and lemon juice and cook, stirring continuously, until hot. Add the cheeses and season with salt and pepper to taste.

Drain the fettuccini and toss with the chicken and sauce. Sprinkle with chopped parsley and serve immediately.

GREEN FETTUCCINI WITH TOMATOES AND MOZZARELLA

Serves 2

½ pound green fettuccini
1 cup Fresh Tomato Sauce (see page 188)
3 fully ripe large tomatoes, peeled, seeded, and chopped
¼ cup chopped fresh basil or oregano leaves, or 1 teaspoon dried basil or oregano
¾ cup diced mozzarella cheese
4 tablespoons freshly grated Parmesan cheese
Freshly ground black pepper

Cook the pasta according to package directions or to taste.

While the pasta is cooking, heat the tomato sauce and stir in the chopped tomatoes and basil.

Drain the fettuccini and toss it with the tomato sauce and the cheeses. Season to taste with pepper and serve immediately.

FETTUCCINI WITH CLAMS AND SHRIMP

Serves 3

½ pound fettuccini

2 cups Fresh Tomato Sauce (see page 188)

2 tablespoons olive oil

2 cloves garlic, finely chopped

Salt

½ cup white wine

12 littleneck clams, well scrubbed (see page 37)

½ pound small shrimp, shelled and deveined

1 cup fresh peas

Freshly ground black pepper

8 cherry tomatoes, quartered

3 tablespoon finely chopped fresh parsley, for garnish

Grated Parmesan cheese, for serving

Cook the pasta according to package directions or to taste.

Meanwhile, simmer the tomato sauce gently in a saucepan. In a separate pan, heat the oil; sauté the garlic until softened, about 3 minutes. Add the oil and garlic to the tomato sauce and season with salt to taste; simmer. While the sauce is simmering, pour the wine into a casserole. Put a steamer basket into the casserole, and steam the clams, shrimp, and peas, covered, until the clams open, about 5 minutes.

Toss the drained fettuccini in the hot tomato sauce using 2 forks, and season to taste with pepper. Stir in the clams, shrimp, peas, the liquid from the casserole, and the cherry tomatoes. Garnish with the parsley and serve immediately. Pass the Parmesan cheese separately.

■ PASTA PRIMAVERA

Serves 6

I pound spaghetti
¼ cup olive oil
4 cloves garlic
2 bunches scallions, finely chopped
I green bell pepper, seeded and cut into strips
I red bell pepper, seeded and cut into strips
I yellow bell pepper, seeded and cut into strips
I head broccoli, broken into florets
I pound fresh green peas, shucked
I small green zucchini, cut into strips
½ cup finely chopped fresh basil
Freshly ground black pepper
Freshly grated Parmesan cheese

Cook the spaghetti according to package directions or to taste.

Meanwhile, heat the oil in a small skillet; sauté the garlic and scalions until softened, about 5 minutes. Set aside.

Put a steamer basket into a large pot that has a tight-fitting lid; add water just up to, but not touching, the bottom of the steamer. Add the peppers, broccoli, peas and zucchini and steam, covered, until the vegetables are crisp-tender, about 10 minutes.

Drain the spaghetti and toss with the hot oil, garlic, and scallions. Add the steamed vegetables and basil and toss again until thoroughly combined. Season to taste with pepper and pass the Parmesan cheese separately.

NOTE: Tomatoes, asparagus, and other firm, brightly colored vegetables can be substituted for or added to the vegetables in this dish. Avoid eggplant, mushrooms, and cauliflower, which do not look attractive in this dish.

VARIATION: Serve as a pasta salad, tossed with an oil and vinegar dressing. Serve at room temperature.

▪ LINGUINI WITH MUSSELS AND PEAS

Serves 6

1 pound linguini

½ cup dry white wine

6 cloves garlic, finely chopped

2 pounds mussels (see pages 37–38), well scrubbed

1¼ cups shelled peas, parboiled for 4 minutes, or 1 10-ounce package frozen peas

2 tablespoons cornstarch dissolved in 3 tablespoons white wine or cold water

2 7-ounce jars whole pimientos or roasted peppers, drained and cut into strips

¼ cup chopped fresh basil

½ cup finely chopped fresh parsley

Grated rind of 2 lemons

Cook the pasta according to package directions or to taste.

While the pasta is cooking, pour the white wine into a large casserole that has a tight-fitting lid. Add the garlic. Put a vegetable steamer into the casserole and put the mussels and peas into the steamer. Cover and steam until the mussels have opened, about 5 minutes. Transfer the mussels and peas to a large heated bowl to keep them warm.

Very quickly, strain the liquid from the casserole into a saucepan through a fine sieve or colander lined with cheesecloth. Stir the dissolved cornstarch into the liquid. Cook over low heat, stirring, until a sauce has formed, about 1 or 2 minutes.

Drain the linguini and toss it with the sauce; then add the mussels and peas and combine thoroughly. Stir in the chopped pimientos, basil, parsley, and grated lemon rind. Serve immediately.

ZITI WITH MEAT AND TOMATO SAUCE

Serves 10

2 tablespoons olive oil
2 large onions, finely chopped
2 cloves garlic, finely chopped
2 pounds good-quality ground beef
½ pound mushrooms, thinly sliced
1 35-ounce can Italian plum tomatoes, drained
1 16-ounce can tomato puree
1 tablespoon tomato paste
¼ teaspoon crushed dried hot red pepper flakes
2 teaspoons dried oregano
Salt
Freshly ground black pepper
1 pound ziti
1 cup fine bread crumbs
¾ cup freshly grated Parmesan cheese
2 tablespoons butter or olive oil

Heat the olive oil in a saucepan; sauté the onions and garlic in the oil over moderate heat until softened, about 3 minutes. Add the beef and cook until lightly browned. Add the mushrooms and cook for 2 minutes. Drain and discard any excess fat. Add the canned tomatoes, tomato puree, tomato paste, red pepper flakes, oregano, and salt and pepper to taste. Simmer, uncovered, over low heat for 30 minutes.

Preheat the oven to 350 degrees.

Cook the pasta according to package directions or to taste. Drain and transfer to a large baking dish (or 2 smaller ones, if you prefer).

Combine the bread crumbs with the Parmesan cheese and sprinkle over the ziti. Dot the crumbs with butter or drizzle with oil, cover the dish (or dishes) with foil, and bake for 30 minutes. Remove the foil and continue baking until the surface is crisp, about 10 minutes more.

HOMEMADE PASTA

Serves 4

3 cups semolina or unbleached all-purpose flour

1 teaspoon salt

4 eggs

1 tablespoon olive oil

2 tablespoons water

Sift the flour and salt onto the counter and make a well in the center. Drop one egg into the well. Using your fingertips, draw part of the flour into the egg. Add the eggs, one at a time, mixing until a soft dough forms.

Add the oil and water and shape the dough into a ball. Knead for 10 minutes, adding a drop or two more water if the dough seems too dry, or a little more flour if it is sticky. (The object is to obtain a pliable dough that is rich in taste, smooth-textured, and easy to cut and shape.) Put the dough in a plastic bag to prevent it from becoming dry; let it rest for 1 hour.

Cut the dough into 4 pieces and return 3 pieces to the bag. Pat the piece of dough into a 4-inch square and dust with flour. Clamp the pasta machine onto the counter and set the rollers to 0 or the widest setting. Pass the dough through the rollers 3 times until it is smooth and evenly shaped. (The dough should be the same width as the roller.) If the dough becomes sticky, dust lightly with flour. Then pass it through increasingly narrower settings until it is the thickness you desire. For most purposes number 4 on a scale of 0 to 6 is ideal.

Use the first cutter on the machine to make wide noodles (fettuccini) and the second for narrow. Cook immediately after cutting, or leave on a lightly floured cloth and toss occasionally until dry, about 1 hour. Or drape over a wooden towel-drying rack or wire hanger to dry. Repeat the process with the remaining pieces of dough.

4

##############

ROASTS—GREAT
AND SMALL

■

ROAST CHICKEN WITH ROSEMARY

ROAST TURKEY WITH GIBLET GRAVY AND CORNBREAD
AND OYSTER STUFFING

SAUSAGE AND CHESTNUT STUFFING

CORNISH HENS WITH RASPBERRY VINEGAR

CORNISH HENS WITH SALT AND PEPPER

ROAST RACK OF LAMB

ROAST VEAL WITH TUNA DRESSING (VITELLO TONNATO)

ROAST PORK LOIN

ROAST PORK WITH BROWN SAUCE AND HONEY-GLAZED PEARS

GLAZED BAKED HAM

STUFFED HONEY-GLAZED DUCKLING

ROAST CHICKEN WITH ROSEMARY

Serves 4

3 tablespoons butter, softened
1 cup seedless green grapes
1 3½-pound roasting chicken
2 teaspoons fresh rosemary, crumbled
Salt
Freshly ground black pepper
1 teaspoon vegetable oil

Preheat the oven to 350 degrees.

Put 1 tablespoon of the butter and the grapes inside the cavity of the chicken and truss it with string. Rub the remaining butter all over the surface skin of the chicken, sprinkle it with rosemary, and season to taste with salt and pepper.

Brush the oil over a rack fitted in a roasting pan. Set the chicken, breast side up, on the rack. Roast it, basting it at 20-minute intervals with the pan juices, until a meat thermometer inserted into the thickest part of the thigh reads 180 degrees or when the juices run clear when a thigh is pierced with a sharp knife, about 1 hour.

Remove the chicken from the oven and cover with foil; let it rest for 10 minutes so that the juices can redistribute themselves through the meat. This will make it much easier to carve.

ROAST TURKEY WITH GIBLET GRAVY AND CORNBEAD AND OYSTER STUFFING

Serves 8 to 12

1 turkey, preferably fresh (for each person, allow 1 pound of turkey for a bird weighing
   less than 12 pounds and ¾ pound for one weighing more)
About 8 tablespoons butter, melted, or vegetable shortening

CORNBREAD AND OYSTER STUFFING
Makes 4 cups (enough for an 8-pound capon or a 12-pound turkey)

4 tablespoons butter
2 cups finely chopped onion
1 cup finely chopped celery, with the leaves
3 tablespoons finely chopped fresh parsley
1 teaspoon oregano
Salt and freshly ground black pepper
7-ounce bag cornbread stuffing
1 cup chicken broth (see page 5)
1 pint shucked oysters (see page 38), with their liquor

GIBLET GRAVY
Makes 2 cups

1 small onion, finely chopped
1 stalk celery, thinly sliced
3 sprigs fresh parsley
Turkey giblets, including the liver, cut into small pieces
3 cups chicken broth (see page 5)
2 tablespoons butter
3 tablespoons all-purpose flour
Salt and freshly ground black pepper
⅓ cup heavy cream (optional)

Preheat the oven to 325 degrees.

To make the stuffing, heat the butter in a large skillet; sauté the onion and celery gently for 10 minutes and pack it loosely into the cavity of the turkey. (Do this no more than 2 hours ahead as the warm, moist environment of the turkey's cavity can quickly become an ideal breeding ground for harmful bacteria. Don't pack the stuffing too tightly; it will expand when it is heated and you don't want it to erupt through the skin.) Seal the cavity with skewers or trussing string.

Massage the skin with melted butter or vegetable shortening. To protect the wings from burning, wrap them in oiled foil. Make sure the wings and legs are secured close to the body of the turkey.

Put the turkey, breast side down, on an oiled rack in a large roasting pan. Allowing 15 minutes to the pound, roast the bird, uncovered, for half of the estimated cooking time. Turn it breast side up for the remaining time or until a meat thermometer inserted sideways into the thickest part of the breast reads 185 degrees.

Allow the turkey to rest for 20 minutes before carving it. This resting period allows the juices that have risen to the surface to redistribute themselves, moistening all of the meat evenly. Wrap the bird loosely in aluminum foil to keep it warm. Be sure the serving platter on which the bird will make its entrance is warmed, too. Meanwhile, make the gravy.

Put the onion, celery, parsley, and giblets in a heavy saucepan. Add the chicken broth and simmer, uncovered, until reduced to 1½ cups, about 1½ hours. Discard the parsley and neck. Strain the liquid and put the onion, celery, and remaining giblets in a food processor. Add ½ cup of the broth and process until finely chopped.

Heat the butter in the saucepan over moderate heat and stir in the flour. Cook until the flour is lightly browned, about 2 minutes. Using a wire whisk, stir in the broth and giblets and season generously with salt and pepper. Add cream, if desired. (It gives the gravy a nice color and enriches its flavor, but the gravy tastes quite good without it.)

(continued on next page)

ROAST TURKEY WITH GIBLET GRAVY AND CORNBREAD AND OYSTER STUFFING *(cont.)*

NOTE: Almost all recipes suggest cooking a turkey at 350 degrees and 20 minutes to the pound. This is why so often the breast meat in particular becomes dried out and tasteless. Instead of stuffing a bird, spread the stuffing in a buttered 11-by-7-inch baking dish, cover with foil, and bake in a preheated 350-degree oven for 30 minutes.

VARIATION: If Cornbread and Oyster Stuffing is not to your taste, try the Sausage and Chestnut Stuffing that follows or substitute one of your own favorites.

SAUSAGE AND CHESTNUT STUFFING
Makes 7 cups (enough for a 14- to 18-pound turkey)

2 pounds fresh chestnuts
4 tablespoons butter
2 cups finely chopped onion
3 cups chopped celery, with the leaves
1 pound bulk sausage
3 cups freshly made bread crumbs (see page 5)
Salt
Freshly ground black pepper

Cut a cross in the flat side of each chestnut, using a sharp paring knife. Put the chestnuts in a large saucepan, cover them with cold water, and simmer them gently over low heat for 1 hour. Drain the chestnuts and peel them while they are still warm, keeping them as whole as possible.

Heat the butter in a large skillet; gently sauté the onion and celery in the butter until they are slightly softened but still quite crisp, about 10 minutes. Set aside.

In another skillet, crumble and fry the sausage until all the fat is rendered, adding about ⅓ cup cold water to the skillet to prevent the sausage from sticking. Drain the sausage and combine it with the onion-celery mixture. Add the peeled chestnuts and bread crumbs and season generously with salt and pepper.

NOTE: If you prefer a softer stuffing, add ½ cup chicken broth or bind the mixture with 2 slightly beaten eggs. You can also add a teaspoon of dried thyme or 2 teaspoons dried sage and 3 tablespoons of chopped fresh parsley with the salt and pepper.

CORNISH HENS WITH RASPBERRY VINEGAR

Serves 4

4 Cornish hens
1 medium onion, sliced
20 peppercorns, crushed
¼ cup raspberry vinegar
½ cup olive oil
Salt

Prepare the hens by removing the backbones with poultry shears or a sharp knife and flattening the hens out. Lay them in a shallow dish that is large enough to hold them all easily.

Add the onion, crushed peppercorns, vinegar, and olive oil and season to taste with salt. Rub the hens all over with the marinade, cover the dish, and refrigerate it overnight.

Preheat the broiler or a charcoal grill.

Lift the hens from the marinade using a slotted spoon, and arrange them on a lightly oiled rack. Broil, brushing frequently with the remaining marinade, until the juices run clear when the thighs are pierced, about 10 to 15 minutes on each side.

CORNISH HENS WITH SALT AND PEPPER

Serves 6

6 Cornish hens, trussed
3 tablespoons vegetable oil
6 teaspoons cracked black pepper
1½ boxes coarse kosher salt (3-pound box)
1 Hard-cooked Egg, preferably a brown one (see page 227)
Watercress, for garnish

Preheat the oven to 350 degrees.

Rub the surfaces of the hens with oil and press the cracked pepper onto the skin. Pour the kosher salt into an ovenproof platter large enough to accommodate all 3 hens. Spread the salt to form a thick bed for the hens coming three-quarters of the way up the dish's sides. Set the hens on the bed of salt, arranging them in a spokelike fashion in the dish with their breasts toward the center.

Roast the hens until the skins are deeply browned, about 50 minutes. Remove the dish from the oven, place the egg in the center, and garnish with sprigs of watercress.

NOTE: The salt keeps the hens wonderfully moist; it also retains the heat. Even if the hens have to be held for 20 minutes after they are cooked, they will stay hot.

ROAST RACK OF LAMB

Serves 6

2 3-pound racks of lamb
3 tablespoons butter, melted
2 tablespoons finely chopped fresh parsley
1 teaspoon dried thyme
2 teaspoons chopped chives
1 clove garlic, finely chopped
¾ cup freshly made bread crumbs
½ teaspoon salt
Freshly ground black pepper, to taste

Preheat the oven to 425 degrees.

Brush the lamb with part of the melted butter. Put the lamb on a roasting rack and roast, uncovered, for 15 minutes.

Meanwhile, combine the remaining butter and all the other ingredients in a bowl, and mix thoroughly. Remove the lamb from the oven and press the mixture over the outside of the meat. (It will form a fine crisp, nicely browned coating.) Return the lamb to the oven, reduce the temperature to 350 degrees, and continue roasting for 20 minutes or until it reads 130 degrees on a meat thermometer. Remove the lamb from the oven, allow it to rest for 10 minutes, then carve it between the ribs.

ROAST VEAL WITH TUNA DRESSING (VITELLO TONNATO)

Serves 8

1 3½-pound loin veal roast, boned, rolled, and tied at 1-inch intervals

1 6-ounce can Italian tuna, packed in oil

1 medium yellow onion, finely chopped

1 carrot, sliced

2 tender stalks celery, sliced

1 bay leaf

½ teaspoon dried thyme

1 teaspoon peppercorns

3 sprigs fresh parsley

1 cup chicken broth (see page 5)

1 cup dry white wine

2 cups Homemade Mayonnaise (see page 186)

4 cups cold cooked All-Purpose Rice (see page 205)

2 teaspoons capers

GARNISH

Fresh parsley sprigs

Sliced tomatoes

Sliced cucumber, finely chopped

Scallions, trimmed and sliced

1 Hard-cooked Egg (see page 227), cut in wedges

Green and black olives

Preheat the oven to 350 degrees.

Put the veal, tuna, onion, carrot, celery, bay leaf, thyme, pepper-corns, parsley, chicken broth, and white wine in a 2½-quart casserole. Bake, covered, for 50 minutes. (Do not overcook or the veal will toughen.) Remove the casserole from the oven and let it cool, without removing the lid. When cooled, refrigerate it for 12 hours.

Remove the veal from the liquid (which will have set into a jelly)

and set aside. Let the casserole return to room temperature, then heat it gently over low heat for 20 minutes. Strain the liquid into a clean, heavy saucepan and boil until it is reduced to about ⅔ cup. Cool then chill the reduced liquid, and, finally, beat it into the mayonnaise. This will become a pouring sauce for the veal.

Slice the veal thinly and arrange it on a platter decorated with the suggested garnishes. Scatter the capers over the veal slices and serve with cold cooked rice and the flavored mayonnaise in a sauceboat.

VARIATION: Serve the veal on a bed of cold rice, with a dressing composed of 3 tablespoons olive oil and 1 tablespoon lemon juice.

■ ROAST PORK LOIN

Serves 6

2 teaspoons salt
1 tablespoon mild dry mustard
2 teaspoons dried thyme
½ cup brown sugar
2 tablespoons butter, melted
1 4-pound boneless pork loin, tied at 2-inch intervals
2 cups apple juice
Peach halves, or applesauce, for garnish

Preheat the oven to 325 degrees.

Combine the salt, mustard, thyme, sugar, and butter in a bowl. Press the mixture firmly over the top and sides of the pork loin.

Set the meat on a rack over a roasting pan and insert a meat thermometer into the center. Pour the apple juice into the roasting pan. Roast, uncovered, until the meat thermometer reads 180 degrees, about 1 hour and 20 minutes (approximately 35 minutes per pound).

Remove the pork from the oven, wrap it loosely in aluminum foil, and allow it to rest for 15 minutes before slicing.

ROAST PORK WITH BROWN SAUCE AND HONEY-GLAZED PEARS

Serves 8

2 teaspoons very finely chopped gingerroot

I 4-pound boneless pork loin

Salt

Freshly ground black pepper

⅓ cup dry sherry

3 tablespoons butter, melted

I tablespoon honey

HONEY-GLAZED PEARS

8 small or 4 medium firm cooking pears

I cup sugar

2 cups water

Pared rind of I lemon

⅓ cup honey

¼ cup chopped sweet gherkins for garnish

BROWN SAUCE

I tablespoon diced pork fat, fatty ham, or blanched bacon

I small onion, finely chopped

I small carrot, diced

½ teaspoon dried thyme

3 tablespoons all-purpose flour

2 cups beef broth (see page 5)

½ cup red wine

3 medium fully ripe tomatoes, peeled, seeded, and chopped

2 teaspoons tomato paste

3 tablespoons red wine vinegar

2 teaspoons Dijon mustard

I tablespoon butter

Preheat the oven to 300 degrees.

Press the ginger over the surface of the pork fat and season it to taste with salt and pepper. Place the pork on a rack set over the roasting pan, insert a meat thermometer into the center of the meat, and roast for about 2 hours (allow 30 minutes per pound). Combine the sherry with the melted butter and honey; baste the pork with this mixture every 20 minutes. Remove the meat from the oven when the meat thermometer reads 185 degrees. The surface will be shiny and golden.

While the pork is roasting, peel, core, and halve each pear. Combine the sugar and water in a medium saucepan and boil over medium-high heat for 5 minutes. Add the lemon rind and then the pears. Reduce the heat to low; simmer the pears until they have softened somewhat—but do not let them become too soft—about 25 minutes. Drain the pears, reserving the poaching syrup; put the pears in a baking dish. Stir together ½ cup of the poaching syrup and the honey and pour the mixture over the pears.

Bake the pears in the oven with the pork for the final 30 minutes of cooking time.

To prepare the brown sauce, put the pork fat in a heavy saucepan; add the onion, carrot, and thyme. Cover the pan and fry over low heat for about 15 minutes. Stir in the flour; gradually whisk in the beef broth. Add the red wine, tomatoes, and tomato paste. Simmer, uncovered, over low heat until thickened and reduced by one third, about 40 minutes. Strain the sauce and return it to the saucepan. Stir in the vinegar and mustard and simmer for a few minutes over low heat until the sauce has thickened.

When ready to serve, swirl the butter into the sauce to make it shine attractively and garnish the glazed pears with the chopped gherkins.

GLAZED BAKED HAM

Serves 12

1 12-pound ham (labeled "cook before eating," "fully cooked" or "smoked")
Whole cloves (optional)

MUSTARD GLAZE
½ cup mild prepared mustard
½ cup brown sugar

FRUIT GLAZE
1 cup apricot preserves, marmalade, or pineapple or plum jam

If you are preparing a ham labeled "cook before eating," first preheat the oven to 325 degrees. Then put the ham, skin side up, on a rack in the roasting pan without any liquid. For a whole ham weighing 12 or more pounds, allow 18 minutes cooking time per pound, or approximately 3½ hours, until the internal temperature on a meat thermometer reaches 160 degrees.

If you are preparing a ham labeled "fully cooked" or "smoked," put the ham in a large casserole and cover it with water, apple cider, or part water and part white wine, immersing it so that the liquid comes to at least 1 inch above the ham. Simmer the ham gently over low heat, allowing 15 minutes to the pound. A 12-pound ham will be cooked in approximately 2½ hours, or when the internal temperature has reached 130 degrees when tested with a meat thermometer.

For any of the types of ham, continue as follows: Take the ham out of the casserole and allow it to cool somewhat. Remove the rind, score the fat, and stud it with cloves.

To prepare the mustard glaze, combine the mustard and brown sugar; to prepare the fruit glaze, strain the apricot preserves. Brush the surface of the ham with the glaze of your choice.

Increase the oven temperature to 400 degrees and return the

ham to the oven until it is nicely browned, about 15 minutes. When you remove it from the oven you should be able to see 2 bones. If the ham is correctly cooked, you will be able to pull out the smaller bone without any effort, making the ham much easier to slice.

Transfer the ham to a serving dish and let it rest for at least 15, or preferably 30, minutes before slicing it thinly.

■ STUFFED HONEY-GLAZED DUCKLING

Serves 4

STUFFING
2 tablespoons butter
1 cup chopped walnuts
1 small yellow onion, finely chopped
3 cups freshly made bread crumbs
Grated rind of 1 lemon
½ teaspoon cinnamon
1 teaspoon dried sage
½ teaspoon salt
Freshly ground black pepper, to taste
2 eggs, slightly beaten

1 4- to 5-pound duckling
3 tablespoons butter, softened
3 tablespoons honey

Preheat the oven to 350 degrees.

To prepare the stuffing, heat the butter in a skillet; sauté the walnuts in the butter over medium-high heat until they have browned, about 3 minutes. Add the onion and sauté until softened, about 3

(continued on next page)

minutes. Remove the pan from the heat and stir in the remaining stuffing ingredients. Lightly pack the stuffing into the duck cavity and secure it with trussing string or poultry lacers.

Set the duck, breast side up, on a rack in a roasting pan. Prick the skin all over with a fork to allow the fat to escape. Combine the butter and honey in a small bowl, then spread it over the duck. Insert a meat thermometer into the plumpest part of the thigh, making sure the tip does not touch the bone. Roast the duck until the meat thermometer reads 190 degrees, about 1½ hours. Don't be alarmed when you open the oven door and find that the duck skin has become almost black. This is how it should be—and the bird will be deliciously sweet and crisp.

Remove the duck and allow it to rest for 15 minutes before serving.

5

IT'S ALL IN THE SAUCE

VINAIGRETTE DRESSING

SPLENDID SALAD DRESSING

ROQUEFORT DRESSING I

ROQUEFORT DRESSING II

HOMEMADE MAYONNAISE

HOLLANDAISE SAUCE

BARBECUE SAUCE FOR SPARERIBS

FRESH TOMATO SAUCE (UNCOOKED)

COCKTAIL SAUCE FOR SHRIMP

PESTO

BOLOGNESE SAUCE FOR PASTA

MARMALADE SAUCE

CRANBERRY SAUCE

CRANBERRY RELISH

CHOCOLATE SAUCE

MELBA SAUCE

VINAIGRETTE DRESSING

Makes ¾ cup

2 tablespoons tarragon vinegar

6 tablespoons olive oil

2 small sweet gherkins, chopped

1 Hard-cooked Egg (see page 227), chopped

1 teaspoon drained capers

½ teaspoon Dijon mustard

Salt and freshly ground black pepper, to taste

Combine the ingredients in the order listed above.

SPLENDID SALAD DRESSING

Makes about 1 ½ cups

1 cup Homemade Mayonnaise (see page 186)

¼ cup heavy cream

1 teaspoon Dijon mustard

2 cloves garlic, crushed

½ cup finely grated Gruyère or Swiss cheese

¼ teaspoon sage

¼ teaspoon thyme

Combine all the ingredients in a blender or food processor. (The cheese will "melt" into the dressing.)

NOTE: This dressing will keep for at least 2 weeks in the refrigerator. If it becomes too thick to toss easily, add a little more vinegar or cream.

■ ROQUEFORT DRESSING I

Makes 1 cup

2 tablespoons good-quality Roquefort cheese
1 cup Homemade Mayonnaise (see page 186)
2 tablespoons whipped cream or sour cream

Crumble the cheese into the mayonnaise and combine with the whipped cream.

■ ROQUEFORT DRESSING II

Makes 1 cup

¼ cup crumbled good-quality Roquefort cheese
4 tablespoons heavy cream
Juice of ½ lemon
½ cup olive oil
3 tablespoons tarragon vinegar
Freshly ground black pepper

Mix the crumbled Roquefort and the cream with a fork; combine the classic mixture with the lemon juice, oil, and vinegar. Season with pepper to taste.

HOMEMADE MAYONNAISE

Makes 2½ cups

3 egg yolks
¼ teaspoon mild mustard
½ teaspoon salt
Freshly ground black pepper, to taste
3 tablespoons lemon juice or white wine vinegar
1½ cups olive oil, or ¾ cup each olive oil and vegetable oil

Put the egg yolks in a bowl; using a wire whisk or an electric mixer, beat them until they are thick and creamy. Beat in the mustard, salt, pepper, and 1 tablespoon of the lemon juice. Add the oil in a slow, steady, continuous stream, beating constantly, until all the oil is incorporated and the mayonnaise is thick. Be sure not to add the oil too quickly or the mayonnaise may curdle. Beat in the remaining lemon juice.

VARIATIONS:
- Puree ½ cup cooked spinach leaves in the food processor and combine with the mayonnaise to make Green Mayonnaise. Add more salt if needed.
- Add 2 to 3 tablespoons fresh mixed chopped herbs (parsley, chives, tarragon, basil, or dill) or half this quantity of dried herbs to the mayonnaise, and serve it with cold fish or hard-cooked egg dishes.
- Add 1 teaspoon curry powder to use with cold egg dishes.
- Add 1 teaspoon each of tomato paste and chopped pimiento to the mayonnaise to accompany cold fish salads.
- Add 1 teaspoon capers and 1 teaspoon finely chopped parsley to the mayonnaise to make a quick caper sauce.
- Give the mayonnaise a thinner pouring consistency by stirring in 1 to 2 tablespoons of hot, but not boiling, water.
- Add a little grated Swiss or cheddar cheese to mayonnaise to make an excellent quick hot sauce. When placed under a

broiler, the sauce will turn golden brown but, amazingly, will not separate.

■ HOLLANDAISE SAUCE

Makes 1 ¼ cups

12 tablespoons butter, chilled
3 egg yolks
3 tablespoons lemon juice
Pinch of salt
Dash of cayenne pepper

Reserve 2 tablespoons of the butter; melt the remaining butter in a small saucepan over low heat until it is bubbling. Turn off the heat at once or the butter will burn. Remove the saucepan from the stove.

In a separate small heavy saucepan, combine the egg yolks, lemon juice, and salt. Put the pan over low heat and add 1 tablespoon of the reserved chilled butter, stirring constantly until it has almost melted. Add the remaining 1 tablespoon butter and, again, stir until melted.

Remove the pan from the heat and add the very hot butter from the first saucepan slowly, stirring madly with a wire whisk. Do not take your eyes off the sauce for a moment. Taste for seasoning, adding cayenne pepper, salt, and lemon juice as necessary. As soon as the sauce has thickened, remove the saucepan from the stove. It must not continue to cook.

VARIATION: Hollandaise can be made in the food processor, but the texture does not compare with that of the handmade version. If you nonetheless prefer to use this method, heat the butter in a small saucepan until it is hot but not boiling. Place the egg yolks, salt, lemon juice, and cayenne in the food processor. Turn on the motor and add the melted butter in a slow stream. Turn off the motor as soon as all the butter has been incorporated and the sauce has thickened.

■ BARBECUE SAUCE FOR SPARERIBS

Makes about ½ cup

¼ cup beer
Juice of ½ lemon
1 tablespoon honey
1 teaspoon salt
1 teaspoon dry English mustard
¼ teaspoon ground ginger
⅛ teaspoon dried red pepper flakes

Combine all the ingredients in a bowl and mix thoroughly.

■ FRESH TOMATO SAUCE (UNCOOKED)

Makes 1 ½ cups

2 pounds fresh, fully ripened plum tomatoes, peeled, seeded, and chopped
6 garlic cloves, peeled and finely chopped
1 4½-ounce jar green olives, pitted and chopped
⅛ to ¼ teaspoon crushed dried hot red pepper flakes
1 tablespoon capers
2 tablespoons finely chopped fresh parsley
⅓ cup olive oil

Combine all the basic ingredients and let stand at room temperature for 4 to 6 hours to mature.

VARIATION: To make the sauce a little sharper, add a touch of freshly squeezed lemon juice.

COCKTAIL SAUCE FOR SHRIMP

Makes 1 ⅓ cups

1 cup tomato ketchup

1 teaspoon prepared horseradish

¼ teaspoon hot pepper sauce, or ⅛ teaspoon cayenne pepper

¾ teaspoon chili powder

2 cloves garlic, finely chopped

1 tablespoon fresh lemon juice

½ teaspoon salt

Combine all the ingredients in a bowl and mix thoroughly.

PESTO

Makes 1 ½ cups

2 cups packed fresh basil leaves

2 teaspoons finely chopped garlic

1 teaspoon salt

¼ cup pine nuts

1 cup light olive oil

¼ cup freshly grated Parmesan cheese

Combine the basil, garlic, salt, and pine nuts in the food processor and process until finely chopped. Add the oil through the top in a slow, steady stream with the motor running. Lastly add the cheese.

NOTE: To store pesto, pour a thin film of olive oil over the surface, cover, and refrigerate. Stir in the olive oil when you are ready to use the sauce.

BOLOGNESE SAUCE FOR PASTA

Makes enough for 1 pound of pasta

3 slices bacon, diced
1 large onion, finely chopped
2 cloves garlic, finely chopped
2 medium carrots, finely chopped
1 pound good-quality ground sirloin
3 pounds fresh or canned plum tomatoes
Salt and freshly ground black pepper, to taste
½ cup red wine
1 teaspoon dried oregano
2 teaspoons tomato juice
1 bay leaf (optional)

Fry the bacon in a skillet over moderate heat until the fat is rendered. Sauté the onion, garlic, and carrots in the bacon fat for 3 minutes. Add the ground beef and cook until what little fat there is is rendered. Drain in a colander, discard the fat, and return the mixture to a large saucepan. Add the remaining ingredients. Cover the pan and simmer gently over low heat for about 1 hour, stirring from time to time.

MARMALADE SAUCE

Makes 1 cup

1 cup orange, lemon, or lime marmalade
Juice of 1 orange, lemon, or lime
Pinch of ground ginger
1 teaspoon prepared horseradish

Put all the ingredients in the food processor and process until well combined, about 1 minute. Serve at room temperature.

CRANBERRY SAUCE

Makes 2 cups

1 cup water
1 cup sugar
½ pound cranberries
Grated rind of 1 orange
1 tablespoon port wine (optional)

Combine the water and sugar in a medium saucepan; boil for 10 minutes. Remove the pan from the heat and add the cranberries. Let stand for 5 minutes, then return the pan to a boil and boil for 3 minutes. Remove the pan from the heat and stir in the orange rind and port. Refrigerate the sauce for 4 hours before serving.

CRANBERRY RELISH

Makes two 8-ounce jars

2 cups fresh cranberries
Juice and grated rind of 1 large navel orange
1 cup sugar
1 teaspoon dry mustard dissolved in 1 teaspoon cold water
1 tablespoon cider vinegar

Wash the cranberries and put them in a heavy saucepan. Add the strained orange juice, grated orange rind, and the sugar. Bring just to a boil, then reduce the heat, and simmer gently for 5 minutes. Remove the pan from the heat; stir in the dissolved mustard and then the vinegar. Refrigerate for 24 hours; pack into jars and store in the refrigerator.

CHOCOLATE SAUCE

Makes 1 ½ cups

6 ounces semisweet chocolate morsels
2 tablespoons butter
1 cup heavy cream
1 teaspoon vanilla extract
2 tablespoons dark rum (optional)

Place the chocolate, butter, and cream in a small heavy saucepan. Stir over low heat until the chocolate has melted, about 10 minutes. Remove the pan from the heat; stir in the vanilla and rum.

MELBA SAUCE

Makes about 1 cup

1 pint fresh raspberries, or 1 10-ounce package frozen raspberries
Grated rind and juice of 1 orange
1 tablespoon lemon juice
2 tablespoons Framboise, kirsch, or Grand Marnier

Thaw the raspberries, if necessary, and put them (with their juice) in the food processor or blender. Add the grated orange rind and juice and the lemon juice and process for 1 minute. Strain the sauce through a sieve to remove the raspberry seeds and stir in the liqueur.

6

VEGETABLES PLUS

GRATED ZUCCHINI

BAKED ACORN SQUASH

CREAMED ONIONS

BRAISED CUCUMBERS AND PEAS

BRAISED BRUSSELS SPROUTS

CUCUMBERS IN YOGURT

WHITE CABBAGE WITH CHESTNUTS

RED CABBAGE WITH BEER

BRAISED CELERY

VEGETABLE STEW (RATATOUILLE)

POTATOES IN CREAM

PAN-FRIED POTATOES

SWEET POTATO CASSEROLE WITH ORANGE

NEW POTATO CASSEROLE

RISOTTO

ALL-PURPOSE RICE

BROILED TOMATOES

BAKED RADICCHIO WITH GOAT CHEESE

BRAISED ENDIVE

SICILIAN-STYLE BROCCOLI WITH CAULIFLOWER

PUREE OF WHITE WINTER VEGETABLES

GLAZED CARROTS

GRATED ZUCCHINI

Serves 6

4 or 5 small zucchini
2 tablespoons olive oil
¼ cup pine nuts
Freshly ground black pepper

Grate the zucchini into a bowl. Put a vegetable steamer in a saucepan that has a lid; put the grated zucchini in the steamer and pour boiling water under the steamer to a depth of ½ inch. Cover the pan and steam for 5 minutes. Heat the oil in a skillet and fry the pine nuts until they are lightly browned, about 2 minutes. Toss the zucchini with the hot oil and nuts and season with pepper to taste.

BAKED ACORN SQUASH

Serves 6

3 acorn squash
3 tablespoons butter, cut into small pieces
1¼ cups applesauce
3 tablespoons maple syrup
1½ teaspoons ground ginger

Preheat the oven to 350 degrees.

Cut each squash in half horizontally and scoop out the seeds and fibrous center. Arrange the squash halves in a baking dish and pour in enough hot water to come halfway up the side of the dish. Combine the butter, applesauce, maple syrup, and ginger; divide the mixture among the squash cavities. Cover the dish with foil and bake until tender, about 1 hour.

CREAMED ONIONS

Serves 8 to 12

2 pounds small whole white onions, or 2 1-pound jars whole white onions
3 tablespoons butter
3 tablespoons all-purpose flour
2 cups milk
½ cup heavy cream
Salt
Freshly ground black pepper
⅛ teaspoon nutmeg

If you are using fresh onions, peel them, trim the root ends and cut a cross in each one. Then cook them in boiling salted water until tender, about 25 minutes. If you are using onions from a jar, warm them over low heat in a saucepan.

Heat the butter in a large heavy saucepan. Whisk in the flour and then the milk and cream to form a smooth white sauce. Season to taste with salt and pepper and stir in the nutmeg. Add the onions and simmer gently for 10 minutes.

BRAISED CUCUMBERS AND PEAS

Serves 6

2 medium cucumbers, peeled
1 tablespoon salt
2 pounds fresh peas (1½ cups shelled peas)
2 tablespoons butter
18 scallions, white part only, chopped
¾ cup chicken broth (see page 5)
1 teaspoon lemon juice
2 tablespoons chopped fresh chives

Cut the cucumbers in half lengthwise and scoop out the seeds with a small teaspoon. Cut each half into ½-inch slices, put in a bowl, and toss with the salt. Refrigerate for 2 hours. Drain of any liquid and rinse the cucumbers in a colander under cold running water. Shell the peas.

Heat the butter in a heavy saucepan. Sauté the scallions in the butter over low heat until softened, about 5 minutes; add the cucumbers, peas, chicken broth, and lemon juice. Simmer, uncovered, until the cucumbers are transparent and the peas are tender, about 5 minutes. Drain and serve, garnished with the chopped chives.

BRAISED BRUSSELS SPROUTS

Serves 6

2 pint-boxes brussels sprouts
3 tablespoons butter
1 small onion, finely chopped
2 carrots, grated
¼ cup white vinegar
1 teaspoon salt
Freshly ground black pepper

Trim the brussels sprouts and cut a cross in the base of each sprout so that it will cook evenly. Set aside.

Heat the butter in a casserole and add the onion and carrots. Cover and cook over low heat for 5 minutes. Remove the lid and add the vinegar and brussels sprouts. Season with the salt and pepper to taste, then cover again and continue cooking over low heat for 15 minutes. Drain the sprouts and serve them immediately.

■ CUCUMBERS IN YOGURT

Serves 6

3 small cucumbers, peeled and cut into small pieces
1 tablespoon salt
1 cup plain yogurt
¼ cup chopped fresh cilantro, dillweed, or parsley

Put the cucumbers in a bowl and toss with the salt. Refrigerate for 40 minutes. Drain off the liquid and discard it. Rinse the cucumbers quickly in a colander under cold running water and pat dry on paper towels. Fold in the yogurt and chopped cilantro.

WHITE CABBAGE WITH CHESTNUTS

Serves 2

½ small head white cabbage
1 10½-ounce can chicken broth (see page 5)
8 peeled cooked whole chestnuts

Remove the core and heavy stems from the cabbage and shred the leaves into thin strips. Put the cabbage into a saucepan, add the chicken broth and simmer, uncovered, over low heat for 18 minutes. Add the chestnuts and allow them to heat through. Drain the cabbage and chestnuts and serve.

NOTE: Do not substitute water chestnuts, as their texture is not compatible with the cabbage in this recipe.

RED CABBAGE WITH BEER

Serves 6

8 slices bacon
2 large onions, chopped
2 green apples, peeled, cored, and sliced
1 small head red cabbage, shredded
2 tablespoons red currant jelly
Pinch of nutmeg
½ cup beer
Salt
Freshly ground black pepper

Fry the bacon in a skillet until crisp; drain on paper towels. Pour off all but 2 tablespoons of the bacon fat. Sauté the onions and apples in the fat until softened. Transfer the onions and apples to a deep casserole and add the shredded cabbage, red currant jelly, nutmeg, beer, and salt and pepper to taste. Cover and simmer over low heat for 1 hour.

■ BRAISED CELERY

Serves 6

3 bunches celery hearts
Salt
1 onion, finely chopped
1 carrot, finely chopped
1 teaspoon tomato paste
1 cup beef broth (see page 5)
1 tablespoon cornstarch dissolved in 2 tablespoons cold water
2 tablespoons finely chopped fresh parsley

Preheat the oven to 350 degrees.

Cut the celery hearts lengthwise into thin strips and then into pieces about 3 inches long. Put the celery in a saucepan and cover with cold water. Add salt to taste. Simmer over low heat for 15 minutes, then drain.

Put the drained celery in a baking dish and add the onion, carrot, and tomato paste. Bring the beef broth to a boil and pour it over the celery. Cover the dish with foil and bake until the vegetables are tender, about 1 hour.

Stir the dissolved cornstarch into the hot liquid in the baking dish. Heat the liquid, stirring, until thickened, about 1 or 2 minutes. Serve the celery hot, sprinkled with chopped parsley.

VEGETABLE STEW (RATATOUILLE)

Serves 6

1 medium or 4 small eggplants
4 tablespoons olive oil
2 large onions, thinly sliced
3 cloves garlic, finely chopped
1 green bell pepper, seeded and cut into strips
1 red bell pepper, seeded and cut into strips
2 thin zucchini, sliced
3 medium fully ripe tomatoes, cut into wedges and seeded
¾ teaspoon salt
¼ cup chopped fresh basil leaves
1 bay leaf
2 tablespoons finely chopped fresh parsley

Cut the eggplant into ¼-inch slices and then into cubes. Heat the olive oil in a large skillet; sauté the eggplant cubes in the oil for 6 or 7 minutes until lightly browned all over. Add the onions, garlic, and peppers; sauté for 3 minutes more. Add the zucchini and the remaining ingredients. Cover the skillet and cook over low heat for 15 minutes; remove the lid and continue cooking until most of the liquid has evaporated, about 10 minutes more. Stir occasionally just to make sure the vegetables are not sticking to the bottom of the skillet and burning. Serve hot, at room temperature, or cold.

■ POTATOES IN CREAM

Serves 6

2½ cups heavy cream
2 tablespoons butter
2 cloves garlic, finely chopped
5 large potatoes
1 teaspoon salt
Freshly ground black pepper
½ cup freshly grated Parmesan cheese

Preheat the oven to 350 degrees.

Pour the cream into a heavy saucepan. Add the butter and garlic and simmer over low heat until the cream has thickened and reduced slightly, about 15 minutes. (It has a tendency to boil over, so keep an eye on it.)

Peel the potatoes, cut them into very thin slices, and dry them on paper towels. Butter a small casserole. Cover the bottom of the casserole with a layer of potatoes; sprinkle a little salt, pepper, and Parmesan cheese over the potatoes and top with a few spoonfuls of the reduced cream. Repeat the layering until all the ingredients are used up. Bake, covered, for 1½ hours.

Before serving directly from the casserole, pour off any cream that has not been absorbed by the potatoes and reserve it to use to enrich another sauce or a soup.

PAN-FRIED POTATOES

Serves 6

8 medium all-purpose potatoes (not Idaho baking potatoes)
2 tablespoons butter
1 tablespoon vegetable oil
Coarse kosher salt
Freshly ground black pepper

Peel the potatoes and cut each one into 8 uniformly sized pieces.

Heat the butter and oil in a large frying pan. Dry the potatoes and fry them over medium-high heat until evenly browned on all sides. Reduce the heat and continue cooking, uncovered, until they are fork-tender, about 30 minutes. Season to taste with salt and pepper.

NOTE: Most recipes for pan-fried potatoes suggest that you use previously cooked potatoes. It is much better to start with raw potatoes.

SWEET POTATO CASSEROLE WITH ORANGE

Serves 12

8 medium sweet potatoes, unpeeled and quartered, or 1 4-pound can sweet potatoes
6 tablespoons butter
½ cup light brown sugar
Grated rind of 2 oranges
¾ cup orange juice
¼ cup dark Jamaica rum
Salt and freshly ground black pepper, to taste
1 teaspoon allspice

Preheat the oven to 350 degrees.

If you are using fresh sweet potatoes, boil them in salted water until tender about 25 minutes. Drain them and slip off the skins. Mash the sweet potatoes with all the remaining ingredients. (The mixture will be softer than regular mashed potatoes.)

Transfer the sweet potatoes to a buttered casserole. Bake, covered, for 30 minutes.

NEW POTATO CASSEROLE

Serves 4

1½ pounds tiny new potatoes
3 tablespoons butter, softened
Salt
Freshly ground black pepper
½ cup dry white wine
Additional unsalted butter
3 tablespoons chopped fresh chives, for garnish
Freshly ground black pepper

Preheat the oven to 350 degrees.

Put the unpeeled potatoes in a bowl and rub them all over with the softened butter. Season with salt and pepper to taste.

Pour the wine into a small casserole that has a tight-fitting lid. Set a vegetable steamer over the wine, put the buttered potatoes into it, and cover the casserole. Bring the wine to simmering point, then put the casserole into the oven. Steam the potatoes until they are fork-tender, about 40 minutes. (There will be some variation in timing depending on how "tiny" the potatoes are.)

To serve, put the potatoes in a warm bowl. Add more butter, garnish with chopped chives, and dust with black pepper.

RISOTTO

4½ cups chicken broth (see page 5)
⅛ teaspoon saffron threads (optional)
5 tablespoons butter
1 tablespoon olive oil
1 onion, finely chopped
2 cups Italian Arborio rice
½ cup freshly grated Parmesan cheese
Freshly ground black pepper

Bring the chicken broth to a simmer in a saucepan. If you are using the saffron, soak it in ¼ cup of the hot chicken broth for 5 minutes. Set the broth and saffron aside.

Heat 3 tablespoons of the butter and the oil in a large heavy skillet. Add the onion and cook over low heat for 5 minutes. Add the rice and cook over medium-high heat, stirring constantly, for 4 minutes. (Do not let the butter get too hot or the rice will burn.) When the rice loses its shine and becomes opaque, add ½ cup of the chicken broth and continue cooking until almost all of the broth has been absorbed. Add the remaining chicken broth and the broth with the saffron, ½ cup at a time, and cook until all the liquid is absorbed and the rice is tender and fluffy.

It will take roughly 30 minutes to complete the cooking. If the rice is not quite tender at the end of this time, add a little more chicken broth and continue cooking. When the rice is done, stir in the remaining 2 tablespoons butter and the Parmesan cheese and season to taste with black pepper. Serve immediately.

NOTE: Arborio is the only kind of rice to use in making risotto. It can be found in specialty-food stores.

VARIATIONS: To make a more elaborate version, add small pieces of any of the following near the end of the cooking period, so they have time to heat through but still retain their individual flavors:

- Cooked sausage
- Meat or chicken livers
- Cooked meats or poultry
- Cooked shellfish
- Cut-up fresh vegetables
- Substitute for the chicken broth the strained liquid and pureed beets from a jar of store-bought borscht. The risotto will be rather sweet and have a sensational color. Add morsels of cooked tender duck breast and snow peas.

ALL-PURPOSE RICE

Serves 2

2 cups water
Pinch of salt
1 teaspoon butter
½ cup long-grain rice

Bring the water to a boil; add the salt and the butter. Add the rice and stir once. Cover with a tight-fitting lid and cook over low heat for 20 minutes. Drain in a colander.

NOTE: To reheat cooked rice, spread it on a buttered baking dish, dot the surface with 1 teaspoon butter, and season to taste with salt and pepper. Cover with foil and bake it in a preheated 350-degree oven for 15 minutes. Alternatively, place a steamer basket in a casserole over hot water and steam the rice until heated through, about 5 minutes.

BROILED TOMATOES

Serves 2

2 medium fully ripe tomatoes
2 tablespoons seasoned Italian bread crumbs
2 tablespoons grated Parmesan cheese
4 teaspoons butter
1 tablespoon vegetable oil
4 teaspoons chopped chives, for garnish

Preheat the oven to 400 degrees.

Cut the tomatoes in half. Combine the bread crumbs and cheese and sprinkle over the tomato halves. Dot with butter. Thoroughly coat a pie plate with the oil; arrange the tomato halves in the pie plate and bake for 5 minutes. Preheat the broiler.

Brown the tomatoes under the broiler for 3 minutes, taking care not to let them burn. Garnish with the chopped chives. Serve the tomatoes hot or at room temperature.

BAKED RADICCHIO WITH GOAT CHEESE

Serves 4

2 heads Radicchio, about ½ pound each
4 teaspoons olive oil
Salt
Freshly ground black pepper
½ cup fine dry bread crumbs
2 teaspoons chopped fresh thyme
6 ounces mild goat cheese, such as Bûcheron or Montrachet

Preheat the oven to 350 degrees. Butter a baking dish.

Cut the Radicchio in half crosswise and drizzle 2 teaspoons of the olive oil over the halves. Sprinkle with salt and pepper to taste, and wrap in aluminum foil. Bake until tender, about 40 minutes.

Meanwhile, mix the bread crumbs with the thyme.

Remove the Radicchio halves from the foil and place them, cut side up, in the prepared baking dish. Spread the goat cheese on the Raddichio to within ½ inch of the edge. Sprinkle the herbed crumbs over the cheese and drizzle the remaining oil over the crumbs.

Return the Radicchio to the oven and bake just until the cheese melts, about 5 minutes. Serve immediately.

BRAISED ENDIVE

Serves 4

4 tablespoons butter
4 tablespoons chopped shallots
8 heads endive, trimmed
Salt
Freshly ground black pepper
1⅓ cups water or chicken broth (see page 5)
2 teaspoons fresh lemon juice

Heat the butter in a skillet over moderate heat; sauté the shallots in the butter, stirring, until soft, about 2 to 3 minutes. Add the endive and cook, turning, until lightly browned, about 2 to 3 minutes. Season to taste with salt and pepper.

Add the broth and lemon juice to the skillet. Reduce the heat to low and simmer until the endive is tender, about 35 to 45 minutes.

SICILIAN-STYLE BROCCOLI WITH CAULIFLOWER

Serves 6

¼ cup olive oil
½ cup thinly sliced red onion
2 cloves garlic, crushed
2 cups small broccoli florets
½ cup thinly sliced carrots
1 cup small cauliflower florets
½ cup thinly sliced red bell pepper
½ cup dry white wine
1 tablespoon white wine vinegar
2 tablespoons chopped fresh parsley
2 tablespoons capers
¼ cup chopped oil-cured pitted black olives
Salt
Freshly ground black pepper

Heat the olive oil in a large skillet; sauté the onion and garlic in the oil over low heat until the onion is soft and golden, about 10 minutes. Discard the garlic.

Add the broccoli, carrots, and cauliflower, and sauté, stirring, over moderate heat for 2 minutes. Cover the pan and cook for 3 minutes more.

Add the red pepper, wine, and vinegar; bring the mixture to a boil. Cover and cook over low heat until the vegetables are tender, about 5 minutes. Stir in the parsley, capers, and olives; season to taste with salt and pepper. Serve warm or at room temperature.

PUREE OF WHITE WINTER VEGETABLES

Serves 6

2 cups chicken broth (see page 5)

2 onions, chopped

2 cloves garlic, finely chopped

2 medium potatoes, peeled and chopped

1 medium turnip, peeled and cut into cubes

1 celeriac root, peeled and cut into cubes

1 bulb fennel, sliced

Salt

Freshly ground black pepper

Freshly grated nutmeg

3 tablespoons butter

⅓ cup heavy cream

2 tablespoons chopped chives

Bring the chicken broth to a simmer in a large saucepan. Add the prepared vegetables and the fennel; cover and cook over low heat until the vegetables are tender, about 20 minutes.

Drain the vegetables and reserve the broth for another use. Season the vegetables to taste with salt, pepper, and nutmeg. Add the butter and mash the vegetables with a potato masher, adding the cream a little at a time, until smooth, or whip the vegetables in a heavy electric mixer.

Return the puree to a heavy saucepan and reheat.

GLAZED CARROTS

Serves 6

12 carrots, peeled and sliced, or 1½ pounds baby carrots, scraped
½ teaspoon salt
Freshly ground black pepper
2 tablespoons butter
1 tablespoon sugar
2 tablespoons white vermouth
2 tablespoons finely chopped fresh parsley or fresh dillweed, for garnish

Simmer the carrots in boiling salted water until almost tender, about 15 minutes. Drain them and season to taste with salt and pepper.

Heat the butter in a skillet until bubbling. Add the carrots, sugar, and white vermouth; toss over medium-high heat until the carrots are tender and shiny. Serve garnished with parsley.

7

SALADS

CAESAR SALAD

Serves 4 to 6

1 head Romaine lettuce

½ pound bacon, sliced

2 tablespoons butter

2 tablespoons vegetable oil

2 slices firm-textured bread, crusts removed, cut into crouton-size cubes

4 Hard-cooked Eggs (see page 227), cut into wedges

8 anchovy fillets

¼ cup freshly grated Parmesan cheese

DRESSING

2 tablespoons tarragon vinegar

6 tablespoons olive oil

Salt and freshly ground black pepper, to taste

½ teaspoon Dijon mustard

2 cloves garlic, crushed

1 small egg, beaten

1 tablespoon chopped fresh parsley

Tear the lettuce leaves into bite-size pieces.

Fry the bacon in a skillet over moderate heat until crisp, then remove and drain on paper towels. Heat the butter and oil in a separate skillet; and fry the bread cubes until crisp and brown. Then remove the cubes and drain on paper towels.

Whisk together the dressing ingredients, beating until thoroughly incorporated. Toss the prepared lettuce in the dressing and arrange the pieces in the bottom of a salad bowl. Crumble the bacon and scatter it on top of the lettuce, then sprinkle with the croutons. Decorate the edge of the salad bowl with the egg wedges and lay anchovy fillets over the eggs. Sprinkle with the Parmesan cheese.

■ SPINACH, BACON, AND MUSHROOM SALAD

Serves 2

¾ pound fresh spinach, carefully washed to remove all the sand

6 slices bacon, fried until crisp and then crumbled

6 scallions, thinly sliced

6 medium firm fresh mushrooms, thinly sliced

DRESSING

2 tablespoons freshly squeezed lemon or lime juice

6 tablespoons olive oil

I clove garlic, crushed

Freshly ground black pepper, to taste

I teaspoon Dijon mustard

I raw egg, slightly beaten

Remove the stems from the spinach; tear the leaves into bite-size pieces and place them in a salad bowl. Toss in the bacon, scallions, and mushrooms. Combine the ingredients for the dressing in a small jar. Cover tightly and shake vigorously to blend.

Just before serving, pour about half the dressing over the spinach and toss thoroughly, adding a little more dressing, if needed, until the leaves are well coated. Serve at once.

GREEK SALAD

Serves 16

8 large tomatoes, cut into wedges

2 large green bell peppers, seeded and cut into strips

2 cucumbers, peeled and diced

1 red Bermuda onion, very thinly sliced

4 bunches scallions, finely chopped

2 2-ounce cans anchovy fillets, drained

2 bunches radishes, thinly sliced

1 cup Greek Calamata olives

1 pound feta cheese, crumbled

2 to 3 heads lettuce, preferably Romaine or red-leaf

DRESSING

1 teaspoon salt

Freshly ground black pepper, to taste

⅓ cup lemon juice

1 cup light olive oil

1 teaspoon dried mint, or 2 tablespoons chopped fresh mint (or substitute dried or fresh oregano)

Place all the salad ingredients in a large bowl. Whisk together the dressing ingredients. Pour the dressing over the salad and toss to combine.

COLESLAW

Serves 6

3 cups crisp shredded cabbage

½ cup grated carrot

DRESSING

1 cup Homemade Mayonnaise (see page 186)

¼ cup sour cream

2 tablespoons vinegar

1 teaspoon dry mustard

1 teaspoon sugar

1 teaspoon salt

Put the cabbage and carrot in a bowl. Blend the dressing ingredients in a food processor. Pour the dressing over the cabbage and carrot, tossing until well combined.

CHEF'S SALAD

Serves 6

2 heads Romaine lettuce

¾ cup Vinaigrette Dressing (page 184)

3 cups thin strips of cold roast chicken

½ pound ham, cut into thin strips

½ pound Swiss cheese, cut into thin strips

3 Hard-cooked Eggs (see page 227), cut into wedges

Tear the lettuce leaves into bite-size pieces.

Toss the lettuce in the dressing, then drain thoroughly and arrange in individual bowls or on plates. Arrange the meats and cheese like the spokes of a wheel on the bed of lettuce and put the egg wedges between the "spokes."

VARIATION: Add some freshly cooked and crumbled bacon or cold diced boiled potatoes or both to the salad.

■ COLD DUCK SALAD WITH ORANGES AND WALNUTS

Serves 4

I 4- to 5-pound duckling, roasted and cooled (see pages 32–33)
3 tender stalks celery
2 oranges (blood oranges are particularly good)
I head Boston or 3 heads Bibb lettuce
Pitted black olives, for garnish
Chopped walnuts, for garnish

DRESSING
2 tablespoons white wine vinegar
6 tablespoons olive oil
Grated rind of I orange
¼ teaspoon Dijon mustard

Remove all the meat from the duck and cut it into bite-size pieces. Chop the celery into small pieces. Peel the oranges and cut them into segments, carefully removing all of the white pith. Combine the duck, celery, and oranges in a bowl.

Place the ingredients for the dressing in a jar with a tight-fitting lid; shake vigorously until thoroughly combined. Moisten the duck and orange mixture with the dressing.

Line a salad bowl with lettuce leaves and mound the duck salad in the center. Garnish with pitted black olives and chopped walnuts.

SALADE NIÇOISE

Serves 4

8 Romaine lettuce leaves

2 Hard-cooked Eggs (see page 227), cut into wedges

2 medium tomatoes, cut into wedges

8 canned anchovy fillets

8 black olives, pitted

1 8-ounce can tuna, flaked

4 small boiled potatoes, sliced

2 teaspoons capers

DRESSING

½ teaspoon salt

Freshly ground black pepper, to taste

1 teaspoon Dijon mustard

2 tablespoons vinegar or lemon juice

½ cup vegetable oil

Line a big wooden salad bowl with the lettuce leaves and arrange all the remaining salad ingredients on the lettuce. Combine the ingredients for the dressing; sprinkle the dressing over the salad just before serving. Toss thoroughly and serve in individual wooden bowls or on serving plates.

■ COUSCOUS SALAD

Makes approximately 8 cups

1 16-ounce box couscous (2½ cups)
3 tablespoons light olive oil
1 small onion, finely chopped
1 green bell pepper, seeded and finely chopped
1 red bell pepper, seeded and finely chopped
2 tablespoons fresh lemon juice
2 cups diced boiled ham
Salt
Freshly ground black pepper
¼ cup finely chopped fresh mint, for garnish

Prepare the couscous according to the package directions (it will be ready in a moment). Heat the oil in a heavy skillet; sauté the onion and peppers in the oil until they have softened, about 4 minutes. Set them aside.

Fluff the couscous with a fork. Add the lemon juice and diced ham to the couscous. Stir in the reserved onion and peppers and season to taste with salt and pepper. Garnish with the chopped mint. Serve hot or cold.

VARIATIONS:
- Substitute chicken or fish for the ham.
- Add tomatoes, cucumbers, and almost any kind of salad vegetables to the couscous base, or flavor with pine nuts and raisins.

PORK SALAD WITH MUSTARD MAYONNAISE

Serves 4

3 cups thin strips cold roast pork

2 small crisp apples, peeled, cored, and thinly sliced

2 tablespoons raisins

1 head Romaine or other lettuce

2 tablespoons chopped fresh chives, scallions, or parsley, for garnish

DRESSING

¾ cup Homemade Mayonnaise (see page 186)

1 teaspoon Dijon mustard

¼ cup heavy cream

1 tablespoon apple brandy

Place the pork, apples, and raisins in a bowl. Combine the ingredients for the dressing, pour the dressing over the pork mixture, and toss to combine. Serve on a bed of lettuce leaves, garnished with chopped chives.

CRAB SALAD

Serves 6

2 pound backfin crabmeat, picked over carefully to remove any stray cartilage
12 small fresh white button mushrooms, sliced
3 tablespoons light olive oil
2 tablespoons lemon juice
3 Hard-cooked Eggs (see page 227), each cut into 6 wedges
3 medium tomatoes, cut into wedges
1 medium green bell pepper, seeded and cut into strips
12 pitted black olives
¼ cup chopped walnuts
Chopped fresh parsley, for garnish

Combine the crabmeat with the mushrooms. Combine the oil and lemon juice, and pour it over the crab-mushroom mixture. Let it stand for 10 minutes, then drain off the excess oil and lemon juice.

Mound the crabmeat in the center of a serving platter. Arrange the eggs, tomatoes, and green pepper around the crabmeat and scatter the olives on top of the vegetables. Sprinkle the mound of crabmeat with chopped walnuts and garnish with parsley. Serve with Danish crispbread or slices of pumpernickel.

NOTE: Use fresh crabmeat from a good fish store for the best texture and flavor.

PINTO BEAN SALAD WITH HAM AND MUSTARD

Serves 4

⅔ cup dried pinto beans
Salt
1 green bell pepper, seeded and chopped
2 tablespoons finely chopped onion
½ pound ham, cut into small pieces
2 tablespoons Dijon mustard
1 tablespoon cider vinegar
3 tablespoons olive oil
Freshly ground black pepper

Pick over the beans and soak them overnight in enough cold water to cover.

Drain the beans and rinse them under cold running water. Transfer them to a saucepan and cover them with water. Bring to a boil over medium-high heat, then reduce the heat to low and cook until the beans are soft, testing after 45 minutes. Add 1 teaspoon salt, stirring to dissolve. Drain the beans again and set aside to cool.

Stir the green pepper, onion, and ham into the beans. Combine the mustard, vinegar, and oil; add the dressing and salt and pepper to taste to the bean mixture. Toss thoroughly and allow the mixture to marinate for at least 1 hour. Serve at room temperature.

8

EGGS, CHEESE, AND PANCAKES—ANY TIME

PIPERADE

SCRAMBLED EGGS WITH HOMEMADE COUNTRY SAUSAGE

EGGS BENEDICT

POACHED EGGS WITH CHICKEN HASH

HARD-COOKED EGGS

STUFFED EGGS

PLAIN OMELETTE

FILLED OMELETTE

SPANISH OMELETTE

CHEESE FONDUE

QUICHE LORRAINE

PANCAKES

APPLE PANCAKES

WHOLE WHEAT PANCAKES

BAKED APRICOT PANCAKE

FRENCH TOAST

■ PIPERADE

Serves 6

3 tablespoons olive oil
2 medium onions, finely chopped
1 clove garlic, finely chopped
2 green bell peppers, seeded and chopped
3 medium mushrooms, sliced
2 medium ripe tomatoes, peeled, seeded, and chopped
6 slices boiled ham, cut into thin strips
10 eggs, slightly beaten
Salt
Freshly ground black pepper
2 tablespoons butter
2 tablespoons finely chopped fresh parsley, for garnish

Heat the oil in a skillet over medium-high heat; sauté the onions, garlic, and peppers until softened, about 10 minutes. Add the mushrooms, tomatoes, and ham; sauté until the tomatoes have softened slightly, about 5 minutes. Do not overcook; all the ingredients should retain their bright colors.

Heat the butter in another frying pan. Meanwhile season the eggs to taste with salt and pepper. Scramble the eggs as directed on page 224.

Arrange the scrambled eggs on a warmed serving dish. Make a trough down the center of the eggs and fill it with the prepared vegetables. Garnish with the chopped parsley.

SCRAMBLED EGGS WITH HOMEMADE COUNTRY SAUSAGE

Serves 2

HOMEMADE COUNTRY SAUSAGE
1 pound ground pork
½ cup freshly made bread crumbs
2 cloves garlic, finely chopped
2 tablespoons finely chopped fresh parsley
1 teaspoon dried thyme
1 teaspoon dried sage
½ teaspoon dried marjoram
½ teaspoon salt
Freshly ground black pepper
3 tablespoons peanut oil

2 tablespoons butter
4 jumbo eggs
Pinch of salt
Freshly ground black pepper, to taste
3 tablespoons milk (optional)

To prepare the Homemade Country Sausage, combine all the ingredients except the oil; shape the mixture into small patties. Fry the patties in hot oil, turning occasionally, until brown and crisp, about 20 minutes. When the sausage is almost done, heat the butter in an 8-inch skillet.

Meanwhile, break the eggs into a bowl and beat them lightly with a fork, adding the salt, pepper, and milk.

When the butter is hot and foaming, add the eggs and cook them *slowly* in a nonstick pan over *low* heat, stirring occasionally, until soft curds have formed. Serve the eggs *immediately* with the sausage.

VARIATIONS: Garnish with any of the items on the following page.

- 2 anchovies, cut in half lengthwise and arranged in a crisscross pattern
- 4 slices smoked salmon, shredded
- 1 teaspoon capers
- 2 tablespoons sour cream
- A combination of smoked salmon, capers, and sour cream

■ EGGS BENEDICT

Serves 6

Hollandaise Sauce (see page 187)
6 eggs
6 slices Canadian bacon or boiled ham
3 English muffins
6 slices black truffle or a dash of paprika, for garnish

Preheat the broiler.

Prepare the hollandaise sauce and set aside.

Poach the eggs, following the instructions on page 226. When cooked to your taste, remove the eggs from the poaching liquid and place them in a bowl of hot water.

Heat the Canadian bacon under the broiler until it is hot but not too browned, about 4 or 5 minutes.

Meanwhile, split and toast the muffins. Place a slice of the Canadian bacon on each muffin half and top with a poached egg. Generously coat each egg with warm hollandaise sauce and garnish with a slice of truffle.

VARIATION: Put a slice of tomato on top of the ham and add a teaspoon of tomato paste to the hollandaise sauce.

POACHED EGGS WITH CHICKEN HASH

Serves 4

1 teaspoon salt
1 teaspoon vinegar or lemon juice
8 fresh eggs
Freshly made buttered toast, for serving

CHICKEN HASH
2 tablespoons butter
1 onion, finely chopped
3 tablespoons all-purpose flour
1 cup chicken broth (see page 5)
½ cup milk
1 teaspoon Dijon mustard
1 teaspoon dried oregano
Salt and freshly ground black pepper
Juice of ½ lemon
3 cups leftover cooked chicken

Fill a large saucepan with water and add the salt and vinegar. Bring the water to a simmer.

Stir the water with a spoon so that it is swirling gently. Break open the eggs and gently lower them, one at a time, into the slowly revolving water. The whites will immediately encase the yolks to form a tidy package.

Reduce the heat until no bubbles appear on the surface of the water. Poach the eggs until set, about 4 to 5 minutes. Set the eggs in a bowl of hot water until needed. They will stay hot as long as the water remains hot, and the yolks will not harden.

To make the Chicken Hash, heat the butter in a saucepan; sauté the onion in the butter until it has softened, about 3 minutes. Stir in the flour and add the broth and milk gradually, stirring with a wire whisk to form a smooth sauce. Season with mustard, oregano, and salt and pepper to taste. Stir in the lemon juice.

Cut the chicken into small pieces and add them to the sauce. Continue cooking over moderate heat until the chicken is hot, about 5 minutes.

Remove the eggs from the bowl with a slotted spoon, drain briefly, and serve with the Chicken Hash on freshly made toast or English muffins.

◼ HARD-COOKED EGGS

6 eggs

Put the eggs in a saucepan with just enough cold water to cover them. Over low heat, and with the saucepan uncovered, bring the water to a boil. Reduce the heat and cook the eggs for 15 minutes. Remove the saucepan from the heat; place the pan of eggs under cold running water for a couple of minutes until the eggs are cool enough to handle.

Take the eggs from the pan one at a time. Rap each one briskly on the counter, then roll it back and forth gently to break the shell. It is easier to remove the shell while the egg is still warm. If you do not plan to use the eggs immediately, store them in the refrigerator immersed in a bowl of cold water.

▪ STUFFED EGGS

Makes 24 egg halves

12 Hard-cooked Eggs (see page 227)
2 tablespoons softened butter
4 tablespoons Homemade Mayonnaise (see page 186)
Salt
Freshly ground black pepper

Cut the eggs in half lengthwise and use your finger to slide out the yolks; reserve the egg whites. Force the yolks through a fine tea strainer into a bowl; combine the butter and mayonnaise with the yolks to form a soft mixture. Season the yolk mixture with a little salt and pepper and add ½ cup of a flavoring from the selection that follows, mashed into the egg mixture or as a garnish. Divide the mixture among the halved egg whites.

- Smoked salmon cut into small pieces
- Smoked trout or other smoked fish
- Chopped chutney
- Cold pureed vegetables, such as asparagus or spinach
- Chopped olives
- Cream cheese
- Mashed sardines
- ¼ cup Tapenade (page 56)

PLAIN OMELETTE

Serves 1

2 eggs
Pinch of salt
1 tablespoon butter
Fresh parsley or watercress sprigs, for garnish

Using a fork, beat the eggs and salt in a bowl until they are well mixed.

Heat the butter in a 7½-inch omelette pan over moderate heat. When the butter bubbles are the size of a tiny, rising beer bubble, add the eggs. Immediately stir them with a fork, holding the tines of the fork parallel with the bottom of the pan. Continue stirring as if you were making scrambled eggs until the eggs separate into soft curds. Spread these across the bottom of the pan to make an even layer.

Tip the pan away from you and slide a spatula under the omelette. Lift it and fold it in half.

Slide the folded omelette back to the center of the pan and continue cooking it for 1 minute to let the underside brown. (The side that is on the bottom will be on top when the omelette is served.)

Hold a warm plate in your left hand, and grip the pan with your right hand with your thumb on top of the pan handle. Tip the plate and the pan at a 45-degree angle to each other, then invert the pan completely over the plate, and the omelette will slide out smoothly.

When the omelette is on the plate, brush the surface with melted butter to make it shine and add a sprig or two of fresh parsley for a contrast of color.

VARIATION: To make a filled omelette, follow the directions provided below, and use any of the fillings from the selection that follows.

(continued on next page)

PLAIN OMELETTE *(cont.)*

Prepare the omelette as in the recipe above until the eggs are spread across the bottom of the pan in an even layer. Spoon the filling over half the eggs in a line on the side opposite the handle of the pan. (If you are making a hot filling, as opposed to a cheese filling, make sure it is piping hot before you tuck it inside the omelette because it will not be inside the omelette long enough to heat through to the correct temperature.)

Tip the pan away from you and slide a spatula under the unfilled half of the omelette. Lift this half and fold it over to cover the filling.

Slide the folded omelette back to the center of the pan and continue as for the plain omelette.

MUSHROOM FILLING

2 tablespoons butter
2 scallions, finely chopped
3 medium mushrooms, thinly sliced
1 teaspoon lemon juice
¼ teaspoon salt
Freshly ground black pepper

Heat the butter in a skillet; sauté the scallions in the butter until softened but not browned, about 3 minutes. Add the mushrooms; sauté them very briefly over moderately high heat. Season the mixture with lemon juice, salt, and pepper to taste.

FRIED POTATO AND BACON FILLING

1 tablespoon butter
1 tablespoon vegetable oil
1 small potato, raw or cooked
3 slices bacon

Heat the butter and oil in a skillet. Peel the raw potato and cut it into cubes a little larger than croutons. Fry the cubes in the combined butter and oil until they are tender, crisp, and brown, about 10–15 minutes. (If you are using cooked potatoes, fry them until they are hot and browned.) Drain them on paper towels.

Fry the bacon until crisp. Drain the slices, then crumble them into the cubed potato and mix well.

TOMATO AND HERB FILLING

¼ cup peeled, seeded, and chopped tomato

1 tablespoon of a combination of finely chopped fresh parsley, fresh chives, and fresh tarragon or basil

Combine the tomato and herbs and mix well.

NOTE: If you do not have all fresh herbs, chop fresh parsley, frozen chives, and the dried herbs together. The tiny amount of moisture from the parsley brings out remarkably more flavor in the dried herbs.

CHEESE FILLING

¼ cup grated cheese, preferably a bold-flavored, sharp cheddar

Sprinkle the cheese over the partially cooked omelette, taking care not to sprinkle it too close to the edges of the pan. (This will prevent the melted cheese from running underneath the eggs and sticking to the surface of the pan.)

■ SPANISH OMELETTE

Serves 4

2 tablespoons butter

1 tablespoon vegetable oil

1 Spanish (red) onion, finely chopped

3 medium potatoes, boiled, peeled, and cut into small cubes

2 cloves garlic, finely chopped

1 large tomato, peeled, seeded, and chopped

4 slices ham, chopped

6 eggs

Salt

Freshly ground black pepper

2 tablespoons finely chopped fresh parsley, for garnish

Heat the butter and oil in a skillet over medium-high heat; sauté the onion in the butter and oil until softened, about 5 minutes. Add the potatoes and garlic; sauté until they are lightly browned. Add the tomato and ham.

Beat the eggs slightly in a bowl, season to taste with salt and pepper, and pour them into the skillet on top of the other ingredients. Cook the eggs until they form a layer covering the bottom of the pan, lifting the edges of the "omelette" to allow the uncooked part to run beneath the surface of the cooked eggs.

Serve garnished with fresh parsley.

■ CHEESE FONDUE

Serves 6

1 clove garlic, halved
2 cups dry white wine
1 pound Gruyère cheese, grated
1 pound top-quality Swiss cheese (such as Emmentaler), grated
Freshly ground black pepper
2 tablespoons cornstarch dissolved in 2 tablespoons kirsch
French bread cut into 1-inch cubes, for dipping

Rub the garlic all over the inside of an enameled cast-iron fondue pot. Add the wine. Place the pot over moderate heat until the wine begins to simmer. Add the cheeses, a little at a time, stirring slowly in a figure-eight pattern. When the cheese has melted, season with pepper to taste.

Stir the dissolved cornstarch into the cheese mixture. Continue stirring until the mixture has thickened, about 2 to 3 minutes. Place the fondue over a small burner at the table and invite everyone to pull up a chair. Spear the bread on fondue forks and dip it into the cheese, which will gradually cook more and more and become crustier on the bottom.

NOTE: If you do not have a fondue pot and the correct long thin forks for dipping into the cheese, you can use a deep heavy saucepan and conventional forks instead. Though a little of the charisma will be lost, the fondue will taste just as good. Serve the fondue with small boiled new potatoes, cornichons, and radishes.

QUICHE LORRAINE

Serves 6

Pastry for a single-crust pie (see page 292)

FILLING
½ pound lean bacon
¾ pound Swiss or Gruyère cheese, cut from a wheel and freshly grated
3 eggs
3 egg yolks
1 tablespoon all-purpose flour
½ teaspoon salt
Dash of cayenne pepper
2 to 2½ cups milk, or 1½ cups milk and 1 cup light or heavy cream

Preheat the oven to 375 degrees.

Roll out the pastry dough on a floured surface and fit it into a 10-inch pie plate. Cover the pastry with a sheet of oiled wax paper or foil, oiled side down; cover the paper with a single layer of pastry weights or dried beans.

Bake the pie shell until the pastry has "set," about 10 minutes; discard the paper. (This step will produce a pastry shell that remains flaky even after the quiche custard is added.) Save the pastry weights or dried beans; they can be reused for years.

Meanwhile, fry the bacon in a skillet until crisp; drain the bacon on paper towels. Crumble the bacon over the bottom of the partially baked pie shell. Sprinkle the grated cheese over the bacon.

Whisk together the eggs, egg yolks, flour, salt, and cayenne pepper in a bowl, until thoroughly mixed. Stir in the milk and cream. Pour this custard slowly over the bacon and cheese in the pie shell, allowing it to settle into the cheese. Carefully slide into the oven and bake until the custard is firm, about 40 minutes. Serve the quiche hot or cold.

VARIATIONS: Omit the bacon and substitute any of the following:

- I cup diced ham plus I cup cooked asparagus tips
- I cup cooked lobster, cut into small pieces, I tablespoon tomato paste, and I tablespoon lemon juice
- I cup cooked Polish sausage and I tablespoon mustard
- 6 shallots, finely chopped and sautéed until soft in 2 tablespoons butter, and ¼ pound smoked salmon, diced. For this variation, also substitute ½ cup white wine and 2 tablespoons white vermouth for ½ cup of the milk.
- ½ pound sliced mushrooms and 3 onions, finely chopped and sautéed until soft in 2 tablespoons butter.

PANCAKES

Makes twelve 3-inch pancakes

2 cups all-purpose flour
2 teaspoons baking powder
½ teaspoon salt
1 tablespoon sugar
2 eggs, slightly beaten
1½ cups milk
2 tablespoons butter, melted
3 to 4 tablespoons vegetable oil
Hot melted butter and hot maple syrup, for serving

Sift together the flour, baking powder, salt, and sugar. Combine the eggs, milk, and butter in a medium bowl. Whisk in the dry ingredients until just barely combined. Do not overmix or the pancakes will be heavy.

Pour a tablespoon of the oil into a heavy skillet, tilt the skillet to distribute the oil evenly over the surface, and heat over high heat until a drop of water sizzles in the pan. Pour ¼ cup batter into the skillet for each pancake. Cook the pancakes until small bubbles appear, about 2 minutes, then flip them over and continue cooking until they are lightly browned. Use more oil to coat the pan as needed to prevent the pancakes from sticking.

To prevent the pancakes from becoming soggy while you make up the entire batch, stack them on a wire cake-cooking rack lined with a kitchen cloth. This will allow the air to circulate and prevent the formation of steam.

Serve the pancakes with the hot butter and hot maple syrup.

NOTE: The pancake batter can be made in the food processor, but it will be lighter if you stir it by hand.

■ APPLE PANCAKES

Makes twelve 3-inch pancakes

2 cups sifted all-purpose flour

1 teaspoon salt

1 tablespoon sugar

2 teaspoons baking powder

2 eggs, slightly beaten

1½ cups milk

2 tablespoons butter, melted

¼ teaspoon nutmeg

¼ teaspoon cinnamon

Grated rind of 1 lemon

1 medium cooking apple, peeled and cored

2 tablespoons vegetable oil

Confectioners' sugar, for serving

Hot maple syrup, for serving

Crisp-fried bacon slices, for serving

Resift the flour with the salt, sugar, and baking powder. Combine the eggs, milk, butter, nutmeg, cinnamon, and grated lemon rind in a bowl. Fold in the dry ingredients, stirring until just barely combined.

Cut the apple into thin slices and fold into the pancake batter.

Pour a tablespoon of the oil into each of 2 large skillets and tilt to distribute the oil. Heat until a drop of water sizzles when dropped on the surface. Pour 2 tablespoons batter into the skillet for each pancake. Cook the cakes until small bubbles appear, about 2 minutes, then flip them over and continue cooking until lightly browned.

To keep the pancakes from becoming soggy while you make the entire batch, stack them on a wire rack lined with a kitchen cloth. This allows air to circulate and prevents the formation of steam.

Sprinkle the pancakes with sifted confectioners' sugar and serve with hot maple syrup and slices of crisp-fried bacon.

WHOLE WHEAT PANCAKES

Makes eight 3-inch pancakes

¾ cup whole wheat flour
¾ cup all-purpose flour
2 teaspoons baking powder
¼ teaspoon salt
I teaspoon cinnamon
½ teaspoon allspice
I egg, slightly beaten
I egg yolk
I tablespoon butter, melted
I¼ cups milk
I tablespoon honey
3 to 4 tablespoons vegetable oil
Applesauce and sour cream or hot melted butter and hot syrup, for serving

Sift together the flours, baking powder, salt, cinnamon, and allspice. Combine the egg, egg yolk, butter, milk, and honey in a bowl. Fold in the dry ingredients, stirring until just barely combined. Do not overmix or the pancakes will be heavy.

Heat a tablespoon of the oil in a heavy skillet until a drop of water sizzles when dropped on the surface. Pour 2 tablespoons of the batter into the skillet for each pancake. Cook the pancakes until small bubbles appear, about 2 minutes, then flip them over and continue cooking them until lightly browned. Use more oil, as needed, to coat the skillet.

To prevent the pancakes from becoming soggy while you make up the entire batch, stack them on a wire cake-cooking rack lined with a kitchen cloth. This will allow the air to circulate and prevent the formation of steam.

Serve the pancakes with applesauce and sour cream or hot butter and maple syrup, as you prefer.

NOTE: It is best to make the pancakes with half whole wheat and half all-purpose flour. If they are made with all whole wheat flour, they are very doughy and heavy.

BAKED APRICOT PANCAKE

Serves 4

3 pieces crystallized ginger
3 eggs
1½ cups milk
¾ cup all-purpose flour
2 tablespoons rum
½ teaspoon vanilla extract
¼ teaspoon salt
1 16-ounce can apricot halves, drained
2 tablespoons sifted confectioners' sugar

Preheat the oven to 375 degrees.

Chop the crystallized ginger in the food processor; set it aside.

Put all the remaining ingredients except the apricots and confectioners' sugar in the food processor and blend until smooth.

Pour half of the batter into an 8-inch baking pan; bake it for 20 minutes. Arrange the apricots and ginger on top of the partially set batter. Pour the remaining batter over the top. Return the pan to the oven and continue baking until the batter has set, about 25 minutes.

Sift the confectioners' sugar over the pancake and serve warm.

FRENCH TOAST

Serves 4

3 eggs
¼ cup milk or cream
Salt
Freshly ground black pepper
⅛ teaspoon grated nutmeg
8 slices French or firm-textured bread
2 tablespoons butter
1 tablespoon vegetable oil
4 tablespoons confectioners' sugar
Hot maple syrup, for serving

In a wide, shallow bowl, combine the eggs with the milk, salt and pepper to taste, and nutmeg. Cut each slice of bread in half diagonally and dip the bread slices into the egg mixture to soak them on both sides.

Divide the butter and oil between 2 heavy skillets so that you can prepare the toast more quickly and serve it piping hot. Heat the butter and oil. Fry the bread slices over moderate heat until golden brown, about 3 to 4 minutes on each side. Dust the toast lightly with sifted confectioners' sugar and serve with hot maple syrup in a pitcher.

9

A BREAD OR TWO

BAKING POWDER BISCUITS

POPOVERS

MUSHROOMS AND BACON IN POPOVERS

CORN MUFFINS

BRAN MUFFINS

BLUEBERRY MUFFINS

PUMPKIN MUFFINS WITH PUMPKIN SEEDS

OATMEAL RAISIN MUFFINS

HONEY SPICE BREAD

ZUCCHINI BREAD

CORN BREAD

PARMESAN BATTER BREAD

FRAGRANT ORANGE BREAD

WALNUT CHEDDAR BREAD

APRICOT NUT BREAD

CRANBERRY BREAD

COFFEE CAKE

SOUR CREAM COFFEE CAKE WITH CHOCOLATE AND WALNUTS

FRAGRANT MULTIGRAIN WAFFLES

BAKING POWDER BISCUITS

Makes 12 biscuits

2 cups all-purpose flour
3 teaspoons baking powder
1 teaspoon salt
5 tablespoons cold butter, cut into small pieces
¾ cup milk

Preheat the oven to 450 degrees.

Sift the flour, baking powder, and salt together into a bowl. Cut in the butter using a pastry blender or 2 knives until the mixture resembles coarse meal. Add the milk. Gather the dough into a ball, and knead on a lightly floured board for a few seconds. (Work the dough as little as possible in order to have the lightest possible biscuits.)

Pat or roll out the dough into a circle ½-inch thick, and cut out as many biscuits as possible, using a glass or a biscuit cutter. Gather the scraps together and roll out again to form the remaining biscuits. Place the biscuits on a baking sheet and bake until golden, about 12 minutes. Serve hot, with plenty of butter and preserves.

VARIATIONS:
- For cheese biscuits, fold ¾ cup grated cheddar cheese into the biscuit dough.
- For sesame seed biscuits, fold ½ cup toasted sesame seeds into the biscuit dough. After baking, sprinkle the surface of the biscuits with a combination of ¼ cup toasted sesame seeds and ¼ cup coarse salt.
- For bacon biscuits, substitute 3 tablespoons bacon fat for 3 tablespoons of the butter and fold ¼ pound bacon, crisp-fried and crumbled, into the biscuit dough.

■ POPOVERS

Makes 12 popovers

1½ cups milk
3 eggs
1½ tablespoons melted butter
1½ cups sifted all-purpose flour
½ teaspoon salt

Preheat the oven to 450 degrees.

Oil 12 muffin pans, preferably cast-iron ones, and heat them in the oven until they are very hot, about 10 minutes.

Whisk together the milk, eggs, melted butter, flour, and salt in a mixing bowl until smooth. Divide the mixture among the muffin pans, filling each one three-quarters full.

Bake the popovers for 15 minutes, then, without opening the oven door, reduce the oven temperature to 400 degrees. Continue baking until the popovers have puffed and doubled in size, about 15 minutes more. They will be firm and nicely browned.

MUSHROOMS AND BACON IN POPOVERS

Serves 12

4 tablespoons unsalted butter
3 small onions, finely chopped
1 pound cultivated white mushrooms, stems removed, thinly sliced
½ pound shiitake mushrooms, stems removed, thinly sliced
1 pound thick-cut sliced bacon
12 Popovers (see page 243)

Melt the butter over moderate heat in a large heavy skillet. Add the onions and gently sauté them until softened but not browned, about 5 minutes. Add the mushrooms; stir well and sauté until they are tender and the juices in the pan have completely evaporated, about 8 minutes.

Cut the bacon strips into small pieces. Fry them in a separate skillet over medium-high heat until crisp. Remove the bacon with a slotted spoon and drain on a wire cake-cooling rack lined with a double thickness of paper towels.

When you are ready to serve, reheat the mushrooms and bacon separately in a preheated 350-degree oven for 15 minutes. Fill the freshly made popovers with the hot mushrooms and serve at once.

NOTE: You can make both the mushrooms and bacon up to 1 hour ahead of time; set aside at room temperature. Do not mix them until you put them into the popovers.

■ CORN MUFFINS

Makes 12 muffins

1½ cups cornmeal

½ cup all-purpose flour, sifted

2 teaspoons baking powder

1 teaspoon salt

2 eggs, slightly beaten

1½ cups milk

3 tablespoons butter, melted

Preheat the oven to 400 degrees.

Butter 12 muffin tins or cups.

Place the cornmeal, flour, baking powder, and salt in a mixing bowl. Combine the eggs, milk, and butter in another bowl. Add the liquid ingredients to the dry ingredients, stirring until just combined.

Fill the prepared muffin tins three-quarters full. Bake in the center of the oven until a cake tester or toothpick inserted into the center comes out clean, about 20 minutes. Serve hot from the oven.

VARIATIONS: Add crumbled bacon, fresh herbs, or ½ cup grated cheddar cheese to the muffin batter.

BRAN MUFFINS

Makes 32 muffins

5 cups bran cereal, such as All-Bran or Bran Buds

1½ cups unprocessed bran

4 cups buttermilk

6 eggs

12 tablespoons butter, melted and cooled

½ cup vegetable oil

½ cup molasses

1 teaspoon vanilla extract

1 cup packed brown sugar

5½ cups all-purpose flour

1 tablespoon baking powder

2 teaspoons baking soda

1½ teaspoons salt

Stir together the bran cereal and bran; stir in the buttermilk and let stand until the buttermilk is absorbed. In another bowl, combine the eggs, butter, oil, molasses, and vanilla. Stir in the brown sugar and then the bran mixture.

Sift the flour with the baking powder, baking soda, and salt into a large bowl. Make a well in the center of the dry ingredients, add the liquid mixture, and stir just to combine.

Preheat the oven to 400 degrees. Oil the muffin cups or tins.

Spoon ⅓ cup of the batter into each prepared muffin cup. Bake the muffins until a cake tester inserted in the center of one of the muffins comes out clean, about 20 minutes. Remove the muffin tins to a wire cake-cooling rack and cool for 5 minutes before removing the muffins from the cups. Serve warm or cool completely on the rack.

NOTE: This recipe is deliberately large because it is so convenient to have the batter on hand; in an airtight container, it keeps for up to 2 weeks in the refrigerator. You can make a batch immediately and chill the rest of the batter, then bake a couple of muffins at a time from the refrigerated batter. (Add about 5 minutes extra baking time when making muffins from chilled batter.)

VARIATION: Stir about 1 cup chopped dried fruit or nuts into 4 cups batter just before baking.

BLUEBERRY MUFFINS

Makes 12 muffins

2 cups all-purpose flour, sifted
4 teaspoons baking powder
1 teaspoon salt
2 tablespoons sugar
¼ teaspoon cinnamon
2 eggs, slightly beaten
1 cup milk
3 tablespoons butter, melted
1 cup blueberries, washed and patted dry with paper towels

Preheat the oven to 400 degrees.

Butter 12 muffin tins.

Place the flour, baking powder, salt, sugar, and cinnamon in a mixing bowl. Combine the eggs, milk, and butter in another bowl. Add the liquid ingredients and blueberries to the dry ingredients, stirring with a fork until just combined. (Do not try to get all the lumps out of the batter; too much stirring will make the mixture heavy and prevent it from rising properly.)

Fill the prepared tins three-quarters full and bake in the center of the oven until well risen and golden brown, about 20 minutes.

PUMPKIN MUFFINS WITH PUMPKIN SEEDS

Makes 12 muffins

2 cups all-purpose flour
¾ cup packed brown sugar
2 teaspoons baking powder
¼ teaspoon baking soda
½ teaspoon salt
1 teaspoon cinnamon
¼ teaspoon ground ginger
⅛ teaspoon ground cloves
Dash of ground nutmeg
1 cup canned pumpkin
4 tablespoons butter, melted and cooled
2 large eggs
¼ cup buttermilk
2 teaspoons vanilla extract
1 cup plus 2 tablespoons pumpkin seeds

Stir together the flour, sugar, baking powder, baking soda, salt, cinnamon, ginger, cloves, and nutmeg. In another bowl combine the pumpkin, butter, eggs, buttermilk, and vanilla. Make a well in the center of the dry ingredients; add the pumpkin mixture and stir just to combine. Stir in 1 cup of the pumpkins seeds.

Preheat the oven to 400 degrees.

Butter 12 muffin cups. Spoon the batter into the prepared muffin cups and sprinkle the remaining seeds on top of the muffins until a cake tester inserted in the center of one of the muffins comes out clean, about 20 minutes. Remove the tins to a wire cake-cooking rack and cool for 5 minutes before removing the muffins from the cups. Serve warm, or cool completely on the rack.

■ OATMEAL RAISIN MUFFINS

Makes 8 muffins

1¼ cups all-purpose flour
¾ cup old-fashioned rolled oats
½ cup sugar
2½ teaspoons baking powder
¼ teaspoon salt
½ cup milk
4 tablespoons butter, melted and cooled
1 egg
1½ teaspoons vanilla extract
¾ cup raisins

Stir together the flour, oats, sugar, baking powder, and salt. In another bowl, combine the milk, butter, egg, and vanilla. Make a well in the center of the dry ingredients and add the milk mixture. Stir just to combine. Stir in the raisins.

Preheat the oven to 400 degrees. Oil 8 muffin cups.

Spoon the batter into the prepared cups. Bake until a cake tester inserted into the center of one of the muffins comes out clean, about 20 minutes. Remove the tins to a wire cake-cooling rack and cool for 5 minutes before removing the muffins from the cups. Serve warm, or finish cooling the muffins on the rack.

VARIATION: Any number of "extras" can be added to sweet muffins for flavor and texture. Try, when the recipe seems appropriate, grated orange rind, almond extract, chocolate chips, butterscotch chips, chocolate-covered peanuts, or one peanut butter cup in each muffin.

HONEY SPICE BREAD

Makes two 9-by-5-inch loaves or one round loaf

¼ cup lukewarm water
I envelope active dry yeast
I egg
½ cup honey
I tablespoon ground coriander
½ teaspoon ground cinnamon
¼ teaspoon ground cloves
1½ teaspoons salt
I cup lukewarm milk
6 tablespoons butter, melted
4½ cups all-purpose flour

Pour the lukewarm water into a small bowl; sprinkle the yeast over it and stir to dissolve.

Combine the egg, honey, spices, and salt in a large bowl and beat with a wire whisk until well combined. Add the yeast mixture, milk, and 4 tablespoons of the melted butter; beat again. Stir in the flour, ½ cup at a time, until the dough can be gathered into a soft ball. Knead in the remaining flour with your hands.

Turn the dough out onto a lightly floured surface and knead it until it is smooth and elastic. Do not add any additional flour; the dough should be rather soft. To prevent its sticking, rub your hands occasionally with some of the remaining melted butter.

Form the dough into a ball and put it in a lightly oiled bowl, turning to coat it all over. Cover the bowl with a damp towel and set the bread in a warm place to rise until doubled in bulk.

When the dough has risen, punch it down a few times with your fist and knead it again for a few minutes. Then either divide the dough in half, shape it into 2 loaves and set these in 2 oiled 9-by-5-inch loaf pans, or form it into a round and put it in a 3-quart oiled casserole.

Cover and let the dough rise again until it almost reaches the top of the pans or casserole.

Preheat the oven to 350 degrees.

Bake the bread until the top is crusty and golden brown, about I hour for the loaves, and I hour 10 minutes for the round. Remove the bread from the pans and cool on a wire cake-cooling rack.

ZUCCHINI BREAD

Makes one 9-by-5-inch loaf

½ cup raisins
2 cups all-purpose flour
½ cup light brown sugar
I tablespoon baking powder
I teaspoon salt
½ teaspoon ground nutmeg
½ cup finely chopped walnuts
2 eggs
½ cup buttermilk
⅓ cup vegetable oil
½ pound zucchini, coarsely chopped (about 2 cups)

Preheat the oven to 350 degrees. Butter a 5-by-9-inch loaf pan.

Toss the raisins in a bowl with 2 tablespoons of the flour. Stir together the remaining flour, brown sugar, baking powder, salt, nutmeg, and walnuts in a large bowl. Beat the eggs with the buttermilk and oil in another bowl; stir in the zucchini and add the raisins. Make a well in the center of the dry ingredients, add the buttermilk mixture and blend well. Turn the batter into the prepared pan.

Bake until a cake tester inserted in the center comes out clean, about I hour. Remove the bread to a wire cake-cooling rack and let it cool in the pan for about 15 minutes, then turn it out onto the rack to cool completely. Leave for 2 hours before slicing.

CORNBREAD

Serves 6

1¼ cups yellow cornmeal
1 teaspoon baking powder
2 eggs, beaten
1 8-ounce can golden creamed corn
8 ounces sour cream
5⅓ tablespoons butter, melted

Preheat the oven to 375 degrees. Butter an 8-inch-square baking pan.

Put all the ingredients in a mixing bowl and stir to combine thoroughly. Transfer to the prepared pan and bake until golden brown, about 25 minutes.

NOTE: The cornbread will be moist.

PARMESAN BATTER BREAD

Makes 1 loaf

1 cup all-purpose flour
1 teaspoon salt
2 eggs, slightly beaten
½ cup milk
1 cup ricotta or cottage cheese
½ cup grated Parmesan cheese
3 tablespoons butter
1 clove garlic, finely chopped
1 onion, finely chopped
3 tablespoons chopped fresh parsley
1 teaspoon marjoram
Freshly ground black pepper

Sift together the flour and salt into a bowl. Stir in the eggs, milk, ricotta, and Parmesan cheese.

Heat the butter in an 8-inch cast-iron skillet or 10-inch flame-resistant baking dish until bubbling. Sauté the garlic and onion in the butter over low heat until softened but not brown, about 5 minutes. Take care not to let the butter burn. Stir in the parsley and marjoram and then the batter from the bowl.

Bake until the bread is slightly puffed, about 20 minutes. Season to taste with pepper and serve immediately.

◼ FRAGRANT ORANGE BREAD

Makes one 9-by-5-inch loaf

1 cup orange juice
1 envelope active dry yeast
2 tablespoons honey
1 tablespoon butter or vegetable oil
1 teaspoon salt
Grated rind of 1 orange
1 teaspoon grated nutmeg
2½ to 3 cups flour
½ cup shredded candied orange peel (optional)

Heat the orange juice until lukewarm. Pour the juice into a large bowl, sprinkle the yeast over it, and stir to dissolve. Add the honey, butter, salt, grated rind, nutmeg, and flour. Combine well, cover the bowl with a damp towel and set it aside in a warm place until doubled in bulk.

When the dough has risen, turn it out onto a floured board and knead in candied peel. Let the dough rest for 5 to 10 minutes. Shape it into a loaf and place it in an oiled 9-by-5-inch loaf pan. Cover and let rise again in the pan until at least doubled in bulk.

Preheat the oven to 375 degrees.

Bake until the bread sounds hollow when tapped on the bottom, about 40 to 50 minutes. Remove from the pan and cool on a wire rack.

WALNUT CHEDDAR BREAD

Makes one 8-by-5-inch loaf

2½ cups all-purpose flour

2 teaspoons baking powder

1 teaspoon salt

½ teaspoon dry mustard

½ teaspoon baking soda

Dash of cayenne pepper

4 tablespoons butter

1 cup grated cheddar cheese

1 teaspoon Worcestershire sauce

2 tablespoons honey

1 egg, slightly beaten

1 cup buttermilk

1 cup chopped walnuts

Preheat the oven to 350 degrees. Butter and flour a 8-by-5-inch loaf pan.

Sift together the flour, baking powder, salt, dry mustard, baking soda, and cayenne. Cut the butter into small pieces and cut into the flour mixture, using a pastry blender or 2 knives. Add the grated cheese. Combine the Worcestershire sauce, honey, egg, and buttermilk in a bowl. Stir the mixture into the flour mixture along with the walnuts. Transfer the batter to the prepared loaf pan.

Bake until a cake tester inserted into the center comes out clean, about 55 minutes. Let the bread cool in the pan for 10 minutes and then turn it out onto a wire cake-cooling rack.

APRICOT NUT BREAD

Makes one 8-by-5-inch loaf

6 tablespoons butter, softened

½ cup brown sugar

2 eggs, slightly beaten

2 cups whole wheat flour

I cup chopped dried apricots

½ cup chopped walnuts

Grated rind of I orange

2 teaspoons baking powder

½ teaspoon baking soda

2 teaspoons cinnamon

½ teaspoon mace or nutmeg

½ teaspoon salt

½ cup milk

½ cup orange juice

Preheat the oven to 325 degrees.

Beat the butter and sugar together until thick and creamy. Stir in the eggs, one at a time. Toss ½ cup of the flour with the dried apricots, walnuts, and orange rind in a small bowl. In a larger bowl, combine the remaining flour with the baking powder, baking soda, cinnamon, nutmeg, and salt. Combine the milk and orange juice. Stir the dry ingredients into the butter mixture alternately with the milk and juice until a stiff batter is formed. Fold in the apricot mixture.

Transfer the batter to the prepared pan and bake for about I hour, 15 minutes; test after I hour with a cake tester. When it comes out clean the bread is done. Leave the bread in the pan for 10 minutes, then turn it out on a wire cake-cooling rack. Leave it for at least 2 hours before slicing.

CRANBERRY BREAD

Makes two 8-by-5-inch loaves

3 cups all-purpose flour

2 cups sugar

2 teaspoons baking soda

4 teaspoons baking powder

1½ teaspoons salt

4 tablespoons butter, softened

3 eggs

1½ cups orange juice

2 cups cranberries

1 cup slivered almonds

½ cup raisins

½ cup chopped glacéed fruit

Preheat the oven to 350 degrees. Butter and flour two 8-by-5-inch loaf pans.

Sift together the flour, sugar, baking soda, baking powder, and salt. Beat the butter and eggs until thick and creamy. Add the flour mixture to the butter mixture alternately with the orange juice, then fold in the cranberries, almonds, raisins, and glacéed fruit.

Divide the batter between the prepared loaf pans and bake until a cake tester inserted into the center comes out clean, about 1 hour. Remove the pans to a wire cake-cooling rack; let the bread cool in the pans for about 15 minutes, then turn it out onto the rack to cool completely. Leave for 2 hours before slicing.

■ COFFEE CAKE

Serves 8

1½ cups all-purpose flour

3 teaspoons baking powder

¼ teaspoon salt

4 tablespoons butter, softened

¾ cup sugar

2 eggs

½ cup milk

1 teaspoon vanilla extract

STREUSEL

2 tablespoons all-purpose flour

1 tablespoon cinnamon

2 tablespoons butter, melted

½ cup chopped walnuts

Preheat the oven to 350 degrees. Butter and flour an 8-inch-square baking pan.

Sift together the flour, baking powder, and salt. Beat the butter and sugar in a large bowl until fluffy. Beat the eggs lightly with the milk and vanilla in another bowl, then add the liquid ingredients to the butter mixture alternately with the flour mixture, folding all the ingredients together gently. The mixture will be quite stiff.

Combine the ingredients for the streusel in a separate bowl. Spread half of the coffee cake batter in the prepared baking pan and cover with half of the streusel mixture. Spread the remaining batter over the streusel and top with the remaining streusel mixture. Bake until a cake tester inserted into the center comes out clean, about 30 minutes. Cut it into squares and serve while it is still warm.

SOUR CREAM COFFEE CAKE WITH CHOCOLATE AND WALNUTS

Serves 12

16 tablespoons unsalted butter, cut into small pieces

¾ cup sugar

2 cups all-purpose flour, sifted

¼ teaspoon salt

1 teaspoon baking soda

2 teaspoons baking powder

3 eggs

1 cup sour cream

2 teaspoons vanilla extract

1 cup chopped walnuts

4 ounces bittersweet chocolate, broken into small pieces

Preheat the oven to 350 degrees.

Butter a 9-inch round cake pan. Dust the pan with 2 tablespoons each of flour and sugar and shake out the excess.

In an electric mixer bowl, at high speed, cream the butter. Add the sugar and continue beating at high speed until light and creamy.

Resift the flour with the salt, baking soda, and baking powder. Add ½ cup of the dry ingredients to the butter mixture and blend in on low speed. Beat in one of the eggs. Continue to blend in another cup of the flour mixture, ½ cup at a time, alternately with the remaining 2 eggs. Fold in the remaining flour, the sour cream, and vanilla extract. Using a spatula, fold in the walnuts and chocolate. Transfer the mixture to the prepared baking pan and smooth the surface.

Bake until the cake begins to shrink from the sides of the pan, about 45 minutes. The surface will crack. Insert a toothpick into the center and if it comes out moist, continue baking for another 5 to 8 minutes until it is fully cooked. Let cool in the pan for 10 minutes, then remove it from the pan and transfer it to a wire rack to cool completely. Allow the cake to stand for at least 2 hours before serving.

FRAGRANT MULTIGRAIN WAFFLES

Serves 4

1½ cups flour

½ cup whole wheat flour

2 teaspoons baking powder

1 teaspoon baking soda

½ teaspoon salt

1 tablespoon sugar (optional)

1 teaspoon powdered cinnamon

¼ teaspoon ground cloves

⅛ teaspoon powdered nutmeg

¼ cup oat bran

3 eggs, separated

1½ cups low-fat milk

6 tablespoons melted butter

Maple syrup, berries, and yogurt, for serving

Preheat the waffle iron according to the manufacturer's directions.

Sift the flours with the next seven ingredients and fold in the bran.

Mix together the egg yolks, milk, and melted butter; stir into the dry ingredients. Do not mix too thoroughly; small lumps will disappear in cooking.

Beat the egg whites until they stand in soft peaks. Fold the egg whites into the batter.

Pour ½ cup of the batter onto the hot waffle iron, covering a little less than three-quarters of the surface. Close the lid and cook until no more steam appears, about 4 minutes. Lift the lid. The waffle will slip off the iron easily if it is completely cooked. Add another minute if it seems reluctant to budge.

Pour on the syrup, garnish with berries, and top with a spoonful of yogurt.

10

DESSERTS AND SUCH

BREAD PUDDING

ZABAGLIONE

LEMON MOUSSE

ALMOST INSTANT CHOCOLATE MOUSSE

CLAFOUTI

CARAMEL CUSTARD

RICE PUDDING WITH MERINGUE

CRÈME BRÛLÉE

APPLE PUDDING AND WHIPPED CREAM

BAKED ALASKA WITH FRUIT

APPLE BROWN BETTY

CHEESECAKE THAT DOES NOT SINK IN THE MIDDLE

BRANDIED POUND CAKE WITH ICE CREAM

UNIMAGINABLY GREAT FRUIT CAKE

POUND CAKE

CARROT CAKE

MOCHA GÂTEAU

GINGERBREAD

CHOCOLATE BIRTHDAY CAKE

CHOCOLATE CHIP COOKIES

BROWNIES

CHOCOLATE TRUFFLES

CANDIED GRAPEFRUIT RIND

APPLE, CRANBERRY, RAISIN, NUT PIE

MIXED FRUIT PIE

APPLE PIE

PECAN PIE

PUMPKIN PIE

PASTRY

CHOCOLATE ICE CREAM

VANILLA ICE CREAM

STRAWBERRY ICE CREAM

MOCHA ICE CREAM

LEMON SHERBET

BREAD PUDDING

Serves 6

¼ cup raisins
¼ cup mixed glacéed fruits
¼ cup kirsch
3 tablespoons butter
8 slices firm-textured white bread

CUSTARD
4 egg yolks
½ cup sugar
1½ cups milk
1 teaspoon vanilla extract
1 cup heavy cream
⅛ teaspoon nutmeg

Preheat the oven to 350 degrees.

Cover the raisins with boiling water and let them soak for 5 minutes. Chop the glacéed fruits into small pieces. Drain the raisins and put them in a buttered 1-quart baking dish with the glacéed fruits. Add the kirsch.

Butter the bread generously and cut it into strips or triangles. Add these to the baking dish.

To make the custard, beat the egg yolks and sugar in a bowl with a wire whisk until well combined. Heat the milk to the simmering point in a saucepan and add it to the egg-sugar mixture. Stir to combine, then return the mixture to the saucepan. Place over low heat, and continue stirring until the sauce has thickened. Stir in the vanilla and cream, then pour the custard into the baking dish. Sprinkle the top with nutmeg.

Bake the pudding until the top is golden brown and the pieces of bread sticking up are crusty and golden, about 30 minutes. Serve at room temperature.

■ ZABAGLIONE

Serves 4 to 6

4 egg yolks
⅓ cup sugar
½ cup Marsala

Using a wire whisk, combine the egg yolks and sugar in a special Zabaglione pan, an unlined copper bowl, or the top of a double boiler. Place over heat. Beat furiously until you feel the egg yolks thickening, increasing in volume and doubling and tripling in bulk.

Start adding the Marsala a drop or two at a time and continue beating until all the Marsala has been added. The mixture will reward your efforts by becoming more and more voluminous and lighter and lighter.

Pour the hot Zabaglione into demitasse cups (it is incredibly rich, so a little goes a long way) and serve immediately.

LEMON MOUSSE

Serves 2

2 egg yolks
2 tablespoons sugar
Grated rind and juice of 1 lemon
2 tablespoons water
1 teaspoon unflavored gelatin
½ cup heavy cream

Beat the egg yolks and sugar together in an electric mixer until they are very thick and lemon colored. Add the grated lemon rind and juice. (The mixture will thin out with the addition of the juice.)

Put the water into a very small saucepan. Sprinkle the gelatin over the surface of the water and let it stand, without stirring, for 3 minutes. Put the pan over low heat and heat gently until the gelatin has completely dissolved.

Whip the cream lightly in a separate bowl.

Combine the egg yolk mixture with the dissolved gelatin and fold in the whipped cream, using a spatula. Transfer the mousse to 2 individual serving dishes and chill for at least 2 hours.

ALMOST INSTANT CHOCOLATE MOUSSE

Serves 4 to 6

6 ounces semisweet chocolate morsels or a top-quality bitter chocolate bar, broken into small pieces
⅓ cup hot, but not boiling, heavy cream
2 tablespoons butter, cut into small pieces
2 eggs, slightly beaten
2 tablespoons dark Jamaica rum or Grand Marnier
1 teaspoon vanilla extract

Put the chocolate pieces in a food processor and add the hot cream and butter. Process until the chocolate has melted. Add the eggs, rum, and vanilla. Chill the mousse in the refrigerator until it is firm, about 2 to 3 hours.

VARIATION: Pour the mousse into tiny pot-de-crème containers or espresso cups. The mousse will chill in the refrigerator in an hour and be ready to serve almost immediately. For a grand dinner, a single violet blossom in each cup adds a special touch.

CLAFOUTI

Serves 6

I pound plums, cherries, peaches, blueberries, or other not too juicy fruit
1¼ cups milk
4 eggs
½ cup granulated sugar
I teaspoon salt
I cup all-purpose flour
1½ tablespoons butter, melted
¼ cup confectioners' sugar
Whipped cream, for serving

Preheat the oven to 350 degrees.

Remove the pits from the fruit and slice the fruit. Put the slices in a 10-inch round shallow baking dish.

Combine the milk, eggs, sugar, salt, flour, and melted butter in the food processor or stir briskly with a wire whisk. Pour the batter over the fruit and bake until the batter has set into a custardlike consistency, about 30 minutes.

Dust the surface with sifted confectioners' sugar, and serve hot with mounds of whipped cream.

■ CARAMEL CUSTARD

Serves 6

FOR THE CARAMEL
½ cup sugar
2 tablespoons cold water

FOR THE CUSTARD
3 eggs
3 egg yolks
½ cup sugar
2 cups milk
½ vanilla bean, or 1 teaspoon vanilla extract

Preheat the oven to 325 degrees.

To prepare the caramel, cook the sugar and water in a small heavy saucepan over low heat, without stirring, until the sugar has melted into liquid caramel, about 10 minutes. Continue cooking, swirling the liquid gently from time to time and watching carefully that it doesn't burn, until it is a rich brown color, about 5 minutes more.

Pour the caramel into a 1-quart soufflé dish. Roll the hot caramel quickly around the bottom and sides of the dish to coat them evenly. (Hold the dish with oven mitts because it gets very hot very quickly.) Set the coated dish aside.

To prepare the custard, whisk together the eggs, egg yolks, and sugar in a bowl. Pour the milk into a saucepan. Split the vanilla bean in half lengthwise and scrape the black particles into the milk. Drop the empty pod into the milk as well and bring to a simmer, then discard the pod. If you are not using the bean, add the vanilla extract.

Pour the hot milk into the egg-sugar mixture; stir to combine the ingredients. Pour the custard into the caramel-coated soufflé dish. Place the dish in a larger baking dish, adding enough hot water to come halfway up the sides of the custard dish. Bake until the custard has set, about 50 minutes.

Remove the custard, allow it to cool, then refrigerate it for 4 hours. When ready to serve, loosen the sides of the custard by depressing the outer edges with your finger, and unmold it onto a serving dish. It will slip out of the baking dish very easily.

NOTE: The custard is baked in a water bath to prevent it from becoming too hot and thus pitted with small holes. When it is unmolded, the caramel forms a sauce around the custard.

RICE PUDDING WITH MERINGUE

Serves 3

1 pound store-bought rice pudding
3 tablespoons raspberry preserves
2 egg whites
⅛ teaspoon salt
⅛ teaspoon cream of tartar
⅓ cup sugar

Preheat the oven to 425 degrees.

Divide the rice pudding between 3 ovenproof dessert dishes and cover each with 1 tablespoon of the preserves. Beat the egg whites with salt and cream of tartar until soft peaks form. Add the sugar and continue beating until the peaks are stiff and shiny. Spread the meringue on top of the preserves and bake the pudding until the top is golden brown, about 10 minutes. Serve immediately.

VARIATION: Applesauce or fresh berries can be substituted for the raspberry preserves.

CRÈME BRÛLÉE

Serves 6

6 egg yolks
½ cup granulated sugar
3 cups heavy cream
½ vanilla bean, or 1 teaspoon vanilla extract
½ cup superfine sugar

Preheat the oven to 300 degrees.

Beat the egg yolks and sugar in a bowl, using a wire whisk.

Pour the cream into a saucepan. Split the vanilla bean in half lengthwise and scrape the black particles into the cream. Drop the empty pod into the cream as well and bring just to a simmer. Do *not* let it boil. Discard the pod. If you are not using the bean, add the vanilla extract.

Pour the hot cream over the egg yolks and sugar, stirring constantly. Return the mixture to the saucepan and stir over low heat until the custard has thickened slightly. Again, be sure to not let the custard boil or it will separate later.

Pour the custard into a 9-inch porcelain pie plate or an 8-inch-square glass baking dish. Bake until a skin has formed on the surface of the custard, about 20 minutes.

Cool the custard and refrigerate it for 12 hours. (It continues to thicken as it stands.)

Preheat the broiler.

Sprinkle the surface of the custard with a thin layer of superfine sugar. Place the dish under the broiler until the sugar has caramelized, about 5 minutes or less. Refrigerate for 2 hours more before serving. The caramel will form a crunchy, brittle layer over the creamy custard.

VARIATION: Infuse the milk with a slice of fresh gingerroot instead of the vanilla or add a teaspoon of freshly grated orange or lemon rind.

APPLE PUDDING AND WHIPPED CREAM

Serves 2

1 large baking apple, peeled, cored, and thinly sliced
Grated rind of 1 lemon
3 tablespoons sugar

TOPPING
2 tablespoons butter
2 tablespoons sugar
2 eggs
½ cup cake flour

½ cup heavy cream, whipped, or ice cream, slightly softened

Preheat the oven to 350 degrees.

Butter 2 individual soufflé dishes. Divide the apple slices between the dishes and add the grated lemon rind and 2 tablespoons of the sugar.

To make the topping, beat together the butter and sugar. Stir in the eggs, one at a time, and finally fold the cake flour into the mixture. Spoon the topping over the sliced apples in the soufflé dishes.

Bake until the pudding is lightly browned, about 35 minutes. Serve topped with whipped cream.

BAKED ALASKA WITH FRUIT

Serves 24

3 1-pound store-bought (or homemade, page 276) pound cakes

4 or more ripe fresh peaches, peeled and sliced

2 cups canned pear halves, sliced thinly

2 large bananas, sliced

12 egg whites

¼ teaspoon cream of tartar

½ teaspoon salt

2 cups sugar

2 quarts vanilla ice cream, softened just enough to be easily scooped

¼ cup brandy, heated

Preheat the oven to 375 degrees.

Cut each of the cakes lengthwise into 3 thick slices and lay them close together on 2 baking sheets, or improvise on the basic idea, cutting them to fit into 3 pie plates. (The firm-textured cakes form the base for the Baked Alaska.) Spread a layer of peach slices on top of the cake. Add a layer of pear slices, and top with a layer of bananas.

To prepare the meringue, put the egg whites into the large mixing bowl of an electric mixer (you may need to do this in 2 batches if you do not have a large enough mixing bowl). Add the cream of tartar and salt. Beat at the highest speed until the egg whites stand in soft peaks. Beat in the sugar gradually and continue beating until the mixture stands in stiff peaks.

Cover the fruit-topped cake with ice cream, mounding it to form a dome. Cover the ice cream with the meringue, taking great care to enclose the ice cream completely. (The meringue will insulate the ice cream and momentarily prevent it from melting when it goes into the hot oven.) Bake until the meringue is very lightly browned, about 4 to 5 minutes.

Bring the Alaska to the table immediately. Light the brandy and pour the flames slowly over the Baked Alaska. Or, for a more spectacular presentation, sink eggshell halves in the baked meringue, fill them carefully with warmed brandy, light the brandy and carry the creation aflame into a darkened room.

■ APPLE BROWN BETTY

Serves 6

1 cup all-purpose flour
¼ teaspoon salt
½ teaspoon cinnamon
¼ teaspoon nutmeg
¾ cup sugar
8 tablespoons butter
4 slices firm-textured bread, crusts removed
1 cup raisins
3 small cooking apples, peeled, cored, and sliced
Whipped cream, for serving

Preheat the oven to 350 degrees.

Butter a 9-inch baking dish.

Sift the flour, salt, cinnamon, nutmeg, and sugar into a bowl. Cut the butter into small pieces; cut it into the flour mixture, using a pastry blender.

Cut the bread into crouton-sized pieces. Soak the raisins in boiling water until plump, about 5 minutes, then drain them. Combine the bread, raisins, and sliced apples in a bowl. Sprinkle the bottom of the prepared baking dish with a third of the flour mixture, add the apple mixture, and top with the remaining flour mixture. Bake, uncovered, until the top of the brown betty is crisp and the apples are tender. Serve hot or cold, with whipped cream.

CHEESECAKE THAT DOES NOT SINK IN THE MIDDLE

Serves 12 or more

CRUST

1½ cups graham cracker crumbs

6 tablespoons butter, melted

¼ cup sugar

1 teaspoon cinnamon

FILLING

3 8-ounce packages cream cheese

½ cup sour cream

3 tablespoons all-purpose flour

1 cup sugar

2 eggs

2 egg yolks

1 tablespoon vanilla extract

Grated rind and juice of 2 lemons

DECORATION

20 or so picture-perfect fresh strawberries

1 cup red-currant jelly, melted

Preheat the oven to 350 degrees.

Make the crust by putting the graham crackers into the blender or food processor and processing into fine crumbs. With the motor on, add the butter, then the sugar and cinnamon. Firmly pat the crumb mixture into an 8¾- or 9-inch springform cake pan or cheesecake pan.

Combine all the filling ingredients using an electric mixer. (If you use the food processor, the mixture becomes too compact.) Pour the filling into the prepared graham cracker shell and bake for 50 minutes. Do *not* open the oven door—trust the recipe. Turn off the oven and leave the cheesecake in it for 30 minutes, to allow it to cool slowly.

Remove the cheesecake and refrigerate it for at least 4 hours. Unmold the cake onto a serving platter by releasing the sides of the springform pan. If you are using a cheesecake pan, run a sharp paring knife around its sides and the cheesecake will slide out without any difficulty. Decorate the cake with the strawberries and glaze with melted red-currant jelly.

BRANDIED POUND CAKE WITH ICE CREAM

Serves 8

1 store-bought (or homemade, page 276) Pound Cake
⅓ cup brandy
1 quart ice cream, slightly softened

Cut the pound cake horizontally into 4 layers. Sprinkle each layer but the top with a little brandy, then cover with scoops of ice cream and reassemble. Serve immediately.

VARIATION: Gild the lily by topping the ice cream with some grated bittersweet chocolate.

UNIMAGINABLY GREAT FRUIT CAKE

Makes 2 fruit cakes

2 cups golden raisins

2 cups dark raisins

4 3½-ounce boxes glacéed cherries, left whole

I cup dried pineapple rings, cut into small pieces

I 8-ounce box chopped glacéed fruit rinds

I pound glacéed dessert apricots, diced

I cup sliced almonds

I cup brazil nuts, very finely chopped

3 cups flour

I teaspoon salt

2 teaspoons baking soda

I teaspoon cinnamon

I teaspoon allspice

½ teaspoon grated nutmeg

½ teaspoon ground cloves

16 tablespoons butter, cut into small pieces

I½ cups dark brown sugar

8 eggs

2 teaspoons vanilla extract

4 ounces dark semisweet chocolate, grated

⅓ cup apple brandy

Preheat the oven to 300 degrees.

Butter and flour two 12-by-4-by-3-inch loaf pans, or coat them with vegetable shortening spray.

Toss all the fruits and nuts with I cup of the flour. (A dishwashing bowl is good for this.) Sift the remaining flour with the salt and spices.

Beat the butter until light and creamy. Beat in the brown sugar. Fold in the eggs alternately with the sifted flour mixture. Add the vanilla, chocolate, and brandy. Fold this mixture into the floured fruits and nuts. Divide the cake mixture between the prepared pans and cover with oiled aluminum foil. Bake for 1¼ hours. Remove the foil and continue baking until a cake tester inserted into the centers comes out clean, about 1 hour 15 minutes more.

Leave the cakes to cool in the pans for 15 minutes, then unmold them onto a wire cake-cooling rack and leave to cool completely. Wrap the cakes tightly in foil and store in the refrigerator.

NOTE: The glacéed apricots are the essential ingredients that keep the cake so moist and create the triumph.

■ POUND CAKE

Makes one 8-by-4-by-3-inch loaf

12 tablespoons unsalted butter

¾ cup sifted cake flour

¾ cup sifted all-purpose flour

1 teaspoon baking powder

¼ teaspoon salt

¼ teaspoon mace

¼ cup milk

3 eggs, at room temperature

¾ cup granulated sugar

¼ cup sifted confectioners' sugar

Preheat the oven to 350 degrees and butter and flour the loaf pan.

Cream the butter in a large mixing bowl until light in color. Sift together the sifted flours, baking powder, salt, and mace. Beat the flour mixture into the butter gradually, scraping the sides of the bowl with a spatula. Beat in the milk.

Wash the beaters and beat the eggs and sugars in a small mixing bowl until very thick and tripled in volume (this will take a full 10 minutes). The mixture should fall from the beaters and form a slowly dissolving ribbon. Fold the egg mixture into the flour mixture, a little at a time, until barely combined—do not overmix. Spread into the pre-pared loaf pan and bake in the center of the oven until a cake tester inserted in the center comes out clean, about 50 to 55 minutes.

Cool the cake in the pan for 10 minutes, then unmold onto a wire rack to cool completely. Do not cut the cake for 12 hours—you will be rewarded by its gratifyingly smooth texture and buttery taste.

VARIATIONS: Substitute dry sherry, brandy, orange juice with grated orange rind or lemon juice with grated lemon rind for the milk.

■ CARROT CAKE

Makes one 8-by-8-inch cake

1½ cups whole wheat flour
1 teaspoon baking powder
1 teaspoon baking soda
1 teaspoon allspice
½ teaspoon cinnamon
¼ teaspoon salt
Grated rind of 2 oranges
8 tablespoons butter
1½ cups granulated or light brown sugar
3 eggs
2 teaspoons vanilla extract
1 cup finely chopped almonds
½ cup currants
2 medium carrots, grated (about 1½ cups)
2 tablespoons confectioners' sugar, sifted
Whipped cream or plain yogurt, for serving

Preheat the oven to 350 degrees. Butter and flour an 8-inch-square baking pan.

Sift together the flour, baking powder, baking soda, spices, and salt. Add the grated orange rind.

Beat the butter and sugar until thick and creamy, scraping down the sides of the bowl occasionally. Beat in the eggs one at a time, alternating with the flour mixture. Fold in the vanilla extract, almonds, currants, and grated carrot. Spread the batter in the prepared pan and bake until a cake tester inserted into the center comes out clean, about 55 minutes.

Leave the cake in the pan for 15 minutes, then unmold onto a wire cake-cooling rack, cut into squares, and dust the surface with the sifted confectioners' sugar. Serve with whipped cream or yogurt.

MOCHA GÂTEAU

Makes one 9-inch layer cake

4 eggs

¾ cup sugar

1 teaspoon almond extract

1 teaspoon powdered instant coffee

1 cup all-purpose flour, sifted

⅔ cup ground almonds

FILLING

1 cup heavy cream

2 tablespoons sugar

1 teaspoon powdered instant coffee

1 teaspoon vanilla extract

DECORATION

½ cup apricot preserves

1 16-ounce can unpeeled apricot halves, drained

Preheat the oven to 375 degrees. Butter and flour a 9-inch layer cake pan.

Beat the eggs and sugar until thick and creamy. Add the almond extract and instant coffee. Fold in the flour and ground almonds. Spread the cake batter in the prepared cake pan and bake until a cake tester inserted into the center comes out clean, about 35 minutes. Cool the cake in the pan for 5 minutes, then unmold onto a wire cake-cooling rack. When the cake is completely cold, split it horizontally into 2 layers.

To prepare the filling, beat the cream until it has thickened. Add the sugar, instant coffee, and vanilla and continue beating until thick. Spread the whipped cream between the cake layers.

Heat the apricot preserves in a small saucepan until hot and then strain. Brush the surface of the cake with some of the warm apricot preserves. Arrange the apricot halves on top of the cake and brush the fruit with the remaining preserves to make the apricots shine attractively.

◼ GINGERBREAD

Makes one 9-inch-square cake

8 tablespoons butter
1 cup sugar
2 eggs
Grated rind of 1 orange
2 cups sifted all-purpose flour
1½ teaspoons ginger
½ teaspoon cinnamon
½ teaspoon nutmeg
½ teaspoon allspice
1 teaspoon baking soda
½ teaspoon salt
¼ cup molasses
¾ cup white corn syrup
½ cup boiling water
Whipped cream, for serving

Preheat the oven to 350 degrees. Butter and flour a 9-inch-square baking pan.

Beat the butter and sugar in a bowl until thick and creamy. Stir in the eggs and orange rind. Sift the dry ingredients together; in a separate bowl, combine the molasses, corn syrup, and boiling water. Add the dry and liquid ingredients alternately to the butter and sugar mixture until a smooth batter has formed. Turn the batter into the prepared pan and bake until a cake tester inserted into the center comes out clean, about 50 minutes.

Cool the gingerbread for a few minutes in the pan, then cut it into squares. Serve it while still warm, with whipped cream.

CHOCOLATE BIRTHDAY CAKE

Makes one 9-inch layer cake

CAKE

3 1-ounce squares baking chocolate

4 eggs

¾ cup sugar

¾ cup sifted all-purpose flour

1 teaspoon almond extract

BUTTER CREAM

½ cup sugar

½ cup water

3 egg yolks

8 tablespoons unsalted butter

DECORATION

6 ounces bittersweet chocolate

½ cup apricot preserves, melted and strained

Preheat the oven to 350 degrees. Butter and flour a 9-inch layer cake pan.

Break the baking chocolate into small pieces and put them on a plate. Cover with another plate and set both plates over a saucepan of simmering water until the chocolate has melted.

Beat together the eggs and sugar in an electric mixer on high speed until thick and creamy. Using a rubber spatula, fold a third of the flour and a third of the melted chocolate into the egg mixture until just combined. Continue alternating the flour and chocolate until all the flour and chocolate are used and the mixtures are barely combined. Add the almond extract. Spread the cake batter in the prepared pan and bake until a cake tester inserted into the center comes out clean, about 45 minutes.

Leave the cake in the pan for 5 minutes, then unmold it onto a wire cake-cooling rack. When the cake is cold, split it horizontally into 2 layers.

To prepare the butter cream, put the sugar and water into a small saucepan. Boil over high heat until a thick syrup has formed or a candy thermometer reads 238 degrees, about 5 minutes.

Beat the egg yolks until thick. Continue beating the yolks at moderate speed while adding the boiling syrup in a slow, steady stream. (Be careful that the syrup does not splash up into your face.) Continue beating until the mixture has more than doubled in bulk, about 5 minutes more.

Beat the butter in a small mixing bowl until light and creamy. Add the butter to the yolk mixture, a little at a time, until all the butter has been incorporated. Spread the butter cream between the cake layers.

To decorate the cake, melt the bittersweet chocolate between 2 plates as before. Line a baking sheet with wax paper and spread the melted chocolate over it in a very thin layer. Chill for 15 minutes in the freezer until the chocolate is cold and brittle.

Brush the warm strained preserves over the top of the cake. Crumple the wax paper to break the chocolate into wafer-thin fragments and scatter the broken chocolate over the top of the cake.

NOTE: When mixing the cake, fold in the flour and chocolate as delicately as possible—on tiptoe, so to speak. If you mix it like a mad scientist, the batter will deflate and the cake will not rise properly.

CHOCOLATE CHIP COOKIES

Makes 3 dozen cookies

8 tablespoons butter

¼ cup granulated sugar

½ cup brown sugar

1 egg

1¼ cups all-purpose flour

½ teaspoon salt

½ teaspoon baking soda

6 ounces top-quality semisweet chocolate, broken with the point of a paring knife into small pieces

Preheat the oven to 375 degrees. Butter 2 baking sheets.

Beat the butter and sugars together in an electric mixer until they are thick and creamy. Add the egg and beat until fluffy. Sift the flour, salt, and baking soda together and add to the butter mixture. Stir in the chocolate pieces. Refrigerate the mixture for an hour.

Drop the dough by teaspoonfuls onto the prepared baking sheets, leaving enough space between the cookies to allow them to spread. Bake until the cookies are lightly browned, about 10 to 12 minutes. Remove them from the sheets while still hot, using a metal spatula, and cool them in a single layer on wire cake-cooling racks.

■ BROWNIES

Makes sixteen 2-inch squares

2 2-ounce squares unsweetened baking chocolate

5⅓ tablespoons butter

1 cup sugar

2 eggs, slightly beaten

⅔ cup all-purpose flour

½ teaspoon salt

½ teaspoon baking powder

½ cup chopped walnuts

Preheat the oven to 350 degrees. Butter an 8-inch-square baking pan.

Melt the chocolate and butter in the top of a double boiler over hot water, stirring until the butter has completely dissolved. Remove the pan from the heat and stir in the sugar and eggs. Sift the flour with the salt and baking powder; fold it into the chocolate mixture. Stir in the chopped walnuts and transfer the batter to the prepared pan. Bake until a toothpick inserted into the center comes out clean, about 30 minutes. Cool the brownies in the baking pan. Cut into squares when completely cold.

■ CHOCOLATE TRUFFLES

Makes 4 dozen

PRALINE
½ cup sugar
½ cup whole almonds
1 tablespoon vegetable oil

FILLING
6 1-ounce squares semisweet or bittersweet chocolate, broken into small pieces
4 tablespoons unsalted butter, cut into small pieces
2 tablespoons Grand Marnier or rum
Grated rind of 1 orange
2 tablespoons heavy cream

COATING
4 ounces semisweet chocolate, broken into small pieces
½ cup good-quality unsweetened cocoa

To make the praline, put the sugar in a small heavy saucepan and heat over low heat until it has melted into caramel. Add the almonds and continue cooking until it becomes a rich dark brown color. Be careful not to let the caramel burn. Brush a baking sheet with the oil. Pour the hot mixture onto the prepared baking sheet and spread it with a metal spatula to form a thin layer. Leave the praline to cool, then grind it to a find powder in a blender or food processor.

Melt the chocolate for the filling in the top of a double boiler over boiling water. Gradually stir in the butter, Grand Marnier, grated orange rind, cream, and the praline powder until all have been incorporated. Cool the mixture, then refrigerate it for 1 hour. Shape the cooled, thickened truffle mixture into balls about the size of a walnut. Set them on a baking sheet lined with wax paper; freeze until firm.

Melt the chocolate for the coating in the double boiler and allow it to cool to lukewarm. Spread the cocoa powder onto a piece of wax paper.

Roll each ice-cold truffle in the melted chocolate. It is best (though messy) to put a little of the melted chocolate in the palm of your hand and roll the truffle around until it becomes very thinly coated. Roll the chocolate-coated truffles in the cocoa to cover them completely. Store the truffles in an airtight container.

CANDIED GRAPEFRUIT RIND

Makes 100 pieces

4 large pink grapefruit
1½ cups water
4½ cups granulated sugar
Granulated sugar, for coating the candied rinds

Cut the grapefruits in half. Remove the fruit from the rind and save for another use. Pull out all the pithy membranes and cut the rind into strips about 2 inches long and ½ inch wide. (There will be some oddly shaped pieces; do not throw them away—they will still taste good.)

Put the water and sugar into a heavy saucepan and cook, stirring, over low heat until the sugar has dissolved. Boil gently for 4 minutes, then add the grapefruit strips. Now simmer until the syrup reaches 240 degrees on a candy thermometer, about 30 minutes. The rind will gradually become clear and transparent when it is fully cooked. The outer rind will remain firm to the bite and the pink-tinged inside will be soft. (Don't be tempted to taste one right out of the pan or you will burn your tongue.) Drain and reserve the syrup for another use.

Lay a piece of wax paper underneath a wire cake-cooling rack and spread out the rinds on the rack. Leave them on the rack until all the thick syrup has dripped away. Put about a cup of granulated sugar onto another sheet of wax paper and roll the strips, one at a time, in the sugar. Set the strips on a long strip of wax paper and let them dry for about 1 hour. When dry, pack them into 2-quart jars with tight-fitting lids. The rinds will keep in a cool place for at least 2 weeks. If they become slightly sticky, roll them again in granulated sugar.

VARIATION: Candied thick-skinned orange rind is made in the same way. This is a good use for the reserved syrup; if you need more syrup to candy the orange rind, increase the reserved syrup by adding water and sugar in the same proportions as in the above recipe.

APPLE, CRANBERRY, RAISIN, NUT PIE

Makes one 10-inch pie

Pastry for a double-crust pie (page 292)
1 egg yolk, for glaze
2 tablespoons milk, for glaze
Confectioners' sugar, sifted, for dusting

FILLING
4 medium cooking apples, peeled, cored, and sliced
2 cups applesauce
2 cups fresh cranberries
1 cup seedless raisins
1 cup chopped walnuts
½ cup freshly made fine bread crumbs
1 teaspoon cinnamon
½ cup brown sugar

Preheat the oven to 350 degrees.

Divide the pastry into 2 slightly unequal halves. Roll out the larger piece into a circle on a floured surface and fit it into a 10-inch pie plate.

Combine all the filling ingredients in a large bowl and spread them over the pastry.

For the top crust, roll out the smaller piece of dough into a circle on a floured surface and cover the pie. Trim and seal the edges. Cut several slits in the top of the crust to allow the steam to escape. Combine the egg yolks and milk and brush it over the pastry crust to form a glaze.

Bake the pie until golden brown, about 45 minutes. Remove the pie from the oven and let it cool on a wire cake-cooling rack. Dust the pie with sifted confectioners' sugar just before serving.

MIXED FRUIT PIE

Makes one 10-inch pie

Pastry for a double-crust pie (page 292)
1 egg yolk, for glaze
2 tablespoons milk, for glaze
Sifted confectioners' sugar, for dusting

FILLING
4 medium cooking apples, peeled, cored, and thinly sliced
1 8-ounce container blackberries, blueberries, strawberries, or raspberries
2 bananas, sliced
½ teaspoon allspice
1 teaspoon cinnamon
⅓ cup granulated sugar
3 tablespoons cornstarch dissolved in 3 tablespoons orange juice or cold water

Preheat the oven to 350 degrees.

Divide the pastry into 2 slightly unequal halves. Roll out the larger piece into a circle on a floured surface and fit it into a 10-inch pie plate.

Combine the fruits in a bowl and toss with the spices and sugar. Stir the dissolved cornstarch into the fruit slices. Spoon the mixed fruit into the pie shell.

For the top crust, roll out the smaller piece of pastry into a circle on a floured surface and cover the fruit. Trim and seal the edges. Cut several slits in the top crust to allow the steam to escape.

Combine the egg yolk and milk in a small bowl and brush over the pastry crust to form a glaze. Bake the pie until golden brown, about 45 minutes. Refrigerate for 4 hours to allow the juices to thicken.

Dust the surface with confectioners' sugar just before serving.

■ APPLE PIE

Makes one 10-inch pie

Pastry for a double-crust pie (see page 292)
1 egg yolk, for glaze
2 tablespoons milk, for glaze
Whipped cream or sharp cheddar cheese, for serving

FILLING

6 medium baking apples, peeled, cored, and thinly sliced
¼ cup sugar
¼ teaspoon nutmeg
½ teaspoon cinnamon
3 tablespoons butter, cut into small pieces
1 tablespoon cornstarch dissolved in 2 tablespoons cold water

Preheat the oven to 350 degrees.

Divide the pastry dough into 2 slightly unequal halves. Roll out the larger piece into a circle on a floured surface and fit it into a 10-inch pie plate.

Put the apple slices in a bowl and toss with the sugar, spices, and butter. Stir the dissolved cornstarch into the apple mixture. Spoon the filling into the pie shell.

For the top crust, roll out the smaller piece of pastry into a circle on a floured surface and cover the pie with it. Trim and seal the edges. Cut several slits in the top crust to allow the steam to escape. Combine the egg yolk and milk and brush over the pastry crust to form a glaze.

Bake until golden brown, about 45 minutes. Serve warm with whipped cream or slices of sharp cheddar cheese.

PECAN PIE

Makes one 9- to 10-inch pie

Pastry for a single-crust pie (see page 292)
Whipped cream, for serving

FILLING
5 eggs
¼ cup sugar
1 teaspoon vanilla extract
2 tablespoons butter, melted
3 tablespoons all-purpose flour
2 cups dark corn syrup
1 cup pecan halves

Preheat the oven to 350 degrees.

Roll out the pastry dough into a circle on a floured surface and fit it into a 9- to 10-inch pie plate.

Whisk together the eggs, sugar, and vanilla in a bowl. Whisk in the melted butter, flour, and corn syrup. Spoon the mixture into the pie shell and cover with the pecans in an even layer. Bake until the filling has set and is well browned, about 50 to 55 minutes. Refrigerate the pie until firm, about 4 hours.

Serve with a heaping bowl of whipped cream, sweetened with a little sugar, if desired.

■ PUMPKIN PIE

Makes one 9- to 10-inch pie

Pastry for a single-crust pie (see page 292)
Sour cream, for serving
Brown sugar, for serving

FILLING
1 30-ounce can pumpkin pie filling
2 eggs, slightly beaten
½ cup heavy cream
3 tablespoons Grand Marnier
Grated rind of 2 oranges
1 cup chopped pecans (optional)

Preheat the oven to 350 degrees.

Roll out the pastry into a circle on a floured surface and fit it into a 9- to 10-inch pie plate.

Combine the pumpkin pie filling, eggs, cream, Grand Marnier, and grated orange rind in a bowl; mix thoroughly. Pour the filling into the pie shell. Add the pecans, if you wish, sprinkling them evenly over the top. Bake the pie until the custardlike mixture has set, about 1 hour 15 minutes. Refrigerate the pie until firm, at least 4 hours.

Serve the pie with sour cream and brown sugar.

■ PASTRY

FOR A SINGLE-CRUST PIE

1¼ cups all-purpose flour

⅛ teaspoon salt

3 tablespoons cold butter, cut into small pieces

3 tablespoons solid vegetable shortening

6 tablespoons cold water

FOR A DOUBLE-CRUST PIE

2½ cups all-purpose flour

½ teaspoon salt

6 tablespoons cold butter, cut into small pieces

6 tablespoons solid vegetable shortening

12 tablespoons cold water

Sift the flour and salt onto a sheet of wax paper. Measure it again, leveling it off with a knife in the measuring cup.

To make the pastry by hand, put the flour in a bowl and cut in the butter and shortening with a pastry blender until of the consistency of cornmeal. Stir in the water gradually with a fork until a ball of dough has formed.

To make the pastry in the food processor, put the flour, salt, butter, and shortening into the workbowl and process until the butter and shortening form small pieces. Add the water gradually through the top, processing only until a ball of dough has just formed.

Shape the dough into a disk, wrap it in wax paper, and chill it for 30 minutes before rolling it out.

■ CHOCOLATE ICE CREAM

Makes 1 ½ quarts

2 2-ounce squares unsweetened baking chocolate

2 cups milk

4 egg yolks

1 cup sugar

¼ teaspoon salt

2 cups heavy cream

2 teaspoons vanilla extract

Put the chocolate on a plate set over a saucepan of simmering water, cover it with an inverted saucer, and simmer over low heat until the chocolate has melted.

Heat the milk to a simmer in another saucepan. Stir together the egg yolks, sugar, and salt in a small bowl. Using a wire whisk, stir the hot milk into the egg yolk mixture, then return it to the saucepan. Stir over low heat until a light custard has formed. Add the melted chocolate, cream, and vanilla; combine thoroughly.

Cool the mixture, then pour it into an ice-cream maker and process it according to the manufacturer's directions.

VARIATIONS:

- Add crushed Heath bars, M & Ms, or crumbled cookies to the mixture when it is to the point of freezing.
- Serve the chocolate ice cream topped with grated chocolate.

VANILLA ICE CREAM

Makes 1 ½ quarts

2 cups milk
¾ cup sugar
¼ teaspoon salt
2 cups heavy cream
1 tablespoon vanilla extract

Bring 1 cup of the milk to a simmer in a medium saucepan. Add the sugar and salt, and cook, stirring, over low heat until they are dissolved. Remove the pan from the heat and stir in the cream and vanilla. Set the mixture aside to cool. Pour the cooked mixture into an ice-cream maker and process it according to the manufacturer's directions.

STRAWBERRY ICE CREAM

Makes about 1 pint

½ pint fresh strawberries, or ½ 10-ounce package frozen strawberries
¾ cup milk
¾ cup heavy cream
⅓ cup superfine sugar
1 teaspoon vanilla extract

Rinse and then hull the fresh berries. Puree them in a blender or food processor. Strain the puree to remove the seeds.

Combine the milk and cream with the sugar. Whisk until the sugar dissolves, about 2 minutes. Stir in the vanilla extract and the strawberry puree. Pour the mixture into an ice-cream maker and process it according to the manufacturer's directions.

VARIATION: Substitute low-fat milk for the milk and whole milk for the cream, reduce the amount of sugar to 1 tablespoon—and serve Strawberry Ice Milk.

NOTE: Though it is against my principles to use food coloring, this is one time when it is useful. No matter how beautiful the strawberries may be, the color of the ice cream becomes "muddy" when it is frozen. Add the coloring a drop at a time after stirring in the vanilla and strawberry puree; too much is worse than none at all.

■ MOCHA ICE CREAM

Makes 1½ quarts

2 cups milk
4 egg yolks
¾ cup sugar
¼ teaspoon salt
1 tablespoon powdered instant coffee
2 6-ounce packages bittersweet *eating* (not baking) chocolate
2 teaspoons vanilla extract
2 cups heavy cream

Bring the milk to a simmer over low heat. Meanwhile, stir the egg yolks and sugar together in a small bowl, then stir in the hot milk and return to the saucepan. Cook over low heat, stirring with a wire whisk, until thickened. Remove the pan from the heat and stir in the salt and instant coffee.

Break the chocolate into squares. Place the squares on a plate over a saucepan of simmering water, cover with an inverted saucer, and simmer over low heat until the chocolate has melted. Scrape the chocolate into the custard, add the vanilla and cream, and stir until thoroughly combined. Cool the mixture, then pour it into an ice-cream maker and process it according to the manufacturer's directions.

LEMON SHERBET

Makes 1 quart

2 cups water
1 cup sugar
1 cup freshly squeezed and strained lemon juice
Grated rind of 1 lemon

Pour the water into a saucepan and add the sugar. Bring it to a boil over medium-high heat. Boil, uncovered, for 5 minutes, then remove the pan from the heat and let it cool. Add the lemon juice and rind. Pour the mixture into an ice-cream maker and process it according to the manufacturer's directions.

11

FRUIT FOR ALL SEASONS

PEACHES IN PORT WINE

PEACHES IN CHAMPAGNE

BAKED RUM PEACHES

PEARS BAKED IN RED WINE

PEARS WITH RASPBERRY SAUCE AND ICE CREAM

ORANGES STUFFED WITH SHERBET

ORANGES IN SWEET MARMALADE SAUCE

ORANGES WITH ORANGES

STEWED RHUBARB

MELON WITH BLUEBERRIES

RASPBERRIES WITH RASPBERRY PUREE

GRAPEFRUIT HALVES FILLED WITH RED AND BLACK FRUIT

PLUM COMPOTE

PRUNE COMPOTE

BANANAS WITH CHOCOLATE SAUCE

STRAWBERRIES ROMANOFF

STRAWBERRY WINE CUP

STRAWBERRIES WITH STRAWBERRY PUREE

GRAPEFRUIT CUPS

BAKED APPLES WITH RUM

BAKED APPLES WITH SWEET YOGURT

PINEAPPLE IN CARAMEL KIRSCH

PEACHES IN PORT WINE

Serves 4

4 fully ripe peaches
½ cup port wine
½ cup red wine
¼ cup red currant jelly
1 tablespoon lemon juice
2 teaspoons cornstarch dissolved in 2 tablespoons cold water
Freshly baked macaroons or other homemade cookies

Bring a saucepan of water to a boil. Plunge the peaches, one at a time, into the water and count slowly to 10. Remove the peaches, dip each one in cold water, and slip off the skins. Cut each peach in half and remove the pit. Put the peach halves into a crystal bowl.

Pour the port, red wine, red currant jelly, and lemon juice into a heavy saucepan and simmer over low heat for 10 minutes. Stir the dissolved cornstarch into the wine sauce and cook until the sauce thickens slightly. Pour the sauce over the peaches in the bowl.

Serve the still-warm peaches with freshly baked macaroons.

NOTE: Good-quality canned peach halves can be used if fresh peaches are not available.

PEACHES IN CHAMPAGNE

Serves 4

6 fully ripe peaches
¼ cup sugar
¼ bottle champagne

Bring a saucepan of water to a boil. Plunge the peaches, one at a time, into the water and count slowly to 10. Remove the peaches, dip them in cold water, and slip off the skins. Cut each peach in half and remove the pit.

Slice the skinned peaches into a crystal bowl. Stir in the sugar and champagne. Refrigerate for 2 hours before serving.

VARIATION: Add a teaspoon of Cassis syrup to each serving to make a very pretty pink color.

BAKED RUM PEACHES

Serves 2

2 fresh ripe peaches
2 tablespoons chopped almonds
4 crisp sugar cookies, crumbled
2 teaspoons sugar
2 tablespoons dark Jamaica rum
½ cup heavy cream, whipped

Preheat the oven to 350 degrees.

Bring a small saucepan of water to a boil. Plunge the peaches, one at a time, into the water and simmer for 2 or 3 minutes. Remove the peaches, then drop them in a bowl of cold water. When the peaches are cool enough to handle, slip the skins off. Cut each peach in half and remove the pit; place the peach halves, cavity side up, in a buttered baking dish.

Combine the almonds, cookie crumbs, sugar, and rum in a bowl. Divide the mixture among the cavities of the peach halves. Pour ⅓ cup water into the dish and bake for 30 minutes. Serve hot, with whipped cream.

■ PEARS BAKED IN RED WINE

Serves 6

6 ripe fresh pears, unpeeled, halved, and cored

1½ cups brown sugar

1 cup red wine

4 cloves

1 cinnamon stick

1 teaspoon lemon juice

WHIPPED CREAM

1 cup heavy cream

2 tablespoons granulated sugar

1 teaspoon vanilla extract

Preheat the oven to 350 degrees.

Arrange the pears in a baking dish. In a small saucepan, combine the brown sugar, wine, cloves, and cinnamon stick; simmer gently over low heat for 10 minutes. Stir in the lemon juice and pour the syrup over the pears. Cover the dish with aluminum foil and bake, occasionally basting the pears with the syrup, for 45 minutes. Remove the baking pan from the oven and allow the pears to cool in the syrup.

To make the whipped cream, beat the cream in a bowl until it has thickened slightly. Add the sugar and continue beating until it stands quite stiffly. Fold in the vanilla extract.

Serve the pears directly from the dish in which they were baked and pass the whipped cream separately.

NOTE: The pears can be peeled for this dish, if you prefer.

PEARS WITH RASPBERRY SAUCE AND ICE CREAM

Serves 6

3 ripe fresh pears, peeled, halved, and cored
6 scoops coffee ice cream
1 10-ounce package frozen raspberries, thawed

Put a pear half in each of 6 individual serving dishes; top each pear half with a scoop of ice cream. Puree the raspberries in the blender. Strain the puree through a fine sieve to remove the seeds and spoon it over the fruit.

NOTE: Canned pear halves, drained, can be used if fresh pears are not available.

ORANGES STUFFED WITH SHERBET

Serves 12

12 navel oranges
1 quart orange, lemon, or other fruit-flavored sherbet, slightly softened
1 cup stiffly whipped cream
24 orange or tangerine sections, or berries (to complement the flavor of the sherbet)
Cinnamon or cocoa powder

Cut the oranges in half, scoop out the pulp, and replace it with sherbet. Freeze the sherbet in the shells. Just before serving, pipe or spoon a rosette of whipped cream in the center. Top with an orange segment or a berry, and sprinkle the edges with cinnamon.

ORANGES IN SWEET MARMALADE SAUCE

Serves 2

2 navel oranges
½ cup orange marmalade
2 tablespoons Grand Marnier
2 tablespoons cold water
1 tablespoon light corn syrup

Peel the oranges and cut them into segments, removing all the white pith and membranes and any seeds. If you do this over a bowl, you can drop the segments into it and save the juice as you go along.

Combine the marmalade, liqueur, cold water, and corn syrup and stir to make the sauce. Pour this over the oranges in the bowl. Chill for at least 2 hours and serve in glass dishes.

ORANGES WITH ORANGES

Serves 6

6 navel oranges
1 cup sugar
1 cup water
2 tablespoons Cointreau, Triple Sec, or Grand Marnier
1 pint orange sherbet

Peel 1 orange, taking care to remove only the brightly colored rind. Cut the rind into fine julienne pieces. Simmer the rind in a saucepan of boiling water for 5 minutes, then drain and reserve the rind.

Remove the rind from the remaining oranges, leaving them whole. Discard every suspicion of white pith. Cut each orange horizontally into 6 slices and reassemble them, securing the slices with long tooth-picks or bamboo skewers. Set aside.

Measure the sugar into a small heavy saucepan. Add 2 table-spoons of the water and cover over low heat without stirring until a dark, clear caramel syrup has formed. Add the remaining water, a little at a time. The syrup will be very hot and the water will surge up and splatter, so be extremely careful not to burn yourself. Continue sim-mering the syrup over low heat until it is a rich, dark color.

Arrange the oranges in a bowl and scatter the rind over them. Pour the syrup and the orange liqueur over the oranges. Serve with scoops of orange sherbet.

■ STEWED RHUBARB

Serves 4

1 pound pink rhubarb, cut diagonally into 1-inch pieces
1 cup sugar
1 cup freshly squeezed orange juice
1 vanilla bean, split in half lengthwise, or 1 teaspoon vanilla extract
1 tablespoon cornstarch dissolved in 2 tablespoons cold water

Place the rhubarb, sugar, orange juice, and vanilla bean, if you are using it, in a heavy saucepan. Simmer, covered, over low heat until the rhubarb is tender but not falling apart, about 15 to 20 minutes.

Stir the dissolved cornstarch into the rhubarb; continue simmering until the juices are slightly thickened, about 2 minutes. Discard the vanilla bean, or add the vanilla extract at this point if you did not use the bean.

Let the rhubarb cool, then cover and refrigerate it.

MELON WITH BLUEBERRIES

Serves 6

1 cup water
2 cups sugar
Juice of 1 lemon
1 cantaloupe
¼ honeydew, cranshaw, Persian, or other melon
¼ small watermelon
1 pint blueberries
Mint leaves, for garnish

In a small saucepan, combine the water and sugar; gently simmer, uncovered, for 30 minutes. Stir in the lemon juice and let the syrup cool.

Meanwhile, form the melons into balls, using a melon ball scoop. Cut the watermelon into small pieces. Put all the melon into a bowl.

Pick over the blueberries to remove any leaves, stems, or geen unripe berries, then wash them and drain thoroughly. Add the blueberries to the bowl of melon. Pour the cooled syrup over the fruit and allow it to macerate in the refrigerator for at least 1 hour.

Serve in a melon half or a glass serving bowl, garnished with mint leaves.

RASPBERRIES WITH RASPBERRY PUREE

Serves 4

4 pints raspberries
2 tablespoons confectioners' sugar
2 tablespoons Framboise or Cassis

Puree 2 of the pints of raspberries in a blender or food processor with the sugar and liqueur. Force the puree through a strainer to remove the seeds.

Divide the remaining raspberries among 4 large wineglasses and pour the puree over them.

■ GRAPEFRUIT HALVES FILLED WITH RED AND BLACK FRUIT

The contrasting colors of the fruit make a dramatic presentation on the table. Choose among pitted red cherries, strawberries, raspberries, red currants, pomegranates, watermelon and red-skinned apples. For the black fruit, select from blueberries, blackberries, black raspberries, pitted black cherries, and pitted black plums. An alternative would be to fill some of the halves with all white, yellow, or green fruit, though green is difficult because after green grapes, you find yourself stumped. Maybe this is why kiwis were invented.

Serves 12

6 grapefruit
Approximately 12 cups pitted, sliced, or diced (as necessary) assorted red and black seasonal fruits
½ cup Crème de Cassis
Fresh violet or nasturtium blossoms

Cut each grapefruit in half; squeeze out the juice and set it aside for another use. Scoop out with a grapefruit spoon and discard the remaining pulp and membranes. Fill each grapefruit shell with part red fruit and part black fruit, or, alternatively, fill 6 of the halves with red fruit and the other 6 with black fruit.

Drizzle a tablespoon or so of Cassis over the fruit in each grapefruit cup. Garnish with the fresh blossoms.

PLUM COMPOTE

Serves 4

2 pounds red or black plums, halved and pitted
½ cup sugar
¼ cup water
Rind and juice of 1 orange
½ cup port wine
2 tablespoons red currant jelly
1 teaspoon almond extract

Place all the ingredients except the almond extract in a saucepan. Cover and simmer over very low heat for 15 minutes, then stir in the almond extract. Refrigerate for 4 hours. Serve in an attractive glass dish.

PRUNE COMPOTE

Serves 4

1 pound pitted prunes
2 cups orange juice
Juice of ½ lemon
1 cinnamon stick
2 tablespoons sugar
Heavy cream, for serving

Put the prunes in a bowl with the orange juice, and let them soak, covered, overnight. Transfer the prunes to a saucepan. Add the lemon juice, cinnamon stick, and sugar; simmer, uncovered, over low heat until the prunes have completely softened, about 20 minutes. Set aside to cool, then refrigerate.

Serve with a small pitcher of heavy cream; the prunes will be mightily improved thereby.

BANANAS WITH CHOCOLATE SAUCE

Serves 4

4 scoops Vanilla Ice Cream (see page 294)
4 bananas, sliced
Chocolate Sauce (see page 192)

Put a scoop of ice cream into each of 4 large wineglasses. Add the sliced bananas and cover with the chocolate sauce. Set each wineglass on a decorative plate and serve with cookies of your choice.

STRAWBERRIES ROMANOFF

Serves 4

I quart fresh strawberries
3 tablespoons superfine sugar
2 large oranges
2 tablespoons Grand Marnier
2 tablespoons Cognac (optional)

Remove the stems from the strawberries and rinse them *quickly* under cold running water. Do not let them soak in a bowl of water or they will become waterlogged and tasteless. Dry the berries on paper towels, arrange them in a serving dish, and sprinkle them with the sugar.

Peel the oranges and cut between the membranes to remove the orange segments. Add the orange segments to the strawberries; squeeze the orange juice remaining in the pulp over the berries. Add the liqueurs, toss lightly, and serve well chilled.

STRAWBERRY WINE CUP

Serves any number

Glasses of red or white wine
Ripe strawberries
Superfine sugar (optional)

Dip the strawberries in the wine and eat them. Sprinkle them with sugar if you have a sweet tooth. That is all. It is enough.

STRAWBERRIES WITH STRAWBERRY PUREE

Serves 4

2 pints fresh strawberries
2 tablespoons confectioners' sugar
2 tablespoons Grand Marnier

Puree half the strawberries in a blender or food processor with the sugar and liqueur. Force the puree through a strainer to remove the seeds. Pour the puree into 4 individual serving dishes or large wineglasses and top each one with a grouping of whole strawberries.

VARIATIONS:

- Use kirsch or a fruit brandy instead of Grand Marnier.
- Flavor the puree with grated orange rind, vanilla extract, or almond extract.
- Use blueberries or orange segments in addition to the whole strawberries to top the puree.

GRAPEFRUIT CUPS

Serves 4

2 grapefruit
4 oranges
2 tablespoons orange marmalade
2 tablespoons hot water
Mint leaves, for garnish

Cut each grapefruit in half. Cut between the membranes to remove the segments. Place the segments and grapefruit juice in a bowl.

Peel the oranges and cut between the membranes to remove the segments. Combine the oranges with the grapefruit.

With a grapefruit spoon, scoop out the pulp and pith from each grapefruit, taking care not to pierce the skin at the base. Divide the grapefruit and orange segments and the juice among the grapefruit shells.

Combine the marmalade with the water and divide it among the shells. Garnish with fresh mint leaves.

BAKED APPLES WITH RUM

Serves 6

6 baking apples
½ cup chopped pecans or walnuts
6 teaspoons honey
6 teaspoons butter
½ cup apple cider or water
½ cup dark Jamaica rum
Sweetened whipped cream or softened ice cream, for serving

Peel the top two-thirds of each apple. Remove the entire core, using an apple corer or a small paring knife. Arrange the apples in a baking dish just large enough to hold them. Place a few chopped nuts and a teaspoon each of honey and butter in each cavity. Pour hot water into the baking dish to a depth of 1 inch, cover the dish with oiled foil, and bake until the apples have softened but are not falling down, about 35 minutes.

Transfer the apples to a serving dish. Heat the rum in a small saucepan. Light it and pour the flames slowly over the apples. Serve with sweetened whipped cream.

BAKED APPLES WITH SWEET YOGURT

Serves 4

4 baking apples
⅓ cup chopped pecans
¼ cup raisins or chopped glacéed fruits
½ cup raspberry preserves
1 cup plain yogurt
2 teaspoons honey
Ground cinnamon or freshly grated nutmeg

Preheat the oven to 350 degrees.

Peel the top two-thirds of each apple. Remove the entire core, using an apple corer or a small paring knife. Arrange the apples in a baking dish just large enough to hold them. Fill the centers with nuts and raisins. Top each apple with enough preserves so that they will run down the sides of the apple. Pour hot water into the baking dish to a depth of 1 inch, cover the dish with oiled aluminum foil, and bake for 15 minutes. Uncover and continue cooking until the apples are softish—but don't cook them for so long that they collapse—about 10 minutes more.

Combine the yogurt and honey in a bowl. Top the apples before serving with spoonfuls of the yogurt mixture and dust them with cinnamon.

PINEAPPLE IN CARAMEL KIRSCH

Serves 2

1 tablespoon butter
2 tablespoons sugar
2 slices fresh pineapple, core removed
2 tablespoons kirsch
2 scoops Vanilla Ice Cream (see page 294), for serving

Heat the butter in a skillet and add 1 tablespoon of the sugar. Add the pineapple rings and sprinkle them with the remaining tablespoons of sugar. Cook over medium-high heat, turning the pineapple rings until they are golden brown and the sugar has caramelized. Add the kirsch to the pan and touch with a lighted match to flame the liqueur.

Serve hot on dessert plates with a scoop of ice cream.

12

CHEERS!

MULLED WINE

SPICED TEA

EGGNOG

HOT BUTTERED RUM

FISH HOUSE PUNCH

HOT TODDY

LEMONADE WITH MINT

BLOODY MARY

FLAVORED VODKA

FRESH GRAPEFRUIT JUICE WITH MANGO AND MINT

MINT JULEP

SANGRIA

■ MULLED WINE

Makes 24 drinks

4 bottles reasonably good quality red wine
8 cups water
⅓ cup sugar
1 teaspoon Angostura bitters
1 teaspoon ground allspice
Freshly grated nutmeg
2 sticks cinnamon
12 whole cloves
Pared rind of 1 orange

Pour the wine and water into a large saucepan. Add the sugar and bitters. Wrap the remaining ingredients in a piece of cheesecloth and tie it with string. Add the cheesecloth bag to the pan and simmer for 10 minutes. (Take care not to let the wine boil or all the alcohol will evaporate and much of its effect will be lost.) Discard the spice bag. Ladle the hot wine into mugs or glasses to be served immediately, or pour the wine into a container such as a large copper stockpot that retains heat for a long time, or keep the wine warm over a Sterno flame.

SPICED TEA

Makes 4 cups

3 cups water
12 whole cloves
I stick cinnamon
I cup strained orange juice
4 good-quality tea bags

Bring the water to a boil in a saucepan. Add the cloves and cinnamon, lower the heat and simmer for 2 minutes. Remove the pan from the heat, cover, and let it stand for 5 minutes. Add the orange juice and return it to a boil. Remove the pan from the heat and add the tea bags. Strain and serve as soon as the tea has steeped.

EGGNOG

Makes 10 drinks

6 eggs, separated
¾ cup sugar
2 cups whipped cream
2 cups light cream or half-and-half
I pint bourbon
¼ cup dark Jamaica rum or brandy
Grated nutmeg

Beat the egg yolks and sugar in a bowl until light and creamy. Fold in the whipped cream and light cream. Transfer the mixture to a punch bowl and stir in the bourbon and rum.

In a separate bowl, beat the egg whites until they stand in soft peaks, then fold them gently into the punch. Sprinkle with grated nutmeg. Chill the eggnog, but do not leave it in the refrigerator for more than I hour. Serve it in small glasses.

HOT BUTTERED RUM

Makes 1 drink

2 ounces dark Jamaica rum
1 teaspoon honey
1 slice lemon
3 whole cloves
1 teaspoon butter
1 cinnamon stick
Boiling water

Rinse a tall glass with hot water and leave a spoon in the glass to prevent it from breaking. Put the rum, honey, lemon slice, cloves, butter, and cinnamon stick in the glass and fill it to the brim with boiling water. Remove the spoon and stir with the cinnamon stick.

FISH HOUSE PUNCH

Makes 30 drinks

2 cups sugar
4 cups lemon juice, strained
8 cups dark Jamaica rum
4 cups brandy
½ cup peach or apple brandy

Stir all the ingredients together and let stand at least 4 hours to mellow. To serve, place a block of ice in a large punch bowl and pour the punch over it. The sugar will dissolve in the alcohol—so may you. This is powerful stuff.

HOT TODDY

Makes 4 drinks

1½ cups bourbon
4 teaspoons sugar
4 teaspoons honey
4 teaspoons lemon juice
2½ cups boiling water
4 long cinnamon sticks

Pour equal amounts of bourbon into each of 4 glasses. Combine the remaining ingredients, divide among the 4 glasses, and stir with cinnamon sticks.

LEMONADE WITH MINT

Makes 2 quarts

12 large lemons
⅓ cup sugar
Small bunch of fresh mint
8 cups water

Squeeze and strain the juice from 11 of the lemons. (There will be about 2 cups of juice.) Pour the juice into a glass container and refrigerate.

Put the empty lemon halves, sugar, and mint into a saucepan. Add the water and simmer gently over low heat for 15 minutes. Strain and chill the lemon-flavored water, and then add it to the chilled lemon juice. Slice the remaining lemon thinly and add the slices to the lemonade.

Serve by ladling the lemonade and lemon slices into tall glasses filled with ice cubes.

VARIATIONS: Make ice cubes from the lemonade too, for a more intense lemon flavor.

- Half fill the ice cube tray and when it has frozen put half a lemon slice on each cube's surface. Top with more water. The lemon slice will be captured, decoratively, in the center of the cube.

■ BLOODY MARY

Makes 4 drinks

1 cup vodka
3 cups tomato juice or spicy V-8 juice
Juice of 1 lemon
Juice of 1 lime
1 teaspoon Worcestershire sauce
1 teaspoon salt
8 drops Tabasco
Freshly ground black pepper
4 lime wedges
4 small stalks celery, with the leaves

Combine the vodka, tomato juice, lemon and lime juices, Worcestershire sauce, salt, and Tabasco; mix thoroughly. Fill 4 glasses with ice cubes; pour the mixture over them and dust with black pepper. Garnish each glass with a wedge of lime and insert a celery stalk as "stirrer."

NOTE: Keep a second pitcher of Bloody Marys in the freezer while sampling the first. If you forget about it long enough for it to freeze, it won't come to any harm.

FLAVORED VODKA

Makes 24 drinks

1 pound dried apricots
1 cup sugar
1 fifth of vodka
3 tablespoons apricot brandy

Cut the apricots into small pieces and put them into a saucepan with the sugar and 1 cup of the vodka. Slowly bring to a boil. Remove the pan from the heat and let the apricots macerate in the vodka for 48 hours. Strain the apricot mixture; pour the resulting flavored vodka, the apricot brandy, and the remaining vodka into a bottle. Cork tightly and keep in the freezer until the right moment arrives.

VARIATIONS: You can make other fruit-flavored vodkas by substituting one of the following fruits for the apricots and an appropriately flavored brandy for the apricot brandy: 1 pound pitted cherries; 2 mangos; 1 pint raspberries; or the grated rind and juice of 3 lemons.

FRESH GRAPEFRUIT JUICE WITH MANGO AND MINT

Makes 12 drinks

4 cups freshly squeezed grapefruit juice (from about 6 grapefruit)
1 12-ounce can mango nectar
1 liter seltzer or club soda
12 sprigs fresh mint or 12 thin slices of unpeeled cucumber, for garnish

Combine the grapefruit juice, mango nectar, and seltzer in a large punch bowl. Stir well. Place a mint sprig or cucumber slice on the edge of each of 12 tall glasses filled with ice, and let guests help themselves.

■ MINT JULEP

A handful of fresh mint leaves
2 teaspoons sugar
¼ cup boiling water
Crushed ice
½ cup bourbon

Chill 2 tall glasses or silver goblets in the freezer for at least 1 hour. Meanwhile, chop 8 mint leaves with the sugar in a bowl and pour the boiling water over them. Leave until cool, then strain to extract the mint essence.

Fill the glasses with crushed ice. Add the mint extract and bourbon. Garnish each glass with a small bunch of mint leaves and serve with a straw.

VARIATION: Rum or brandy may be used instead of bourbon.

■ SANGRIA

Makes 18 drinks

3 cups water
1½ cups sugar
6 bottles Rioja or a decent California red jug wine
½ cup or more Cointreau or Grand Marnier (optional)
Sliced oranges, lemons, limes, peaches, berries, or other fresh fruit (except bananas, which
   become mushy)

Heat the water and add the sugar, stirring until all the sugar has dissolved. Let it cool. Combine with all the remaining ingredients and serve in a tall pitcher filled with ice cubes.

PART THREE

CREATIVE COMBINATIONS

Recipes preceded by a ■ are found in this book.

Fruit Juice

- Scrambled Eggs with Homemade Country Sausage

- Popovers

- Grapefruit Cups

- Piperade

Croissants and French Bread

Fresh Berries

- Fragrant Multigrain Waffles

- Baked Apples with Sweet Yogurt

Fresh Grapefruit Juice with Mango and Mint

- Eggs Benedict

Hot Beef Consommé

- Omelette with Fried Potato and Bacon Filling

- Broiled Tomatoes

MORE IDEAS FOR BREAKFAST AND BRUNCH

- Bloody Mary

Champagne with Fresh Orange Juice

Hot Apple Cider with Cinnamon Sticks

- Hot Buttered Rum

Freshly Squeezed Fruit Juices

Winter Tomato Consommé

Hot or Cold Beef Broth

Hot Chicken Broth

Hot or Cold V-8 Juice

- Melon with Blueberries
- Stewed Rhubarb
- Prune Compote
- Grapefruit Halves Filled with Red and Black Fruit
- Plum Compote

- Mushrooms and Bacon in Popovers
- Baking Powder Biscuits
- Corn Muffins
- Blueberry Muffins
- Bran Muffins
- Pumpkin Muffins with Pumpkin Seeds
- Oatmeal Raisin Muffins
- Fragrant Orange Bread
- Honey Spice Bread
- Corn Bread
- Walnut Cheddar Bread
- Apricot Nut Bread
- Cranberry Bread
- Coffee Cake
- Sour Cream Coffee Cake with Chocolate and Walnuts

- Pan-Fried Potatoes

- Plain Omelette

with Mushroom Filling

with Tomato and Herb Filling

with Cheese Filling

- Spanish Omelette
- Quiche Lorraine
- Pancakes
- Baked Apricot Pancake
- Whole Wheat Pancakes
- Apple Pancakes
- French Toast

LOAVES AND FISHES BRUNCH

A variety of breads including muffins, croissants, brioches, pumpernickel, sour dough, rye and other dark and multigrain breads, and bagels go well with the fish or shellfish dishes below. Serve with sliced onions, sliced tomatoes, olives, sour cream, and/or sweet butter.

Oysters on the Half Shell with Small Pork Sausages

Clams on the Half Shell

- New England Clam Chowder
- Manhattan Clam Chowder
- Fish Soup

Smoked Salmon

- Gravad Lax

Smoked Sturgeon

Smoked Trout

- Poached Trout

Herring

Whitefish

SAUSAGE AND HAM BRUNCH

- Glazed Baked Ham ·
- Baking Powder Biscuits with Country Ham
- Prosciutto with Figs

A variety of American, German, and Italian Sausages

A variety of mustards and pickles

- Vegetable Stew (Ratatouille)
- Potato Salad I or II

Many breads and a cheese and fruit platter

QUICK DINNERS FOR TWO

- Cornish Hens with Salt and Pepper
- Red on Red Salad
- Tossed Salad with Splendid Salad Dressing
- Lemon Sherbet

- Calves Liver with Lemon and Thyme Sauce

Boiled Potatoes

- Grated Zucchini
- Broiled Tomatoes

Fresh Fruit

Watercress and Endive Salad

- Broiled Chicken with Mustard
- Vegetable Stew (Ratatouille)
- Bread Pudding

Steamed Asparagus with Oil and Vinegar Dressing

- Tortellini with Scallops and Bacon

Tossed Salad

- Oranges Stuffed with Sherbet

- Fried Chicken in Beer Batter

Fresh Corn

Sliced Tomatoes and Bermuda Onion with Oil and Vinegar

Fresh Peaches

- Crisp-Fried Turkey Breast

- Sicilian-Style Broccoli with Cauliflower

French Bread

- Melon with Blueberries

- Stir-Fried Chicken with Walnuts

Cellophane Noodles

Mango with Lime Juice

- Stir-Fried Turkey Breast with Sesame Oil

- All-Purpose Rice

- Pineapple in Caramel Kirsch

MORE INSPIRATIONS FOR QUICK DINNERS

Mix and match as you wish

- Guacamole

- Sautéed Almonds

- Basic Dip

Store-Bought Pâté

Cheeses

- Green Fettuccini with Pesto and Zucchini
- Green Fettuccini with Prosciutto and Cream
- Fettuccini in a Warm Bath
- Hot Shrimp with Coarse Salt

- Broiled Chicken with Mustard
- Red Snapper with Tomatoes
- Baked Red Snapper with Tarragon Sauce
- Swordfish Steak with Shrimp
- Shrimp in Crisp Batter
- Broiled Shrimp with Garlic
- Moules Marinières

CANDLELIT DINNERS

- Artichokes with Grebiche Dressing
- Poached Salmon Steaks
- Braised Cucumbers and Peas
- Boiled New Potatoes
- Raspberries with Raspberry Puree

- Chicken in Champagne
- White Cabbage with Chestnuts
- Glazed Carrots
- Almost Instant Chocolate Mousse

- Pepper Steak
- Braised Endives

String Beans
- Mocha Gâteau

- Veal with Lemon and Brandy

Saffron Rice
- Hollandaise Sauce over Asparagus

Fresh Fruit with Sorbets
- Tomato Tartare
- Cornish Hens with Raspberry Vinegar

Roast Potatoes
- Grated Zucchini
- Zabaglione and Sliced Peaches

- Fresh Tomato Soup
- Roast Rack of Lamb
- Potatoes in Cream
- Vegetable Stew (Ratatouille)
- Apple Brown Betty

- Cold Curried Avocado Soup
- Lobster Mayonnaise
- Peaches in Champagne

Mesclun (mixed baby leaves and blossoms) Salad
- Cornish Hens with Salt and Pepper
- Red on Red Salad

- Yellow on Yellow Salad
- Green on Green Salad
- Mocha Ice Cream with Chocolate Sauce

MORE INSPIRATIONS FOR CANDLELIT DINNERS

Mix and match as you wish

- Stuffed Artichokes
- Liver Pâté with Vermouth and Currants
- French Country Terrine
- Shrimp with Marmalade Sauce
- Bay Scallops with Lime and Cream
- Mousse of Smoked Trout
- Curried Mussels and Cucumber Polonaise
- Pear and Prosciutto Salad
- Lichee and Mushroom Salad

- Cream of Asparagus Soup
- Cream of Chestnut Soup
- Chilled Claret Consommé
- Billi Bi Soup with Crab
- Onion Soup
- Vichyssoise
- Clear Vegetable Soup

- Veal and Prosciutto Rolls (Saltimbocca alla Romana)
- Baked Veal Chops with Ham and Cheese
- Sautéed Pork Loin
- Chicken with Citrus Fruits
- Chicken with Prosciutto

- Chicken with Almonds and Garlic
- Chicken Breasts Stuffed with Ricotta and Herbs
- Tuna with Red Wine and Tomatoes
- Lobster Newburg
- Roast Veal with Tuna Dressing (Vitello Tonnato)
- Roast Pork with Brown Sauce and Honey-Glazed Pears
- Roast Pork Loin
- Stuffed Honey-Glazed Duckling

COCKTAIL PARTY

- Stuffed Mushrooms
- Stuffed Cherry Tomatoes
- Sautéed Almonds
- Basic Dip
- Cheddar Cheese Spread
- Tapenade
- Marinated Mushrooms
- Guacamole
- Shiny Fresh Vegetables
- Liver Pâté with Vermouth and Currants
- French Country Terrine
- Bay Scallops with Lime and Cream
- Mousse of Smoked Trout
- Curried Mussels and Cucumber Polonaise

CELEBRATION DINNERS

- Liver Pâté with Vermouth and Currants
- Roast Rack of Lamb
- Potatoes in Cream

- Vegetable Stew (Ratatouille)
- Chocolate Birthday Cake

- Lobster Mayonnaise
- Baked Alaska with Fruit

- Winter Tomato Consommé
- Stuffed Honey-Glazed Duckling
- White Cabbage with Chestnuts
  String Beans
- Oranges with Oranges

- Fresh Tomato Soup
- Roast Veal with Tuna Dressing (Vitello Tonnato)
  Saffron Rice
- Peaches in Champagne

LUNCH

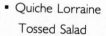

- Cold Duck Salad with Oranges and Walnuts
  Three Sorbets with Fresh Fruit

- Quiche Lorraine
  Tossed Salad
- Strawberries with Strawberry Puree

  Cold Roast Cornish Hen
- Watercress and Endive Salad

- Yellow on Yellow Salad
  - Plum Clafouti

- Pasta Primavera
  Tossed Salad
- Pears Baked in Red Wine

- Crab Salad
  Pumpernickel Bread
- Baked Rum Peaches

- Gingered Chicken
  - Couscous Salad
- Baked Apples with Sweet Yogurt

PASTA DINNERS

- Spaghetti with Garlic and Herbs
- Tortellini with Scallops and Bacon
- Green Fettuccini with Tomatoes and Mozzarella
- Fettuccini with Clams and Shrimp
- Spaghetti with Butter and Cheese
- Pasta Primavera
- Linguini with Mussels and Peas
- Ziti with Meat and Tomato Sauce
- Green Fettuccini with Pesto and Zucchini
- Green Fettuccini with Prosciutto and Cream
- Fettuccini in a Warm Bath
- Linguini with a Tempest of Mixed Vegetables

- Belgian Carbonnade of Beef
- Beef in Red Wine (Boeuf Bourguignon)
- Sauerbraten
- New England Boiled Dinner
- Meat Loaf
- Chili
- Braised Veal Shanks (Osso Buco)
- Fruit-Stuffed Pork Loin with Red Cabbage
- Lamb Stew
- Lamb Shanks with Yellow Split Peas and Lemon
- Chicken in the Pot
- Chicken Potpie
- Chicken in Red Wine
- Chicken Paprikash
- Chicken with Rice (Arroz con Pollo)
- Pot-Roasted Roulade of Turkey
- Sunday Night Chicken Supper
- Curried Chicken
- Smoked Fish Casserole
- Swordfish with Capers
- Roast Chicken with Rosemary
- Lasagne
- Cioppino

- Sangria
- Mulled Wine

THANKSGIVING DINNER

■ Cream of Chestnut Soup

or

■ Winter Tomato Consommé

■ Roast Turkey with Giblet Gravy and Cornbread and Oyster Stuffing

or

■ Sausage and Chestnut Stuffing

■ Baked Acorn Squash

■ Creamed Onions

■ Puree of White Winter Vegetables

■ Sweet Potato Casserole with Orange

■ Cranberry Relish

■ Apple, Cranberry, Raisin, Nut Pie

■ Pumpkin Pie

■ Unimaginably Great Fruit Cake

INDEX

IRENA CHALMERS is a graduate of the *Cordon Bleu* Cooking School in her native London. Before founding her own publishing company in 1980, she wrote over 100 single-subject cookbooks, ran a cooking school and kitchenwares shop, taught neuroanatomy and neurophysiology at New York's Columbia Presbyterian Hospital, and served as a midwife in Scotland.

Recognized as a brilliant commentator on lifestyle and food trends, Irena Chalmers is often referred to as the "Guru of Food." She has received nine Tastemaker Awards honoring outstanding cookbooks and writing on food and wine, was inducted into the Who's Who of Cooking in America in 1988, and received the New York University Woman of the Year in Food Award in 1989. Ms. Chalmers is a former president of *Les Dames d'Escoffier* and is currently serving a second term on the board of directors of the Society for American Cuisine. She is also on the board of directors of the International Association of Cooking Professionals and a member of the Company of the Culinary Institute of America.

Irena Chalmers makes her home in New York City.